Oracle8™ DBA: Backup & Recovery The Cram Sheet

This Cram Sheet contains the distilled, key facts about Oracle8 in the area of backup and recovery. Review this information last thing before you enter the test room, paying special attention to those areas where you feel you need the most review. You can transfer any of these facts from your head onto a blank sheet of paper before beginning the exam.

BACKUP AND RECOVERY CONSIDERATIONS

1. Planning and implementation of an effective backup and recovery strategy are critical tasks performed by Oracle Database Administrators (DBAs).
2. A thorough understanding of the business, operational, and technical requirements will help you develop an effective backup and recovery strategy that will protect the database from different types of failures, and ensure high availability, minimal downtime, and complete data recovery.
3. It is important to test regularly your backup and recovery strategy, because it ensures the integrity of backups, the validity of the backup and recovery methods, the reduction of problems before they occur in a production environment, and the streamlining of the overall backup and recovery process.

Oracle Recovery Structures And Processes

4. The Oracle backup and recovery functionality relies on many components of the Oracle Server architecture, including memory structures, background processes, and the physical database structure.
5. The System Global Area (SGA) contains database buffers, redo log buffers, shared pool, large pool, and optionally the Program Global Area (PGA). The shared pool holds the library cache and the data dictionary cache. Use of a Multi-Threaded Server (MTS) causes the shared pool to house the PGA. The *large pool* is an optional Oracle8 memory area that is used to allocate sequential I/O buffers from shared memory. **RMAN** uses the large pool for performing backup and recovery operations. The **LARGE_POOL_SIZE** *initSID.ora* parameter sets the size of memory allocated from the SGA.
6. The essential background processes are **SMON**, **PMON**, **DBWR**, **LGWR**, and **CKPT**. The **ARCH** background process is an optional process that is used by databases operating in **ARCHIVELOG** mode. The **ARCH** process copies the redo log files to the designated area specified by the **LOG_ARCHIVE_DEST** parameter. The **LGWR** checks if a redo log file has been archived before overwriting it. The archived logs are essential for recovery operations.
7. The physical database structure consists of three main OS file types: one or more control files, one or more data files, and two or more redo log files. Other auxiliary files include initialization parameter file, password file, archive logs, and so on.
8. The checkpoint event synchronizes the write operations of **DBWR** and **LGWR**. Checkpoints occurs under the following circumstances:

ORACLE RECOVERY WITHOUT ARCHIVING

35. When operating in **NOARCHIVELOG** mode, recovery from media failure is limited to the most recent full database backup.
36. You need to restore all data files, redo log files, and control files from your backup even if only one file is lost.
37. The recovery process is as follows:
    - Shut down the database with the **SHUTDOWN ABORT** statement.
    - Restore all files from the most recent offline database backup using OS copy commands or a third-party media manager. Use the **ALTER DATABASE RENAME FILE** command to specify new locations of data files or redo log files when applicable.
    - Open the database with the **STARTUP OPEN PFILE=init_SID.ora**.
38. **RMAN** uses the recovery catalog or the target database control file to determine which full and incremental backups or image copies it will use in the restore operation. Use the **RESTORE** command to restore files from backup sets or from image copies on disk to the specified location.

COMPLETE ORACLE RECOVERY WITH ARCHIVING

39. In complete recovery, the database is restored and recovered through the application of all redo information generated since the most recent available backup.
40. You can recover your database manually by executing the **RECOVER** or the **ALTER DATABASE RECOVER** commands. Alternatively, you can use **RMAN** to automate recovery.

INCOMPLETE ORACLE RECOVERY WITH ARCHIVING

41. In an incomplete recovery, the database is restored from a valid backup and recovered through the application of only some of the redo information generated since the valid backup. The database is essentially rebuilt to a point in time before the time of failure.
42. To perform incomplete recovery, you must have a valid offline or online backup of all the database files, and all the archived redo log files from the valid backup, until the designated time of recovery. Under all circumstances, the database must be opened with the **RESETLOGS** option.
43. Incomplete recovery types include the following:
    - Cancel-based recovery
    - Time-based recovery
    - Change-based recovery
    - Recovery using a backup control file
    - Tablespace point-in-time recovery (TSPITR)

ORACLE EXPORT AND IMPORT UTILITIES

44. The **EXPORT** utility enables DBAs to perform logical backups of the database. A logical backup involves making a copy of the logical database structures with or without the associated business data. A logical backup does not involve the physical database files. There are three export modes: full database, user, and table.
45. The **IMPORT** utility enables DBAs to read a valid file generated by the **EXPORT** utility for moving data into an Oracle database and for the recovery of database objects and business data. There are three export modes: full database, user, and table.

ADDITIONAL ORACLE RECOVERY ISSUES

46. There are several ways to minimize downtime and enhance recovery performance, including the following:
    - *Fast warmstart*—A database feature that enables the database to be opened as soon as cache recovery is complete.
    - *Starting Oracle with missing data files*—Oracle enables you to bring the unaffected parts of the database up for normal use while you perform recovery on the tablespace containing the lost or damaged data file.
    - *Parallel recovery*—A database feature that enables you to use several processes to apply changes from the redo log files to improve recovery performance. It can be accomplished by setting the **RECOVERY_PARALLELISM** parameter or issuing the **RECOVER** command with the **PARALLEL** keyword.

DELETE, and **PRINT** commands for stored script maintenance. Use the **RUN** command to run OS commands, SQL scripts, backup commands, stored scripts, and so on.

PHYSICAL BACKUPS WITHOUT RMAN

21. A closed (offline) database backup is an OS backup of all the data files, control files, redo log files, and other auxiliary files when the database is shut down using **SHUTDOWN NORMAL**, **SHUTDOWN IMMEDIATE**, or **SHUTDOWN TRANSACTIONAL**.
22. An open (online) database backup is a backup of the database, tablespaces, or individual data files while the **ARCHIVELOG** mode database is in use. This type of backup supports high availability and 24×7 operations.
23. Use the **ALTER DATABASE BACKUP CONTROLFILE TO <filename>** command to create a binary backup of the control file. Use the **ALTER DATABASE BACKUP CONTROLFILE TO TRACE** command to create a script text file that can be run to create the binary control file.
24. Use the **ALTER TABLESPACE** command to set a tablespace to read-only. You only need to take one backup after the tablespace is set to read-only, because no subsequent updates are performed. Resume normal backups should the tablespace become read-write.
25. Oracle provides two logging modes—**LOGGING** and **NOLOGGING**—to support direct-load and some Data Definition Language (DDL) operations that can be performed with or without logging of redo or undo information. When the **NOLOGGING** option is in effect for a direct-load operation, you should back up the data file pertaining to the direct-load operation upon load completion.

PHYSICAL BACKUPS USING RMAN

26. There are two types of **RMAN** backups: image copies and backup sets. An *image copy* is a copy of a single file on disk generated by an Oracle server process similar to an OS-generated file copy. A *backup set* multiplexes several files and typically contains one backup piece.
27. Use the **COPY** command to create an image copy. Use the **BACKUP** command to create backup sets.
28. There are two types of backup sets: data file backup set and archivelog backup set.
29. **RMAN** incremental and cumulative backups can be used to increase backup and recovery performance.
30. Use the **ALLOCATE CHANNEL** command to start a server process on the target database. Every backup, restore, and recover command requires at least one channel. The degree of parallelism is dependent on the number of channels allocated. Channels can write to different device types such as disk or tape via a media manager.

TYPES OF FAILURES AND TROUBLESHOOTING

31. Know these types of failures:
    - *Statement failure*—When an SQL statement fails. Oracle handles statement failures automatically and returns control to the user with an error message.
    - *User process failure*—When an Oracle user process ends abnormally. The **PMON** process takes care of recovery from user process failure.
    - *Instance failure*—When the Oracle instance fails. The **SMON** process performs instance recovery at startup using the online redo logs.
    - *User error failure*—When a user makes a mistake. Manual recovery is required for most user errors.
    - *Media failure*—When files needed by the database are no longer accessible. Oracle provides several options to recover from media failure.
32. The **DBVERIFY** utility can be used to perform physical data structure integrity checks on the data files.
33. Use **DB_BLOCK_CHECKSUM** and **LOG_BLOCK_CHECKSUM** to configure Oracle to use **CHECKSUM** to verify blocks in the data files and in the online redo log files.
34. Use the alert log file and trace files in the location specified by the **BACKGROUND_DUMP_DEST** to help troubleshoot system problems.

- A log switch
- The time specified in the **LOG_CHECKPOINT_TIMEOUT** parameter passed after the last checkpoint
- The number of OS blocks specified in the **LOG_CHECKPOINT_INTERVAL** parameter have been written since the last checkpoint
- A DBA manually used the **ALTER SYSTEM CHECKPOINT** command
- A tablespace is taken offline
- An online backup is initiated
- During instance shutdown when the **NORMAL IMMEDIATE,** or **TRANSACTIONAL** option has been specified.

9. Redo log files record all changes made to the database and are used to recover the database to a desired point in time. There must be at least two redo log groups with each group having the same size and the same number of members. To multiplex the redo logs, you should make sure each group has at least two redo log members, with each member on a different disk.

10. The multiplexing of control files protects them against a single point of failure. An instance cannot start with a corrupted control file. Oracle recommends at least two control files on different disks.

BACKUP AND RECOVERY CONFIGURATION

11. When a database is in **ARCHIVELOG** mode, a history of redo information is maintained through the archiving of the online redo logs. The **ARCH** background process must be explicitly started to support automatic archiving. This mode supports backups made while the database is open for normal use and complete recovery up to the point of failure. If the archiving destination runs out of space, the database will hang until sufficient free space is available for more archived redo log files.

12. When a database is set up for **NOARCHIVELOG** mode, no redo history is maintained. In **NOARCHIVELOG** mode, an online redo log group becomes available for reuse by the **LGWR** process as the checkpoint at the log switch completes. Media recovery is limited to the last full database backup. **NOARCHIVELOG** mode is the default database configuration.

13. Use the **ALTER DATABASE [ARCHIVELOGINOARCHIVELOG]** command to change the archiving mode of the database while the database is in **MOUNT** state.

14. For **ARCHIVELOG** mode databases, you can enable automatic archiving by the **ARCH** process when the database is **OPEN** or you can specify an initialization parameter.
    - When the database is open, use the **ALTER SYSTEM ARCHIVE LOG START TO <destination>** command to enable automatic archiving by the **ARCH** process. You must restart the **ARCH** process upon each instance startup.
    - You can set the initialization parameter **LOG_ARCHIVE_START=<TRUEIFALSE>** to automatically start the **ARCH** process upon instance startup.

15. Use the **ALTER SYSTEM ARCHIVE LOG** command to archive selectively redo log files.

16. An Oracle8 new feature enables the DBA to multiplex or duplex the archived redo log files to protect them against media failure. You need to set two *initSID.ora* parameters: **LOG_ARCHIVE_DUPLEX_DEST** and **LOG_ARCHIVE_MIN_SUCCEED_DEST**.

RECOVERY MANAGER (RMAN)

17. The Recovery Manager (**RMAN**) is an Oracle-provided utility that enables DBAs to manage the backup, restore, and recovery processes in an automated fashion. **RMAN** features can be accessed using the command line interface or the GUI interface via OEM's Backup Manager tool.

18. **RMAN** components include the following: **RMAN** executable, **RMAN** interface, target database, recovery catalog, and channels.

19. When performing backup and recovery operations, you can choose to use only OS mechanisms, **RMAN**, or a combination of the two.

20. Use the **REGISTER DATABASE**, **RESET DATABASE**, and **RESYNC CATALOG** commands to register, resync, and reset a database. Use the **CHANGE**, **DELETE**, and **CATALOG** commands to maintain the recovery catalog. Use the **REPORT** and **LIST** commands to generate reports and lists from the recovery catalog contents. Use the **CREATE**, **REPLACE**,

Oracle8™ DBA: Backup and Recovery

Debbie Wong

Oracle8™ DBA: Backup and Recovery Exam Cram

Limits Of Liability And Disclaimer Of Warranty

The author and publisher of this book have used their best efforts in preparing the book and the programs contained in it. These efforts include the development, research, and testing of the theories and programs to determine their effectiveness. The author and publisher make no warranty of any kind, expressed or implied, with regard to these programs or the documentation contained in this book.

The author and publisher shall not be liable in the event of incidental or consequential damages in connection with, or arising out of, the furnishing, performance, or use of the programs, associated instructions, and/or claims of productivity gains.

Trademarks

Trademarked names appear throughout this book. Rather than list the names and entities that own the trademarks or insert a trademark symbol with each mention of the trademarked name, the publisher states that it is using the names for editorial purposes only and to the benefit of the trademark owner, with no intention of infringing upon that trademark.

The Coriolis Group, LLC
14455 N. Hayden Road
Suite 220
Scottsdale, Arizona 85260

480/483-0192
FAX 480/483-0193
http://www.coriolis.com

Library of Congress Cataloging-in-Publication Data
Wong, Debbie
Oracle8 DBA: backup and recovery exam cram / Debbie Wong
p. cm.
Includes index.
ISBN 1-57610-623-3
1. Electronic data processing personnel--Certification. 2. Database management--Examinations--Study guides. 3. Oracle (Computer file) I. Title.
QA76.3.W66 2000
005.75'85--dc21 00-025760
CIP

Printed in the United States of America
10 9 8 7 6 5 4 3 2 1

President, CEO
Keith Weiskamp

Publisher
Steve Sayre

Acquisitions Editor
Jeff Kellum

Marketing Specialist
Cynthia Caldwell

Project Editor
Greg Balas

Technical Reviewer
Eugenio Reis

Production Coordinator
Laura Wellander

Cover Designer
Jesse Dunn

Layout Designer
April Nielsen

CORIOLIS

14455 North Hayden Road • Suite 220 • Scottsdale, Arizona 85260

Coriolis: The Smartest Way To Get Certified™

To help you reach your goals, we've listened to readers like you, and we've designed our entire product line around you and the way you like to study, learn, and master challenging subjects.

In addition to our highly popular *Exam Cram* and *Exam Prep* books, we offer several other products to help you pass certification exams. Our *Practice Tests* and *Flash Cards* are designed to make your studying fun and productive. Our *Audio Reviews* have received rave reviews from our customers—and they're the perfect way to make the most of your drive time!

The newest way to get certified is the *Exam Cram Personal Trainer*—a highly interactive, personalized self-study course based on the best-selling *Exam Cram* series. It's the first certification-specific product to completely link a customizable learning tool, exclusive *Exam Cram* content, and multiple testing techniques so you can study what, how, and when you want.

Exam Cram Insider—a biweekly newsletter containing the latest in certification news, study tips, and announcements from Certification Insider Press—gives you an ongoing look at the hottest certification programs. (To subscribe, send an email to **eci@coriolis.com** and type "subscribe insider" in the body of the email.) We also sponsor the Certified Crammer Society and the Coriolis Help Center—two other resources that will help you get certified even faster!

Help us continue to provide the very best certification study materials possible. Write us or email us at **cipq@coriolis.com** and let us know how our books have helped you study. Tell us about new features that you'd like us to add. Send us a story about how we've helped you; if we use it in one of our books, we'll send you an official Coriolis shirt!

Good luck with your certification exam and your career. Thank you for allowing us to help you achieve your goals.

Keith Weiskamp

Keith Weiskamp
President and CEO

Look For These Other Books From The Coriolis Group:

Oracle8 DBA: SQL and PL/SQL Exam Cram
by Michael R. Ault

Oracle8 DBA: Performance Tuning Exam Cram
by Michael R. Ault and Josef Brinson

Oracle8 DBA: Database Administration Exam Cram
by Paul Collins

Oracle8 DBA: Network Administration Exam Cram
by Barbara Ann Pascavage

Oracle8 Black Book
by Michael R. Ault

To my parents, who gave my brothers and I the greatest gift of all—life. You will always be the wind beneath our wings.

To you, the reader, I hope you will find what you are looking for, and I urge you to remember that in the electronic virtual world, it is those who help the most, who receive the most benefit.

❧

About The Author

Debbie Wong is an IT professional whose experience includes system analysis and design, application development, database administration, customer support, and project management. She has spent the majority of her career developing and maintaining host, PC-LAN, and Web-based database systems to accommodate her client's distinct business needs.

Debbie began her Oracle certification history with Oracle6's certification exams for Database Administration and Application Developer, and then served as one of the cut-score committee members and recipients of the Chauncey/ETS Oracle7 certification. She is currently an Oracle Certified Professional (OCP) for Oracle7.3, Oracle8, and Oracle8i.

Debbie is an active participant in local, regional, and international Oracle user groups. In addition, she has also presented at MAOP, ECO, ODTUG, IOUW/IOUG-A, and Oracle Open World conferences.

Acknowledgments

I would like to thank, in particular, the dedicated professionals at The Coriolis Group: Jeff Kellum, Greg Balas, Laura Wellander, and Jesse Dunn. Without their patience, excellent support, and know-how, this book would never have gotten off the drawing board.

In addition, thanks to Eugenio Reis for tech reviewing the book, Jennifer Huntley Mario for copyediting, Mary Cullen for proofreading, Janet Perlman for indexing, and Kim Scott for typesetting the book.

Sincere thanks to Jason Evans, VP of Communications at Self Test Software, for providing some of the sample questions.

Special thanks to Elaine Schuetz, a great friend and an Oracle expert, who patiently mentored me over the years. Your thoughtfulness, encouragement, and support provided the solid foundation upon which I stand.

Special thanks also to Marlene Theriault, my Oracle, for your encouragement, inspiration, and willing support. Your passing along of this project opportunity, and your believing in me (more than I've believed in myself) makes this book a reality.

Heartfelt thanks to my uncle for bringing our family to this land of opportunity.

Thank you to my family, friends, and co-workers, for tolerating my stressful moments, for putting up with me through months of grouchy days and sleepless nights, and for making this book a reality. Your encouragement, positive attitude, and unparalleled moral support, have kept me motivated throughout this challenging project. You guys are the greatest!

Last, but not least, thanks to you for purchasing this book.

Contents At A Glance

Table Of Contents

Introduction

Welcome to *Oracle8 DBA Backup and Recovery Exam Cram*! This book will help you get ready to take—and pass—the third of the five part series of exams for Oracle Certified Professional-Oracle8 Certified Database Administrator (OCP-DBA) certification. In this Introduction, I talk about Oracle's certification programs in general and how the *Exam Cram* series can help you prepare for Oracle8's certification exams.

Exam Cram books help you understand and appreciate the subjects and materials you need to be familiar with to pass Oracle certification exams. The books are aimed strictly at test preparation and review. They do not teach you everything you need to know about a topic. Instead, I present and dissect the questions and problems that you're likely to encounter on a test.

Nevertheless, to completely prepare yourself for any Oracle test, I recommend that you begin by taking the Self-Assessment included in this book immediately following this Introduction. This tool will help you evaluate your knowledge base against the requirements for an OCP-DBA under both ideal and real circumstances.

Based on what you learn from the Self-Assessment, you might decide to begin your studies with some classroom training or by reading one of the many DBA guides available from Oracle and third-party vendors. I also strongly recommend that you install, configure, and fool around with the software or environment that you'll be tested on, because nothing beats hands-on experience and familiarity when it comes to understanding the questions you're likely to encounter on a certification test. Book learning is essential, but hands-on experience is the best teacher of all!

The Oracle Certified Professional (OCP) Program

The OCP program for DBA certification currently includes five separate tests. A brief description of each test follows, and Table 1 shows the required exams for the OCP-DBA certification:

Table 1 OCP-DBA Requirements*

All 5 of these tests are required		
Test 1	Exam 1Z0-001	Introduction to Oracle: SQL and PL/SQL
Test 2	Exam 1Z0-013	Oracle8: Database Administration
Test 3	Exam 1Z0-015	Oracle8: Backup and Recovery
Test 4	Exam 1Z0-014	Oracle8: Performance Tuning
Test 5	Exam 1Z0-016	Oracle8: Network Administration

* If you are currently an OCP certified in Oracle7.3, you need take only the upgrade exam (Oracle8: New Features for Administrators, Exam 1Z0-010) to be certified in Oracle8.

- *Introduction to Oracle: SQL and PL/SQL (Exam 1Z0-001)*—Test 1 is the base test for the series. Knowledge tested in Test 1 will also be used in all other tests in the DBA series. Besides testing knowledge of SQL and PL/SQL language constructs, syntax, and usage, Test 1 covers Data Definition Language (DDL), Data Manipulation Language (DML), and Data Control Language (DCL). Also covered in Test 1 are basic data modeling and database design.

- *Oracle8: Database Administration (Exam 1Z0-013)*—Test 2 deals with all levels of database administration in Oracle8 (primarily version 8.0.5 and above). Topics include architecture, startup and shutdown, database creation, managing database internal and external constructs (such as redo logs, rollback segments, and tablespaces), and all other Oracle structures. Database auditing, use of National Language Support (NLS) features, and use of SQL*Loader and other utilities are also covered.

- *Oracle8: Backup and Recovery (Exam 1Z0-015)*—Test 3 covers one of the most important parts of the Oracle DBA's job: database backup and recovery operations. Test 3 tests knowledge in backup and recovery motives, architecture as it relates to backup and recovery, backup methods, failure scenarios, recovery methodologies, archive logging, supporting 24x7 shops, and troubleshooting. The test also covers the use of Recovery Manager (**RMAN**), new in Oracle8.

- *Oracle8: Performance Tuning (Exam 1Z0-014)*—Test 4 covers all aspects of tuning an Oracle8 database. Topics in both application and database tuning are covered. The exam tests knowledge in diagnosis of tuning problems, database optimal configuration, shared pool tuning, buffer cache tuning, Oracle block usage, tuning rollback segments and redo mechanisms, monitoring and detection lock contention, tuning sorts, tuning in OLTP, DSS, and mixed environments, and load optimization.

- *Oracle8: Network Administration (Exam 1Z0-016)*—Test 5 covers all parts of the Net8 product: NET8, Oracle Names Server, the listener process, **lsnrctl** (the listener control utility), and the NET8 configuration files sqlnet.ora, tnsnames.ora, and listener.ora.

To obtain an OCP certificate in database administration, an individual must pass all five exams. You do not have to take the tests in any particular order. However, it is usually better to take the examinations in order, because the knowledge tested builds from each exam. The core exams require individuals to demonstrate competence with all phases of Oracle8 database lifetime activities. If you already have your Oracle7.3 certification, you need to take only one exam—Oracle8: New Features for Administrators (Exam 1Z0-010)—to upgrade your status.

It's not uncommon for the entire process to take a year or so, and many individuals find that they must take a test more than once to pass. The primary goal of the *Exam Cram* series is to make it possible, given proper study and preparation, to pass all of the OCP-DBA tests on the first try.

Finally, certification is an ongoing activity. Once an Oracle version becomes obsolete, OCP-DBAs (and other OCPs) typically have a six-month time frame in which they can become recertified on current product versions. (If an individual does not get recertified within the specified time period, his or her certification becomes invalid.) Because technology keeps changing and new products continually supplant old ones, this should come as no surprise.

The best place to keep tabs on the OCP program and its various certifications is on the Oracle Web site. The current root URL for the OCP program is at **http://education.oracle.com/certification**. Oracle's certification Web site changes frequently, so if this URL doesn't work, try using the Search tool on Oracle's site (**www.oracle.com**) with either "OCP" or the quoted phrase "Oracle Certified Professional Program" as the search string. This will help you find the latest and most accurate information about the company's certification programs.

Taking A Certification Exam

Alas, testing is not free. You'll be charged $125 for each test you take, whether you pass or fail. In the United States and Canada, tests are administered by Sylvan Prometric. Sylvan Prometric can be reached at 800-891-3926, any time from 7:00 A.M. to 6:00 P.M., Central Time, Monday through Friday. If you can't get through at this number, try 612-896-7000 or 612-820-5707.

To schedule an exam, call at least one day in advance. To cancel or reschedule an exam, you must call at least one day before the scheduled test time (or you may be charged the $125 fee). When calling Sylvan Prometric, have the following information ready for the telesales staffer who handles your call:

- Your name, organization, and mailing address.
- The name of the exam you want to take.
- A method of payment. (The most convenient approach is to supply a valid credit card number with sufficient available credit. Otherwise, payments by check, money order, or purchase order must be received before a test can be scheduled. If the latter methods are required, ask your order-taker for more details.)

You will be sent an appointment confirmation by mail if you register more than five days before an exam, or by fax if you register less than five days before the exam. A Candidate Agreement letter, which you must sign to take the examination, will also be provided.

On the day of the test, try to arrive at least 15 minutes before the scheduled time slot. You must supply two forms of identification, one of which must be a photo ID.

All exams are completely closed book. In fact, you will not be permitted to take anything with you into the testing area. I suggest that you review the most critical information about the test you're taking just before the test. (*Exam Cram* books provide a brief reference—The Cram Sheet, located inside the front of this book—that lists the essential information from the book in distilled form.) You will have some time to compose yourself, to mentally review this critical information, and even to take a sample orientation exam before you begin the real thing. I suggest you take the orientation test before taking your first exam; they're all more or less identical in layout, behavior, and controls, so you probably won't need to do this more than once.

When you complete an Oracle8 certification exam, the testing software will tell you whether you've passed or failed. Results are broken into several topical areas. Whether you pass or fail, I suggest you ask for—and keep—the detailed report that the test administrator prints for you. You can use the report to help you prepare for another go-round, if necessary, and even if you pass, the report shows areas you may need to review to keep your edge. In the event you failed the test, try to write down all the questions that you can remember so you can incorporate them into your retake test preparation. If you need to retake an exam, you'll have to call Sylvan Prometric, schedule a new test date, and pay another $125.

Tracking OCP Status

Oracle generates transcripts that indicate the exams you have passed and your corresponding test scores. After you pass the necessary set of five exams, you'll be certified as an Oracle8 DBA. Official certification normally takes anywhere from four to six weeks (generally within 30 days), so don't expect to get your credentials overnight. Once certified, you will receive a package with a Welcome Kit that contains a number of elements:

- An OCP-DBA certificate, suitable for framing.
- A credit-card sized card with your name, the certification track, and the effective date, suitable for your wallet and can be used as a proof of certification.
- An OCP-pin for your decorative needs.
- A license agreement to use the OCP logo. Once it is sent into Oracle and your packet of logo information is received, the license agreement allows you to use the logo for advertisements, promotions, documents, letterhead, business cards, and so on. An OCP logo sheet, which includes camera-ready artwork, comes with the license.

Many people believe that the benefits of OCP certification go well beyond the perks that Oracle provides to newly anointed members of this elite group. I am starting to see more job listings that request or require applicants to have an OCP-DBA certification, and many individuals who complete the program can qualify for increases in pay and/or responsibility. As an official recognition of hard work and broad knowledge, OCP certification is a badge of honor in many IT organizations.

How To Prepare For An Exam

At a minimum, preparing for OCP-DBA exams requires that you obtain and study the following materials:

- The Oracle8 Server version 8.0.5 Documentation Set on CD-ROM.
- The exam preparation materials, practice tests, and self-assessment exams on the Oracle certification page (**http://education.oracle.com/certification**). Find the materials, download them, and use them!
- This *Exam Cram* book. It's the first and last thing you should read before taking the exam.

In addition, you'll probably find any or all of the following materials useful in your quest for Oracle8 DBA expertise:

- *OCP resource kits*—Oracle Corporation has a CD-ROM with example questions and materials to help with the exam; generally, these are provided free by requesting them from your Oracle representative. They have also been offered free for the taking at most Oracle conventions, such as IOUGA-Alive! and Oracle Open World.
- *Classroom training*—Oracle, TUSC, LearningTree, and many others offer classroom and computer-based training-type material that you will find useful to help you prepare for the exam. But a word of warning: These classes are fairly expensive (in the range of $300 per day of training). However, they do offer a condensed form of learning to help you brush up on your Oracle knowledge. The tests are closely tied to the classroom training provided by Oracle, so I would suggest taking at least the introductory classes to get the Oracle-specific (and classroom-specific) terminology under your belt.
- *Other publications*—You'll find direct references to other publications and resources in this book, and there's no shortage of materials available about Oracle8 DBA topics. To help you sift through some of the publications out there, I end each chapter with a "Need To Know More?" section that provides pointers to more complete and exhaustive resources covering the chapter's subject matter. This section tells you where to look for further details.
- *The Oracle Support CD-ROM*—Oracle provides a Support CD-ROM on a quarterly basis. This CD-ROM contains useful white papers, bug reports, technical bulletins, and information about release-specific bugs, fixes, and new features. Contact your Oracle representative for a copy.
- *The Oracle Administrator and PL/SQL Developer*—These are online references from RevealNet, Inc., an Oracle and database online reference provider. These online references provide instant lookup on thousands of database and developmental topics and are an invaluable resource for study and learning about Oracle. Demo copies can be downloaded from **www.revealnet.com**. Also available at the RevealNet Web site are the DBA and PL/SQL Pipelines, online discussion groups where you can obtain expert information from Oracle DBAs worldwide. These applications run about $400 each (current pricing is available on the Web site) and are worth every cent.

These required and recommended materials represent a nonpareil collection of sources and resources for Oracle8 DBA topics and software. In the section that follows, I explain how this book works and give you some good reasons why this book should also be on your required and recommended materials list.

About This Book

Each topical *Exam Cram* chapter follows a regular structure, along with graphical cues about especially important or useful material. Here's the structure of a typical chapter:

- *Opening hotlists*—Each chapter begins with lists of the terms, tools, and techniques that you must learn and understand before you can be fully conversant with the chapter's subject matter. I follow the hotlists with one or two introductory paragraphs to set the stage for the rest of the chapter.
- *Topical coverage*—After the opening hotlists, each chapter covers a series of topics related to the chapter's subject. Throughout this section, I highlight material most likely to appear on a test using a special Exam Alert layout, like this:

This is what an Exam Alert looks like. Normally, an Exam Alert stresses concepts, terms, software, or activities that will most likely appear in one or more certification test questions. For that reason, any information found offset in Exam Alert format is worthy of unusual attentiveness on your part. Indeed, most of the facts appearing in The Cram Sheet appear as Exam Alerts within the text.

Occasionally in *Exam Crams*, you'll see tables called "Vital Statistics." The contents of Vital Statistics tables are worthy of an extra once-over. These tables contain informational tidbits that might show up in a test question.

Even if material isn't flagged as an Exam Alert or included in a Vital Statistics table, *all* the contents of this book are associated, at least tangentially, to something test-related. This book is tightly focused for quick test preparation, so you'll find that what appears in the meat of each chapter is critical knowledge.

I have also provided tips that will help build a better foundation of data administration knowledge. Although the information may not be on the exam, it is highly relevant and will help you become a better test-taker.

This is how tips are formatted. Keep your eyes open for these, and you'll become a test guru in no time!

- *Practice questions*—A section at the end of each chapter presents a series of mock test questions and explanations of both correct and incorrect answers. I also try to point out especially tricky questions by using a special icon, like this:

  Ordinarily, this icon flags the presence of an especially devious question, if not an outright trick question. Trick questions are calculated to "trap" you if you don't read them carefully, and more than once at that. Although they're not ubiquitous, such questions make regular appearances in the Oracle8 exams. That's why exam questions are as much about reading comprehension as they are about knowing DBA material inside out and backward.

- *Details and resources*—Every chapter ends with a section titled "Need To Know More?" This section provides direct pointers to Oracle and third-party resources that offer further details on the chapter's subject matter. If you find a resource you like in this collection, use it, but don't feel compelled to use all these resources. On the other hand, I recommend only resources I use on a regular basis, so none of my recommendations will be a waste of your time or money.

The bulk of this book follows this chapter structure slavishly, but I would like to point out a few other elements. Chapter 15 includes a sample test that provides a good review of the material presented throughout the book to ensure you're ready for the exam. Chapter 16 provides an answer key to the sample test. In addition, you'll find a handy glossary and an index.

Finally, look for The Cram Sheet, which appears inside the front of this *Exam Cram* book. It is a valuable tool that represents a condensed and compiled collection of facts, figures, and tips that I think you should memorize before taking the test. Because you can dump this information out of your head onto a piece of paper before answering any exam questions, you can master this information by brute force—you need to remember it only long enough to write it down when you walk into the test room. You might even want to look at it in the car or in the lobby of the testing center just before you walk in to take the test.

How To Use This Book

If you're prepping for a first-time test, I've structured the topics in this book to build on one another. Therefore, some topics in later chapters make more sense after you've read earlier chapters. That's why I suggest you read this book from front to back for your initial test preparation.

If you need to brush up on a topic or you have to bone up for a second try, use the index or table of contents to go straight to the topics and questions that you need to study. Beyond the tests, I think you'll find this book useful as a tightly focused reference to some of the most important aspects of topics associated with being a DBA, as implemented under Oracle8.

Given all the book's elements and its specialized focus, I've tried to create a tool that you can use to prepare for—and pass—the Oracle OCP-DBA set of examinations. Please share your feedback on the book with me, especially if you have ideas about how I can improve it for future test-takers. I'll consider everything you say carefully, and I try to respond to all suggestions. You can reach me via email at **dw4ocpbook@yahoo.com**. Also, be sure to check out the Web pages at **www.certificationinsider.com**, where you'll find information updates, commentary, and certification information.

Thanks, and enjoy the book!

Self-Assessment

I've included a Self-Assessment in this *Exam Cram* to help you evaluate your readiness to tackle Oracle Certified Professional-Oracle8 Certified Database Administrator (OCP-DBA) certification. It should also help you understand what you need to master the topic of this book—namely, Exam 1Z0-015 (Test 3), "Oracle8 Background Recovery." But before you tackle this Self-Assessment, let's talk about the concerns you may face when pursuing an Oracle8 OCP-DBA certification, and what an ideal Oracle8 OCP-DBA candidate might look like.

Oracle8 OCP-DBAs In The Real World

In the next section, I describe an ideal Oracle8 OCP-DBA candidate, knowing full well that only a few actual candidates meet this ideal. In fact, my description of that ideal candidate might seem downright scary. But take heart; although the requirements to obtain an Oracle8 OCP-DBA may seem pretty formidable, they are by no means impossible to meet. However, you should be keenly aware that it does take time, requires some expense, and consumes a substantial effort.

You can get all the real-world motivation you need from knowing that many others have gone before you. You can follow in their footsteps. If you're willing to tackle the process seriously and do what it takes to obtain the necessary experience and knowledge, you can take—and pass—the certification tests. In fact, the *Exam Crams* are designed to make it as easy as possible for you to prepare for these exams. But prepare you must!

The same, of course, is true for other Oracle certifications, including the following:

- Oracle7.3 OCP-DBA, which is similar to the Oracle8 OCP-DBA certification but requires only four core exams.
- Application Developer, Oracle Developer Rel 1 OCP, which is aimed at software developers and requires five exams.
- Application Developer, Oracle Developer Rel 2 OCP, which is aimed at software developers and requires five exams.

- Oracle Database Operators OCP, which is aimed at database operators and requires only one exam.
- Oracle Java Technology Certification OCP, which is aimed at Java developers and requires five exams.

The Ideal Oracle8 OCP-DBA Candidate

Just to give you some idea of what an ideal Oracle8 OCP-DBA candidate is like, here are some relevant statistics about the background and experience such an individual might have. Don't worry if you don't meet these qualifications (or if you don't even come close), because this world is far from ideal, and where you fall short is simply where you'll have more work to do. The ideal candidate will have the following:

- Academic or professional training in relational databases, Structured Query Language (SQL), performance tuning, backup and recovery, and Net8 administration.
- Three-plus years of professional database administration experience, including experience installing and upgrading Oracle executables, creating and tuning databases, troubleshooting connection problems, creating users, and managing backup and recovery scenarios.

I believe that well under half of all certification candidates meet these requirements. In fact, most probably meet less than half of these requirements (that is, at least when they begin the certification process). But, because all those who have their certifications already survived this ordeal, you can survive it, too—especially if you heed what this Self-Assessment can tell you about what you already know and what you need to learn.

Put Yourself To The Test

The following series of questions and observations is designed to help you figure out how much work you'll face in pursuing Oracle certification and what kinds of resources you may consult on your quest. Be absolutely honest in your answers, or you'll end up wasting money on exams you're not ready to take. There are no right or wrong answers, only steps along the path to certification. Only you can decide where you really belong in the broad spectrum of aspiring candidates.

Two things should be clear from the outset, however:

- Even a modest background in computer science will be helpful.

- Hands-on experience with Oracle products and technologies is an essential ingredient to certification success.

Educational Background

It is also important to assess your educational background:

1. Have you ever taken any computer-related classes? [Yes or No]

   If Yes, proceed to question 2; if No, proceed to question 4.

2. Have you taken any classes on relational databases? [Yes or No]

   If Yes, you will probably be able to handle Oracle's architecture and backup and recovery discussions. If you're rusty, brush up on the basic concepts of databases and backup and recovery. If the answer is No, consider some basic reading in this area. I strongly recommend a good Oracle database administration book such as *Oracle8 Administration and Management* by Michael Ault (Wiley, 1998). Or, if this title doesn't appeal to you, check out reviews for other, similar titles at your favorite online bookstore.

3. Have you taken any backup and recovery classes? [Yes or No]

   If Yes, you will probably be able to handle Oracle's backup and recovery terminology, concepts, and technologies (but brace yourself for frequent departures from normal usage). If you're rusty, brush up on basic backup and recovery concepts and terminology. If your answer is No, you might want to check out the Oracle Technet Web site (**http://technet.oracle.com**) and read some of the white papers on backup and recovery. If you have access to the Oracle MetaLink Web site or the Technet Web site, download the Oracle8 Backup and Recovery Guide manual.

4. Have you done any reading on relational databases or backup and recovery? [Yes or No]

   If Yes, review the requirements from questions 2 and 3. If you meet those, move to the next section, "Hands-On Experience." If you answered No, consult the recommended reading for both topics. This kind of strong background will be of great help in preparing you for the Oracle exams.

Hands-On Experience

Another important key to success on all of the Oracle tests is hands-on experience. If I leave you with only one realization after taking this Self-Assessment, it should be that there's no substitute for time spent installing, configuring, and using the various Oracle products upon which you'll be tested repeatedly and in depth.

5. Have you installed, configured, and worked with Oracle8, OEM, and RMAN under Windows NT or Unix? [Yes or No]

   If Yes, make sure you understand basic concepts as covered in Exam 1Z0-001, "Introduction to Oracle: SQL and PL/SQL" and advanced concepts as covered in Exam 1Z0-013, "Oracle8: Database Administration" (Test 2). You should also study the Net8 configuration and administration for Exam 1Z0-001 (Test 1), "Introduction to Oracle: SQL and PL/SQL."

You can download the candidate certification guide, objectives, practice exams, and other information about Oracle exams from the company's Training and Certification page on the Web at **http://education.oracle.com/certification**.

If you haven't worked with Oracle, you must obtain a copy of Oracle8. Then, learn about the database, Net8, and backup and recovery. Optionally, Personal Oracle8 can be used to learn about basic database administration before going to Oracle8.

For any and all of these Oracle exams, the candidate guides for the topics involved are a good study resource. You can download them free from the Oracle Web site (**http://education.oracle.com**). You can also download information on purchasing additional practice tests from Self Test Software (**www.stsware.com**) for $99 per exam.

If you have the funds or your employer will pay your way, consider taking a class at an Oracle training and education center.

Before you even think about taking any Oracle exams, make sure you've spent enough time with Oracle8 and Net8 to understand how they may be installed and configured, how to maintain such an installation, and how to troubleshoot that software when things go wrong. This will help you in the exam—as well as in real life.

Testing Your Exam-Readiness

Whether you attend a formal class on a specific topic to get ready for an exam or use written materials to study on your own, some preparation for the Oracle certification exams is essential. At $125 a try, pass or fail, you want to do everything you can to pass on your first try. That's where studying comes in.

I have included in this book several practice exam questions for each chapter and a sample test, so if you don't score well on the chapter questions, you can study more and then tackle the sample test at the end of the book. If you don't earn a score of at least 70 percent after this test, you'll want to investigate the other practice test resources I mention in this section.

For any given subject, consider taking a class if you've tackled self-study materials, taken the test, and failed anyway. If you can afford the privilege, the opportunity to interact with an instructor and fellow students can make all the difference in the world. For information about Oracle classes, visit the Training and Certification page at **http://education.oracle.com**.

If you can't afford to take a class, visit the Training and Certification page anyway, because it also includes free practice exams that you can download. Even if you can't afford to spend much, you should still invest in some low-cost practice exams from commercial vendors such as Self Test Software, because they can help you assess your readiness to pass a test better than any other tool.

6. Have you taken a practice exam on your chosen test subject? [Yes or No]

   If Yes—and you scored 70 percent or better—you're probably ready to tackle the real thing. If your score isn't above that crucial threshold, keep at it until you break that barrier. If you answered No, obtain all the free and low-budget practice tests you can find (or afford) and get to work. Keep at it until you can comfortably break the passing threshold.

There is no better way to assess your test readiness than to take a good-quality practice exam and pass with a score of 70 percent or better. When I'm preparing, I shoot for 75-plus percent, just to leave room for the "weirdness factor" that sometimes shows up on Oracle exams.

Assessing Your Readiness For Exam 1Z0-015 (Test 3)

In addition to the general exam-readiness information in the previous section, other resources are available to help you prepare for the Oracle8: Backup and Recovery exam. For starters, visit the RevealNet pipeline (**www.revealnet.com**) or **http://technet.oracle.com**. These are great places to ask questions and get good answers, or simply to observe the questions that others ask (along with the answers, of course).

Oracle exam mavens also recommend checking the Oracle Knowledge Base from RevealNet. You can get information on purchasing the RevealNet software at **www.revealnet.com**.

For Oracle8: Backup and Recovery preparation in particular, I'd also like to recommend that you check out one or more of these books as you prepare to take the exam:

- Dialeris, Connie. *Oracle8 Backup and Recovery Guide Release 8.0*, Part No. A58396-01, Oracle Corporation, 1997.
- Loney, Kevin. *Oracle8 DBA Handbook*, Oracle Press, 1999.
- Velpuri, Rama. *Oracle Backup and Recovery Handbook*, Oracle Press, 1998.

Stop by your favorite bookstore, online bookseller, or the Oracle store to check out one or more of these books. In my opinion, these books are the best general all around references on Oracle8 backup and recovery available.

One last note: Hopefully, it makes sense to stress the importance of hands-on experience in the context of the Oracle8: Backup and Recovery exam. As you review the material for this exam, you'll realize that hands-on experience with Oracle8 commands, tools, and utilities is invaluable.

Onward, Through The Fog!

Once you've assessed your readiness, undertaken the right background studies, obtained the hands-on experience that will help you understand the products and technologies at work, and reviewed the many sources of information to help you prepare for a test, you'll be ready to take a round of practice tests. When your scores come back positive enough to get you through the exam, you're ready to go after the real thing. If you follow my assessment regime, you'll not only know what you need to study, but you'll also know when you're ready to make a test date at Sylvan. Good luck!

Oracle OCP Certification Exams

Terms you'll need to understand:

- √ Radio button
- √ Checkbox
- √ Exhibit
- √ Multiple-choice question formats
- √ Careful reading
- √ Process of elimination

Techniques you'll need to master:

- √ Assessing your exam-readiness
- √ Preparing to take a certification exam
- √ Practicing (to make perfect)
- √ Making the best use of the testing software
- √ Budgeting your time
- √ Saving the hardest questions until last
- √ Guessing (as a last resort)

As experiences go, test-taking is not something that most people anticipate eagerly; no matter how well they're prepared. But in most cases, familiarity helps ameliorate test anxiety. In plain English, this means you probably won't be as nervous when you take your fourth or fifth Oracle certification exam, as you will be when you take your first one.

No matter whether it's your first test or your tenth, understanding the exam-taking particulars (how much time to spend on questions, the setting you'll be in, and so on), and the testing software will help you concentrate on the material rather than on the environment. Likewise, mastering a few basic test-taking skills should help you recognize—and perhaps even outfox—some of the tricks and gotchas you're bound to find in the Oracle test questions.

In this chapter, I'll explain the testing environment and software, as well as describe some proven test-taking strategies you should be able to use to your advantage.

Assessing Exam-Readiness

Before you take any Oracle exam, I strongly recommend that you read through and take the Self-Assessment included with this book (it appears just before this chapter, in fact). This will help you compare your knowledge base to the requirements for obtaining an Oracle Certified Professional (OCP) certification, and it will also help you identify the areas of your background or experience that may benefit from improvement, enhancement, or further learning. If you get the right set of basics under your belt, obtaining Oracle certification will be that much easier.

Once you've gone through the Self-Assessment, you can work on those topical areas where your background or experience may not measure up. You can also tackle subject matter for individual tests at the same time, so you can continue making progress while you're catching up in some areas.

Once you've worked through an *Exam Cram*, have read the supplementary materials, and have taken the practice test at the end of the book, you'll have a pretty clear idea of when you'll be ready to take the real exam. Although I strongly recommend that you keep practicing until your scores top the 70 percent mark, 75 percent would be an even better goal to give yourself some margin for error in a real exam situation (where stress will play more of a role than when you practice). Once you hit that point, you should be ready to go. If you get through the practice exam in this book without attaining that score, you should keep taking practice tests and studying the materials until you get there. You'll find more information about other practice test vendors in the Self-Assessment, along with even more pointers on how to study and prepare. But now, on to the exam itself!

The Testing Situation

When you arrive at the Sylvan Prometric Testing Center where you scheduled your test, you'll need to sign in with a test coordinator. He or she will ask you to produce two forms of identification, one of which must be a photo ID. Once you've signed in and your time slot arrives, you'll be asked to leave any books, bags, or other items you brought with you, and you'll be escorted into a closed room. Typically, that room will be furnished with anywhere from one to half a dozen computers, and each workstation is separated from the others by dividers designed to keep you from seeing what's happening on someone else's computer.

You'll be furnished with a pen or pencil and a blank sheet of paper, or in some cases, an erasable plastic sheet and an erasable felt-tip pen. You're allowed to write down any information you want on this sheet, and you can write on both sides of the page. I suggest that you memorize as much as possible of the material that appears on The Cram Sheet (inside the front of this book), and then write that information down on the blank sheet as soon as you sit down in front of the test machine. You can refer to the sheet any time you like during the test, but you'll have to surrender it when you leave the room.

Most test rooms feature a wall with a large window. This allows the test coordinator to monitor the room, to prevent test-takers from talking to one another, and to observe anything out of the ordinary that might go on. The test coordinator will have preloaded the Oracle certification test you've signed up for, and you'll be permitted to start as soon as you're seated in front of the machine.

All Oracle certification exams permit you to take up to a certain maximum amount of time (usually 90 minutes) to complete the test (the test itself will tell you, and it maintains an on-screen counter/clock so that you can check the time remaining any time you like). Each exam consists of between 60 and 70 questions, randomly selected from a pool of questions.

The passing score varies per exam and the questions selected. For Exam 1Z0-015, "Oracle8: Backup and Recovery," the passing score is 70 percent.

All Oracle certification exams are computer generated and use a multiple-choice format. Although this might sound easy, the questions are constructed not just to check your mastery of basic facts and figures about Oracle8 database administrator (DBA) topics, but also to require you to evaluate one or more sets of circumstances or requirements. Often, you'll be asked to give more than one answer to a question; likewise, you may be asked to select the best or most effective solution to a problem from a range of choices, all of which technically are correct. The tests are quite an adventure, and they involve real thinking. This book will show you what to expect and how to deal with the problems, puzzles, and predicaments you're likely to find on the tests—in particular, Exam 1Z0-015, "Oracle8: Backup and Recovery."

Test Layout And Design

A typical test question is depicted in Question 1. It's a multiple-choice question that requires you to select a single correct answer. Following the question is a brief summary of each potential answer and an explanation as to why it was either right or wrong.

Question 1

What is the DBA's most important responsibility?

- ❍ a. Keeping the database organized
- ❍ b. Keeping up-to-date backups
- ❍ c. Maximizing database availability for user
- ❍ d. Preventing users from corrupting the database

The correct answer is c. The database is of no value to the organization if it is not available for use. Answers a, b, and d are incorrect, because although they are responsibilities of the DBA, they are not the most important responsibility.

This sample question corresponds closely to those you'll see on Oracle certification tests. To select the correct answer during the test, you would position the cursor over the radio button next to answer c and click the mouse to select that particular choice. The only difference between the certification test and this question is that the real questions are not immediately followed by the answers.

Next, I'll examine a question where one or more answers are possible. This type of question provides checkboxes, rather than radio buttons, for marking all appropriate selections.

Question 2

The Oracle server automatically handles which of the following recovery operations? [Choose two answers]

- ❑ a. Backup file restorations
- ❑ b. Roll-forward operations
- ❑ c. Rollback operations
- ❑ d. Control file creation

The correct answers for this question are b and c. The Oracle server automatically performs instance recovery at instance start when required. The recovery process involves two stages: the roll-forward phase and the rollback phase. In the roll-forward phase, the Oracle server applies changes in the redo log files to the data files. During the rollback phase, the Oracle server removes any uncommitted data from the data files. Answer a is incorrect, because backup file restorations are typically handled by the DBA, not by the Oracle server. Answer d is incorrect, because control file creation is performed by the DBA, not by the Oracle server.

For this type of question, you must select one or more answers to answer the question correctly. For Question 2, you would have to check the checkboxes next to items b and c to obtain credit for a correct answer.

These two basic types of questions can appear in many forms. They constitute the foundation on which all the Oracle certification exam questions rest. More complex questions may include so-called "exhibits," which are usually tables or data-content layouts of one form or another. You'll be expected to use the information displayed in the exhibit to guide your answer to the question.

Other questions involving exhibits may use charts or diagrams to help document a workplace scenario that you'll be asked to troubleshoot or configure. Paying careful attention to such exhibits is the key to success—be prepared to toggle between the picture and the question as you work. Often, both are complex enough that you might not be able to remember all of either one.

Using Oracle's Test Software Effectively

A well-known test-taking principle is to read over the entire test from start to finish first, but to answer only those questions that you feel absolutely sure of on the first pass. On subsequent passes, you can dive into more complex questions, knowing how many such questions you have to deal with.

Fortunately, Oracle test software makes this approach easy to implement. At the bottom of each question, you'll find a checkbox that permits you to mark that question for a later visit. (Note that marking questions makes review easier, but you can also return to any question by clicking on the Forward and Back buttons repeatedly until you get to the question.) As you read each question, if you answer only those you're sure of and mark for review those that you're not, you can keep going through a decreasing list of open questions as you knock the trickier ones off in order.

There's at least one potential benefit to reading the test over completely before answering the trickier questions: Sometimes, you find information in later questions that shed more light on earlier ones. Other times, information you read in later questions might jog your memory about Oracle8 DBA facts, figures, or behavior that also help with earlier questions. Either way, you'll come out ahead if you defer those questions you're not absolutely sure of.

Keep working on the questions until you are absolutely sure of all your answers or until you know you'll run out of time. If you still have unanswered questions, zip through them and guess. No answer guarantees you'll receive no credit for a question, and a guess has at least a chance of being correct. (Oracle scores blank answers and incorrect answers as equally wrong.)

At the very end of your test period, you're better off guessing than leaving questions blank or unanswered.

Taking Testing Seriously

The most important advice I can give you about taking any Oracle test is this: Read each question carefully. Some questions are deliberately ambiguous—some use double negatives, others use terminology in incredibly precise ways. I've taken numerous practice tests and real tests myself, and in nearly every test, I've missed at least one question because I didn't read it closely or carefully enough.

Here are some suggestions on how to deal with the tendency to jump to an answer too quickly:

- Make sure you read every word in the question. If you find yourself jumping ahead impatiently, go back and start over. Pay special attention to questions that ask for what is/are NOT true, because the human mind tends to see what is/are true.
- As you read, try to restate the question in your own words. If you can do this, you should be able to pick the correct answer(s) much more easily.
- When returning to a question after your initial read-through, reread every word again—otherwise, the mind falls quickly into a rut. Sometimes seeing a question afresh after turning your attention elsewhere lets you see something you missed before, but the strong tendency is to see what you've seen before. Try to avoid that tendency at all costs.
- If you return to a question more than twice, try to articulate to yourself what you don't understand about the question, why the answers don't appear to make sense, or what appears to be missing. If you chew on the subject for a while, your subconscious might provide the details that are lacking, or you may notice a "trick" that points to the right answer.

Above all, try to deal with each question by thinking through what you know about being an Oracle8 DBA—utilities, characteristics, behaviors, facts, and figures involved. By reviewing what you know (and what you've written down on your information sheet), you'll often recall or understand things sufficiently to determine the answer to the question.

Question-Handling Strategies

Based on the tests I've taken, a couple of interesting trends in the answers have become apparent. For those questions that require only a single answer, usually two or three of the answers will be obviously incorrect, and two of the answers will be plausible. But, of course, only one can be correct. Unless the answer leaps out at you (and if it does, reread the question to look for a trick; sometimes those are the ones you're most likely to get wrong), begin the process of answering by eliminating those answers that are obviously wrong.

Things to look for in the "obviously wrong" category include spurious command choices or table or view names, nonexistent software or command options, and terminology you've never seen before. If you've done your homework for a test, no valid information should be completely new to you. In that case, unfamiliar or bizarre terminology probably indicates a totally bogus answer. As long as you're sure what's right, it's easy to eliminate what's wrong.

Numerous questions assume that the default behavior of a particular Oracle utility (such as Server Manager, **IMPORT**, or **EXPORT**) is in effect. It's essential, therefore, to know and understand the default settings for Server Manager, **IMPORT**, and **EXPORT** utilities. If you know the defaults and understand what they mean, this knowledge will help you cut through many Gordian knots.

Likewise, when dealing with questions that require multiple answers, you must know and select all of the correct options to get credit. This, too, qualifies as an example of why careful reading is so important.

As you work your way through the test, another counter that Oracle thankfully provides will come in handy—the number of questions completed and questions outstanding. Budget your time by making sure that you've completed one-fourth of the questions one-quarter of the way through the test period (between 13 and 17 questions in the first 22 or 23 minutes). Check the time again three-quarters of the way through the test (between 39 and 51 questions in the first 66 to 69 minutes).

If you're not finished after 85 minutes, use the last five minutes to guess your way through the remaining questions. Remember, guesses are potentially more valuable than blank answers, because blanks are always wrong, but a guess might turn out to be right. If you haven't a clue with any of the remaining questions, pick answers at random, or choose all a's, b's, and so on. The important thing is to submit a test that has an answer for every question.

Mastering The Inner Game

In the final analysis, knowledge breeds confidence, and confidence breeds success. If you study the materials in this book carefully and review all of the questions at the end of each chapter, you should be aware of those areas where additional studying is required.

Next, follow up by reading some or all of the materials recommended in the "Need To Know More?" section at the end of each chapter. The idea is to become familiar enough with the concepts and situations that you find in the sample questions to be able to reason your way through similar situations on a real test. If you know the material, you have every right to be confident that you can pass the test.

Once you've worked your way through the book, take the practice test in Chapter 15. This test will provide a reality check and will help you identify topics you need to study further. Make sure you follow up and review materials related to the questions you miss before scheduling a real test. Only after you've covered all the ground and feel comfortable with the whole scope of the practice test should you take a real test.

If you take the practice test (Chapter 15) and don't score at least 70 percent, you'll want to practice further. At a minimum, download the practice tests and the Self-Assessment tests from the Oracle Education Web site's download page (**http://education.oracle.com/certification/**). If you're more ambitious or better funded, you might want to purchase a practice test from one of the third-party vendors that offers them.

Armed with the information in this book and with the determination to augment your knowledge, you should be able to pass the certification exam. But if you don't work at it, you'll spend the test fee more than once before you finally do pass. In the event you fail the exam, you should write down all the questions you can remember, because this will help you prepare for the retake exam. If you prepare seriously, the execution should go flawlessly. Good luck!

Additional Resources

By far, the best source of information about Oracle certification tests comes from Oracle itself. Because its products and technologies—and the tests that go with them—change frequently, the best place to go for exam-related information is online.

If you haven't already visited the Oracle certification pages, do so right now. As I'm writing this chapter, the certification home page resides at **http://education.oracle.com/certification/** (see Figure 1.1).

> *Note: It might not be there by the time you read this, or it may have been replaced by something new and different, because things change regularly on the Oracle site. Should this happen, please read the section titled "Coping With Change On The Web," later in this chapter.*

The menu options in the left column of the page point to the most important sources of information in the certification pages. Here's what to check out:

- *FAQs*—Frequently Asked Questions, yours may get answered here.
- *What's New*—Any new tests will be described here.
- *Test Information*—This is a detailed section that provides many jumping-off points to detailed test descriptions for the several OCP certifications.
- *Assessment Tests*—This section provides a download of the latest copy of the assessment test after you fill out an online questionnaire.

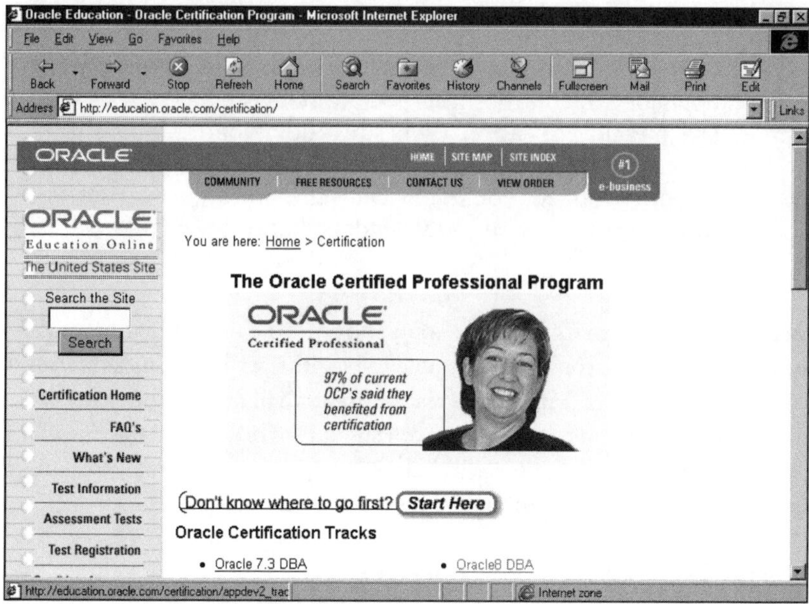

Figure 1.1 The Oracle certification page should be your starting point for further investigation of the most current exam and preparation information.

- *Test Registration*—This section provides information for phone registration and a link to the Prometric Web page for online registration. Also, this section provides a list of testing sites outside the United States.
- *Candidate Agreements*—Just what are you agreeing to be by becoming Oracle certified?
- *Oracle Partners*—This link provides information about test discounts and other offers for Oracle partner companies.

Of course, these are just the high points of what's available in the Oracle certification pages. As you browse through them—and I strongly recommend that you do—you'll probably find other things I didn't mention here that are every bit as interesting and compelling.

Coping With Change On The Web

Sooner or later, all the specifics I've shared with you about the Oracle certification pages, and all the other Web-based resources I mention throughout the rest of this book will go stale or be replaced by newer information. In some cases, the URLs you find here might lead you to their replacements; in other cases, the URLs will go nowhere, leaving you with the dreaded "404 File not found" error message.

When that happens, please don't give up. There's always a way to find what you want on the Web—if you're willing to invest some time and energy. To begin with, most large or complex Web sites—and Oracle's site qualifies on both counts—offer a search engine. As long as you can get to Oracle's home page (and I'm sure that it will stay at **www.oracle.com** for a long while yet), you can use this tool to help you find what you need.

The more particular or focused you can make a search request, the more likely it is that the results will include information you can use. For instance, you can search the string "training and certification" to produce a lot of data about the subject, in general, but if you're looking for the Preparation Guide for the Oracle DBA tests, you'll be more likely to get there quickly if you use a search string such as this:

```
"DBA" AND "preparation guide"
```

Likewise, if you want to find the training and certification downloads, try a search string such as this one:

```
"training and certification" AND "download page"
```

Finally, don't be afraid to use general search tools such as **www.search.com**, **www.altavista.com**, or **www.excite.com** to search for related information. Even though Oracle offers the best information about its certification exams online, there are plenty of third-party sources of information, training, and assistance in this area that do not have to follow a party line like Oracle does. The bottom line is this: If you can't find something where this book says it lives, start looking around. If need be, you can always email me! I just might have a clue. My email address is **dw4ocpbook@yahoo.com**.

Backup And Recovery Considerations

Terms you'll need to understand:

- √ Availability
- √ Downtime
- √ Backup
- √ Recovery
- √ Disaster
- √ Disaster recovery plan

Techniques you'll need to master:

- √ Understanding business considerations
- √ Understanding operational considerations
- √ Understanding technical considerations
- √ Understanding the importance of testing your backup and recovery strategy

In today's complex networked computing environments, enterprise databases house data that represents a valuable asset for public and private organizations. Data takes many forms—purchase orders, customer names, inventory items, taxes due, and so on. The loss of data, even for a short period of time, can translate to thousands of dollars of lost revenue and productivity.

In every database system, system failure is always a possibility. In the event of a system failure or catastrophe, the data must be recovered accurately and quickly. An Oracle database backup makes this possible; it is a copy of data that can be used to recover the original data if it is lost. The recovery process varies depending on the type of failure, the component of the database affected by the failure, and the availability of backups. Planning and implementation of an effective backup and recovery strategy are critical tasks performed by the Oracle Database Administrators (DBAs). Without an effective backup strategy, the recoverability of the database will be severely limited. To protect organizations against system failures and related data loss, a large percentage of planning, developing, and testing efforts on any computing system should be spent on backup and recovery considerations.

Creating An Effective Backup And Recovery Strategy

Every database computing environment is unique and has its own requirements. Business, operational, and technical considerations are important factors in defining an effective backup and recovery strategy for a particular site. It is important that these considerations are communicated to the appropriate level of management so that corporate resources are dedicated to ensuring a successful backup and recovery strategy. An effective backup and recovery strategy will protect the database from different types of failures and ensure high availability, minimal downtime, and complete data recovery.

When you're creating an effective backup and recovery strategy, you should keep in mind three important factors:

- Business considerations
- Operational considerations
- Technical considerations

Whatever backup approach you choose, it is important that you gain appropriate management support. All parties involved should understand the ramifications of the different backup approaches and their potential effects on recoverability.

An effective backup and recovery strategy should evolve with the business to meet ongoing needs.

Business Considerations

Any level of system downtime affects a business. To determine the costs associated with downtime and data loss, database administrators should address three business issues:

- What is the minimum downtime an organization can tolerate?
- What is the maximum amount of data an organization can afford to lose?
- How critical is the data to the business?

Once the costs of downtime and data loss have been determined, DBAs can direct their efforts toward maximizing database availability, minimizing data loss, and preventing system failure. Maximizing database availability can be accomplished using effective recovery techniques and procedures. Minimizing data loss can be achieved through effective backup methodologies. Failure can be prevented through enhanced understanding of backup and recovery structures and appropriate database configuration. As business needs change over time, an organization should regularly review its backup and recovery strategy to incorporate new or changed business needs.

Operational Considerations

Two issues affect operational needs for backup and recovery:

- Business needs
- Database volatility

Business Needs

Different types of businesses have different operational needs. An online catalog business, for instance, may require around-the-clock database availability—it must be continuously available 24 hours a day, 7 days a week. Every second the database is not operational could lead to lost revenues and dissatisfied customers. In such a case when no downtime is tolerated, *online (hot) backups*, in which the database is backed up while it is still online, should be considered. On the other hand, the database for a professional membership organization is less mission-critical and there are periods of time the database could be shut down for maintenance operations. In this case, the DBA should consider *offline (cold) backups*, in which the database is first shut down and then the database files are backed up. Database backup and recovery configurations should be tailored to support different business operational needs.

Database Volatility

Database volatility concerns how often changes occur to the data and the structure of the database. Changes can be triggered from the following database operations:

- Inserting, updating, or deleting of rows in existing tables
- Adding new tables
- Creating or dropping tablespaces
- Adding or renaming data files
- Adding, renaming, or dropping an online redo log group or member

Frequent backups are critical for any recovery approach. The frequency of backups should be based on how often changes occur to the data and the structure of the database. If the database sustains high update activity, database backup frequency should be proportionally high. On the other hand, if the database is static, the database can be backed up less frequently. Highly volatile databases generally require more frequent backups than static read-only databases.

Technical Considerations

Effective use of system resources is the key element in the technical needs for backup and recovery. The types of backups affect available system storage space. The two types of backups are typically referred to as physical or logical backups. The physical backups can be taken while the database is online (open) or offline (closed). The physical backups involve making physical copies of operating system files associated with the database. The logical backups are copies of data and structural definitions in a proprietary Oracle binary format other than the format of the physical database files. The logical backups are typically generated by the Oracle EXPORT utility and used by the Oracle IMPORT utility. These utilities are covered in more detail in Chapter 13. Physical backups require greater storage space requirements than logical backups. Logical backups may affect the load on system resources, because they are performed while the database is online and is being accessed by other database users.

The amount of modification activity sustained by the database will affect how frequently backups are made. If frequent backups must be made, as for a 24×7 business, this will increase the load on system resources. If the data can be recreated easily or the data is available from an alternate source such as a flat file, then less frequent backups are required and therefore have less impact on system resources. Different database configurations have different needs for system resources.

A thorough understanding of the business, operational, and technical requirements will ensure an effective backup and recovery strategy that will protect the database from different types of failures and ensure high availability, minimal downtime, and complete data recovery.

Disaster Recovery Plans

As organizations deploy a greater number of mission-critical applications over distributed networks, they become more vulnerable to potential disasters. A *disaster* is any event that creates an inability on an organization's part to provide critical business functions for some predetermined period of time. A disaster could be one of the following representative incidents:

- Natural disasters (e.g., flood, fire, snow storm, earthquake, and so on)
- Blackouts
- Hardware failure
- Viruses
- Theft
- Key personnel departure/critical illness of essential staff

Disaster recovery is the ability to recover from a disaster and to resume business functions in a timely manner. Disaster recovery has gained importance in recent years due to the expanding role of computers and the increasing occurrence of various types of disasters.

A *disaster recovery plan* is the document that defines the resources, actions, tasks, and data required to manage the business recovery process in the event of a business interruption. The plan is designed to assist in restoring the business process following a catastrophic event by minimizing risk and optimizing recovery time. Many people don't bother creating disaster recovery plans because they believe their business is not at high risk for disaster. The World Trade Center and the Oklahoma Federal Building were not high-risk areas, but each was hit with events that crippled many businesses. Any disaster can affect the availability, integrity, and confidentiality of critical business resources and leave an organization paralyzed.

A disaster recovery plan should include these four components:

- Data
- Equipment
- Facilities
- Personnel

Data

One of the cardinal rules in using computers is to back up your files regularly. Even the most reliable computer is apt to break down eventually. Backups should include data files, as well as complete system backups. It is also prudent to perform a backup before and after a major upgrade. The type of media to be used depends on your needs. Common choices are tapes and CDs. Tapes support large capacity and are reusable. CDs have lower storage capacity, but are more durable and easier to use for partial restorations. To protect these archive storage media from damage, a sturdy fire- and waterproof box should be acquired. To be especially safe, you should keep one backup in a different location from the others. You should select an offsite storage facility that allows rapid access to your data. You will also need to have a reasonable schedule for regularly updating the offsite data.

Equipment

Critical machines used by the organization should be documented. Vital information should include what it does, the vendor, CPU, hard drive, controller, type of power supply, serial number, operating system, and so on. Determine how long replacements will take to acquire and from whom you will acquire them. Depending on the organization's system availability, you may need to consider an alternate replacement system.

Facilities

Determine what processes you will have to go through if a building-wide disaster takes place. A timeline for safety inspection and restoration of data and power should be developed. Make sure the processes fit within your business's operational requirements. An organization should also investigate alternate facilities in case of total destruction.

Personnel

Personnel are the most important resource in an organization. How will the loss of key personnel like the DBA affect the business? During a disaster, knowledgeable personnel can save the company time and money. Key personnel should not be totally irreplaceable in case of an unexpected emergency. Properly documented processes and cross training for redundancy will not only minimize the effects of a disaster, but also typically improve business processes. Educate everyone in the organization on the existence, location, and use of the Disaster Recovery Plan so that everyone will be prepared to cope if disaster strikes.

Disaster recovery plans should be a key part of any system setup. The time and money it takes to set one up is worth it in the long run. Testing the disaster recovery plan is at least as critical as developing the plan in the first place. An untested disaster recovery plan is of little or no value. Testing enables organizations to assess the effectiveness of a disaster recovery plan before a real disaster strikes.

Testing A Backup And Recovery Strategy

To ensure the effectiveness of a backup and recovery strategy, a DBA should test the backup and recovery strategy in a dummy test environment before and after moving to a production environment. Testing offers numerous benefits:

- It ensures the integrity of backups.
- It ensures that the backup and recovery methods are sound.
- It ensures that the backup and recovery strategy meets ongoing business needs.
- It minimizes problems before they occur in a production environment.
- It helps the DBA staff maintain familiarity with backup and recovery procedures so they can react quickly and effectively, and errors are less likely to occur in a crisis situation.
- It enables streamlining of the overall backup and recovery process.

A test plan should be developed and executed in support of this testing effort. The purpose of a test plan is to define the test domain, test strategy, test exit and entrance criteria, and test configurations to verify and validate functionality. When creating a test plan, you should generally accomplish the following:

- Set test objectives.
- Describe items to be tested.

- Determine testing resources.
- Compose schedules.
- Design test process/create test case design specification.
- Define test cases/create scenarios.
- Create test procedures specification.
- Evaluate scripts using walkthrough or inspection.
- Execute test cases.
- Record test results.
- Analyze test results.
- Generate management-level summary reports.

Upon successful execution of a backup and recovery test plan, the backup and recovery methodology can be promoted to the production environment.

Practice Questions

Question 1

Which of the following statements is true?

- ❍ a. Your backup strategy will not affect recoverability.
- ❍ b. Your backup strategy will determine if rollback segments are needed.
- ❍ c. Your backup strategy will help you obtain greater level of support from management.
- ❍ d. Your backup strategy will determine whether a complete or incomplete recovery is possible.

The correct answer is d. Your backup strategy will determine the types of recovery that are possible in the event of a failure. Answer a is incorrect because a backup strategy affects recoverability. Answer b is incorrect because rollback segments are not dependent on the backup strategy. Answer c is incorrect because backup strategy will not help you obtain greater support from management.

Question 2

Trick! question

What is the DBA's most important responsibility?

- ❍ a. Keeping the database organized.
- ❍ b. Keeping up-to-date backups.
- ❍ c. Maximizing database availability for users.
- ❍ d. Preventing users from corrupting the database.

The correct answer is c. The database is of no value to the organization if it is not available for use. Answers a, b, and d are responsibilities of the DBA but not the most important responsibility.

Question 3

What is needed to successfully recover an inoperative database?

- ❍ a. A valid control file.
- ❍ b. A database parameter file.
- ❍ c. A valid backup.
- ❍ d. Online log files.

The correct answer is c. For any type of recovery, a valid backup is required for the successful restoration of the database. Answer a, b, and d are incorrect because each is only a component of a valid backup.

Question 4

How will offline physical backups affect your database?

- ❍ a. It will increase disk space requirements.
- ❍ b. The backups will not be valid.
- ❍ c. It will increase recovery time from a media failure.
- ❍ d. It will increase the DBA staff's maintenance effort.

The correct answer is a. A physical backup copies each database file to the target backup location. The number of files involved in the copy operation can affect available disk space. Answer b is not correct because offline physical backups are valid backups unless testing indicates they are not valid. Answer c is incorrect because offline physical backups don't increase recovery time from a media failure. Answer d is incorrect because offline physical backups are easier to manage than online backups.

Question 5

Your company has a relatively static database that is refreshed monthly. Recovery time is not an issue with the business users. Which backup approach should you follow?

❍ a. Perform backups less frequently than a company with high data update activity.

❍ b. Perform backups more frequently than a company with high data update activity.

❍ c. Perform backups each time the database is changed.

❍ d. Backups are not necessary because the data does not change frequently.

The correct answer is a. Depending on the required recovery time, a fairly static database will need less frequent backups than a highly volatile database. Answer b is incorrect because a static database does not require more frequent backups than a volatile database. Answer c is incorrect because a static database that is refreshed monthly does not require taking a backup each time the database is changed. Answer d is incorrect because backups are still necessary but not as frequent for a static database that doesn't change frequently.

Question 6

What is the main objective for conducting a thorough analysis of the business, operational, and technical needs for backup and recovery?

❍ a. To facilitate effective management decision-making by providing information that fosters understanding of all backup and recovery ramifications.

❍ b. To maintain optimal database configuration.

❍ c. To ensure the backup and recovery strategy is sound.

❍ d. To prepare a static backup and recovery strategy.

The correct answer is a. A thorough analysis of the business, operational, and technical needs provides management with information so that an effective decision can be made and appropriate resources can be dedicated for the execution of the backup and recovery strategy. Answer b and c are incorrect because they are secondary objectives. Answer d is incorrect because a backup and recovery strategy should not be static—it should evolve with the business.

Question 7

How will minimizing recovery time affect the business?

- ❍ a. It reduces the need to regularly update the backup and recovery strategy.
- ❍ b. It reduces the cost of downtime.
- ❍ c. It reduces the amount of data loss.
- ❍ d. It helps to prevent failures from occurring.

The correct answer is b. A reduction in recovery time will shorten total downtime and thus reduce the costs associated with downtime. Answer a is incorrect because minimizing recovery time does not affect how often the backup and recovery strategy is updated. Answer c is incorrect because the amount of data loss depends on the availability of valid backups. Answer d is incorrect because appropriate database configuration and not minimization of recovery time prevents failures from occurring.

Question 8

What are the components to develop in a disaster recovery plan? [Choose all correct answers.]

- ❑ a. Data
- ❑ b. Equipment
- ❑ c. Facilities
- ❑ d. Personnel
- ❑ e. None of the above

The correct answers are a, b, c, and d. There are four components to develop in a disaster recovery plan: data, equipment, facilities, and personnel.

Question 9

You are the newly hired DBA for a pizza delivery company. What should you do to ensure that the previous DBA's backup and recovery plan is valid?

❍ a. Place 100% reliance on the documentation for the plan if it looks like it should work.

❍ b. Throw away the previous DBA's plan and write your own from scratch.

❍ c. Test the backup and recovery plan to make sure that a complete recovery is possible.

❍ d. Make sure that the documentation is correct.

The correct answer is c. All backup and recovery plans should be tested to ensure their validity and effectiveness. Answer a is incorrect because a DBA should not rely solely on documentation to determine validity. Answer b is incorrect because only testing can validate the backup and recovery plan. Answer d is incorrect because testing is required before a DBA can be sure that the documentation is correct.

Question 10

What is the main goal of backup and recovery?

❍ a. Performing backups only when absolutely necessary.

❍ b. Backing up all files.

❍ c. Keeping backed up files off-site.

❍ d. Minimizing data loss and downtime.

The correct answer is d. An effective backup and recovery strategy will minimize data loss and downtime. Answers a, b, and c are incorrect because they are supplementary goals.

Question 11

What is management's role in the development and execution of your backup and recovery strategy?

- ❍ a. To provide the necessary corporate resources and support for implementation.
- ❍ b. To provide recommendations on how to minimize downtime.
- ❍ c. To provide recommendations on how to minimize data loss.
- ❍ d. To implement the strategy.

The correct answer is a. Management is responsible for approving the appropriate resources and support for implementation. Answers b, c, and d are incorrect because they are DBA's roles.

Question 12

What is the benefit of regularly testing the validity of your backup and recovery strategy?

- ❍ a. Testing reduces the likelihood of media failures.
- ❍ b. Testing helps to identify business, operational, and technical needs that may have changed over time.
- ❍ c. Testing is the only way to ensure optimal database configuration.
- ❍ d. Testing helps management determine the costs associated with downtime.

The correct answer is b. Testing helps to assess the effectiveness of the backup and recovery strategy and to identify any new or changed requirements. Answer a is incorrect because testing does not affect the likelihood of media failures. Answer c is incorrect because testing is not the only way to ensure optimal database configuration. Answer d is incorrect because the costs associated with downtime depends on business, operational, and technical factors and not testing.

Need To Know More?

Arnold, Richard. *Disaster Recovery Plan*, John Wiley & Sons, 1993. ISBN: 0-47155-696-3.

Dialeris, Connie. *Oracle8 Backup and Recovery Guide Release 8.0*, 1997, Part No. A58396-01, Oracle Corporation.

Loney, Kevin. Oracle8 *DBA Handbook, 8.0 edition*, Oracle Press, 1997. ISBN 0-07882-289-0.

Velpuri, Rama. *Oracle Backup and Recovery Handbook*, Oracle Press, 1998. ISBN: 0-078-82389-7.

Oracle Recovery Structures And Processes

Terms you'll need to understand:

- √ Oracle database
- √ Oracle instance
- √ Database buffers
- √ Redo log buffers
- √ Shared pool
- √ Large pool
- √ Program Global Area
- √ Background processes
- √ User process
- √ Server process
- √ Online redo log
- √ Redo log group
- √ Checkpoint
- √ Log switch
- √ Archived redo log
- √ System global area
- √ Multiplexed online logs
- √ Multiplexed control files

Techniques you'll need to master:

- √ Understanding architectural components for backup and recovery
- √ Understanding the importance of redo logs, checkpoints, and archives
- √ Understanding the file synchronization process during checkpoints
- √ Understanding the benefits of multiplexing control files and redo logs

The backup and recovery functionality of Oracle relies on many components of the Oracle Server architecture. The pertinent architectural components include memory structures, background processes, and the physical database structure, as shown in Figure 3.1. A good understanding of key database structures and backup and recovery concepts will help you protect data against potential failure and facilitate an effective recovery process in the event of a problem. Key database structures and backup and recovery concepts you should focus on include the following:

- Architectural components of the Oracle server architecture
- Importance of redo logs, checkpoints, and archived redo logs
- File synchronization process during checkpoints
- Multiplexing control files and redo logs

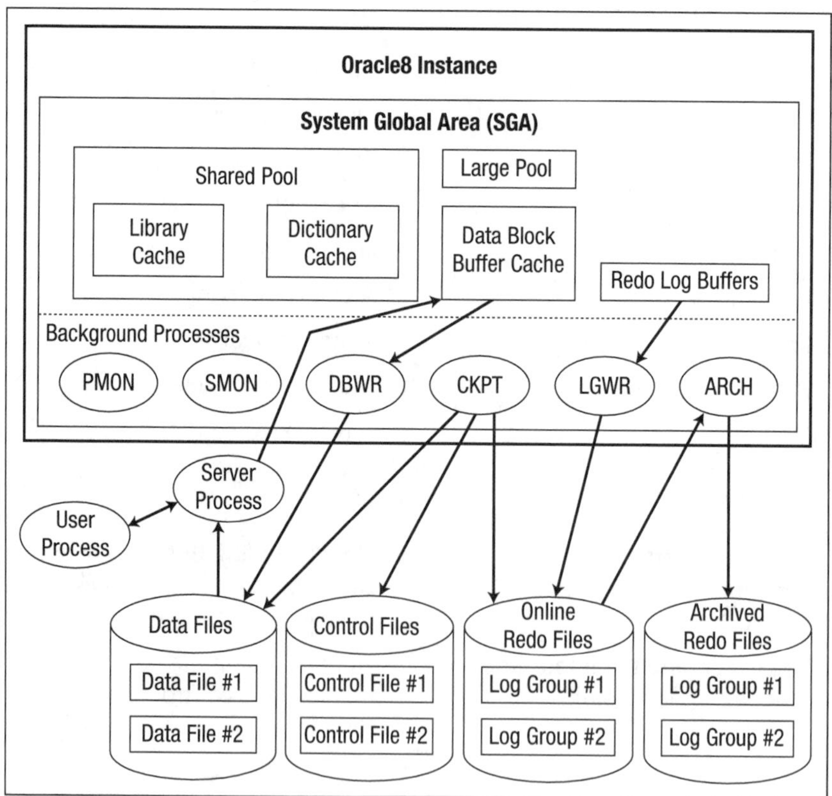

Figure 3.1 The basic Oracle8 architecture.

Architectural Components For Backup And Recovery

An Oracle server is comprised of an *Oracle instance* and an *Oracle database*. An Oracle instance is a set of memory structures and background processes that access a set of database files. An instance is not operationally effective without the user processes that submit information requests and the server processes that fulfill the requests. Multiple database instances could access a single database by using the Parallel Server option. An Oracle database is subdivided into a *physical* and a *logical* structure. This division enables the management of physical data storage to be independent from the access to logical storage structures. Oracle provides numerous data dictionary views to get information on the database and the instance.

Memory Structures

Oracle creates and uses memory structures to accomplish many tasks. One of the main tasks is to share program code and data among users. The System Global Area (SGA) is a shared memory region that holds data and control information for a database instance. Oracle allocates the SGA when an instance is started. The SGA is deallocated when the instance is shut down. The SGA is composed of the following memory elements:

- Database buffers
- Redo log buffers
- Shared pool
- Large pool
- Program Global Area (PGA)

Database Buffers

Database buffers in the SGA hold the most recently used data blocks that are read from the database files. *Database buffer cache* refers to the set of database buffers in an instance. The database buffer cache contains modified and unmodified blocks. Because the database buffer cache cannot hold all of the database's data blocks in memory concurrently, Oracle uses the Least Recently Used (LRU) algorithm to manage the available memory space. The LRU algorithm allows the most frequently used data blocks to remain in memory, which reduces the amount of disk I/O and improves database performance.

Redo Log Buffers

The redo log buffer of the SGA holds redo entries that contain the changes made to the database by database transactions. Redo entries are written to the online redo log files so they can be used in the roll-forward operations if database recovery is needed. Oracle optimizes the writing of the redo log entries to the online redo log files using batch writes. The size in bytes of the redo log buffers is specified in the **LOG_BUFFER** parameter of the init.ora file.

Shared Pool

The shared pool holds the library cache and the data dictionary cache. The library cache contains information about statements that are issued against the database. The parse tree and the execution plan for the issued statement are kept in the library cache. The library cache fosters the sharing of commonly used SQL statements. The data dictionary cache holds information about database objects that are stored in the data dictionary tables. Data dictionary information includes table descriptions, index descriptions, data file name, user account details, privileges, and the like. Oracle manages the data dictionary cache using the LRU algorithm. If the size of the data dictionary cache is inadequate, then Oracle repetitively queries the data dictionary tables for information needed by the database. These repetitive queries are known as *recursive calls*. Recursive calls affect database performance because if the data dictionary information is not found in memory due to limited cache size and cache management using the LRU algorithm, Oracle will need to get the same information repetitively, and these additional queries require additional consumption of system resources which will affect database performance. The size in bytes of the shared pool is specified in the **SHARED_POOL_SIZE** parameter of the init.ora file.

Large Pool

The large pool is an optional Oracle8 memory area. It is used to allocate sequential I/O buffers from shared memory. Recovery Manager (RMAN) uses the large pool for performing backup and restore operations. The large pool does not have an LRU list. If the **LARGE_POOL_SIZE** init.ora parameter is not set, then Oracle will attempt to allocate shared memory buffers from the shared pool in the SGA. If the **LARGE_POOL_SIZE** is set but is not adequate, the allocation fails and the buffer requester responds as follows:

- Log archiving operation fails and an error is returned.
- RMAN writes a message to the alert file and I/O slaves are not used for the operation.

The large pool has the following init.ora parameters:

- *LARGE_POOL_SIZE*—If unspecified, the large pool does not exist. If specified, the size of memory is allocated from the SGA.
- *LARGE_POOL_MIN_ALLOC*—Specifies the smallest chunk of memory to be allocated from the large pool.
- *BACKUP_DISK_IO_SLAVES*—If nonzero, the I/O slaves are employed to read and write disk files for RMAN copy, backup, and restore operations. This is recommended if Oracle doesn't support native asynchronous I/O on the platform.
- *BACKUP_TAPE_IO_SLAVES*—If set to **TRUE**, RMAN's backup and restore operations will use an I/O slave to perform asynchronous I/O when reading and writing to tape. If not specified, then synchronous tape I/O will be in effect.
- *ARCH_IO_SLAVES*—If set to nonzero, then log archiving will use I/O slaves. This is recommended if Oracle doesn't support native asynchronous I/O on the platform.

Program Global Area—PGA

The Program Global Area (PGA) is a memory area reserved for a user process. The PGA memory is private to the user process and is not shareable. If the Multi-Threaded Server (MTS) configuration is in effect, then part of the PGA may exist in the SGA. The MTS configuration allows multiple user processes to use the same server process, resulting in reduction of the overall database memory requirements. If the MTS configuration is utilized, then the user session information is stored in the SGA as opposed to the PGA, and the size of the shared pool will need to be increased to accommodate the additional share memory requirements.

Background Processes

Oracle creates a set of background processes for each database instance. The number of background processes vary depending on the database's configuration. The processes are automatically managed by Oracle. The main background processes include the following:

- System Monitor (SMON)
- Process Monitor (PMON)
- Database Writer (DBWR)

- Log Writer (LGWR)
- Checkpoint (CKPT)
- Archiver (ARCH)

System Monitor—SMON

Upon starting the database, the SMON process performs instance recovery and will utilize the online redo log files when needed. Under the Parallel Server configuration, SMON of one instance can also perform instance recovery for other failed instances. SMON performs garbage collection by eliminating transactional items that are no longer needed by the system. SMON also coalesces contiguous free extents into larger free chunks.

SMON coalesces free space only in tablespaces whose default **PCTINCREASE** storage value is nonzero.

Process Monitor—PMON

The PMON background process performs process recovery for failed user processes. It frees up the resources that the failed process was holding. PMON wakes up periodically to check on dispatcher and server processes and restarts them as needed.

Database Writer—DBWR

The DBWR process manages the database buffer cache. It writes changed blocks from the database buffer cache to the data files in batch. Multiple DBWR processes can be configured to run concurrently for systems that sustain high data modification rates. The init.ora parameter **DB_WRITER_PROCESSES** can be used to specify the number of DBWR processes. Using multiple DBWR processes improves write performance and reduces contention for systems that are heavily modified. When using multiple DBWR processes, the operating system names of the processes should follow this convention: DBWn, DBWn+1, DBWn+2, and so on. If you run three DBWR processes, for instance, then the names could be DBW0, DBW1, and DBW2.

Log Writer—LGWR

The LGWR process writes the redo log entries from the redo log buffer to the online redo log files. The LGWR performs writes in batches. LGWR writes are triggered when transactions commit and the log buffer fills up. The online

redo log files are sequentially written. If the online redo log files are mirrored, LGWR writes to the mirrored sets of logs simultaneously.

Checkpoint—CKPT

The CKPT process is responsible for notifying DBWn at checkpoints so all modified data blocks in the SGA from the last checkpoint are written out to the data files. The CKPT process is always enabled. The CKPT process records the most recent checkpoint in the data file headers and the control file upon checkpoint completion.

Archiver—ARCH

The archiver is an optional process. The archiver copies the online redo log files to a designated archival destination. This process is critical in the backup and recovery of a database in **ARCHIVELOG** mode where 24×7 availability needs to be maintained.

The archiver process is triggered when a log switch occurs. When a database is run in **ARCHIVELOG** mode, the database makes a copy of each redo log file before overwriting it. When using the archiver, contention may be experienced on the redo log disk during heavy transaction processing, because LGWR is trying to write to one redo log file while ARCH is trying to read from another. Placing redo log groups on different disks can resolve this issue. If the archive log destination disk is full, the database freezes until free space is available for the archived redo log files. The init.ora parameter **LOG_ARCHIVE_DEST** can be set to specify the archival destination location.

User Processes

A user process is created when a tool such as SQL*Plus, Oracle Forms, and the like is invoked by the user. A user process could exist on the client machine or the server machine. User processes provide the interface for database users to interact with the database.

Server Processes

Oracle creates server processes to receive requests from the user processes and to carry out the requests. For example, if a user requests data that is not currently in the database buffer cache of the SGA, the associated server process will read the pertinent data blocks from the data files into the SGA. When a valid database connection is established with a database that is not using the Multi-Threaded Server (MTS) option, a server process is created on the machine holding the instance.

Physical Database Structure

An Oracle database's physical structure consists of the physical operating system files. An Oracle instance comprises three main file types: one or more control files, one or more data files, and two or more redo log files. These files must be considered when you're creating the backup strategy.

Control Files

Control files are binary files used by the Oracle server to store its configuration information. Control files record the physical structure and state of the database, while preserving internal consistency and integrity. Additionally, control files guide recovery operations. The following information exists within a control file:

- The name of the database
- The name and location of all the database files
- The name and location of all the redo log files
- The timestamp of database creation
- Checkpoint synchronization information
- Log sequence information
- Redo thread information
- Auxiliary backup information when Recovery Manager is used

An Oracle instance typically uses only one redo thread unless the parallel option is in effect.

Control files are required to mount, open, and maintain the database. These files are critical to the database, so multiple copies are typically stored online. Control files should be backed up every time structural changes are made to the database.

Control files are typically stored on different physical disks to minimize the potential loss due to disk failures. Oracle recommends a minimum of two control files on different disks.

The names of the database's control files are specified in the **CONTROL_FILES** init.ora parameter.

Data Files

Data files are the backbone of the database instance. They are the physical files that make up the tablespaces—the logical structures in which tables, indexes, and the like exist. Each tablespace consists of one or more separate physical data files. Each Oracle database has one or more physical data files, but a data file can be associated with only one database.

Every database instance must contain at least one data file for the **SYSTEM** tablespace. Once a data file has been added to a tablespace, the data file cannot be removed from the tablespace, and it cannot be associated with any other tablespace. Data files can be resized after they are created. Data files can also be set to extend automatically when the database runs out of space.

A database's data files contain all the data for the database. The data may be in one of two states: committed or uncommitted. The data files contain only committed data when the Normal or Immediate option is exercised for a clean instance shutdown. During a clean instance shutdown, all uncommitted data is rolled back and a database checkpoint event is triggered to force all committed data to disk. During a running instance, data files can contain uncommitted data when data in the memory cache has been modified but not committed and has been forced to disk when more space is needed in the memory cache. Redo logs and rollback segments may be used to synchronize the data files during the recovery process from a failure condition.

Redo Log Files

The redo log files contain all changes made to the database. The database changes that generate redo entries in the redo log files may be triggered by the following sample database transactions:

- INSERT
- UPDATE
- DELETE
- CREATE TABLE
- DROP TABLE
- CREATE INDEX
- DROP INDEX

Redo log files include online redo logs and archived redo logs.

Online redo logs record redo log entries as they occur. Redo log entries are used to reconstruct all changes made to the database. Redo log entries are stored in the redo log buffer of the System Global Area (SGA) of an Oracle instance. Whenever a transaction is committed, the Log Writer (LGWR) background process writes the committed transaction's redo log entries from the redo log buffer to the current online redo log file. Redo log entries can also be written to an online redo log file when the redo log buffers are full. Every Oracle database instance must contain at least two online redo log files. One of the required online redo log files must be available for writing. If a member of a redo log group is unavailable for writing, messages are written to the LGWR trace file and to the alert file.

Figure 3.2 illustrates the online redo log writing process. The LGWR process writes to the online redo log files in a circular fashion. The LGWR process starts by writing to the current online redo log file. When the current online redo log file is filled, the LGWR process starts writing to the next available online redo log file. A log switch occurs when LGWR stops writing to one redo log and begins writing to another. At a log switch, the current redo log group is assigned a log sequence number that identifies the information stored in that redo log group and is also used for synchronization. When the last available redo log file is filled, the LGWR process returns to the first online redo log file and overwrites the content. A DBA can manually force a log switch using the **ALTER SYSTEM SWITCH LOGFILE** command.

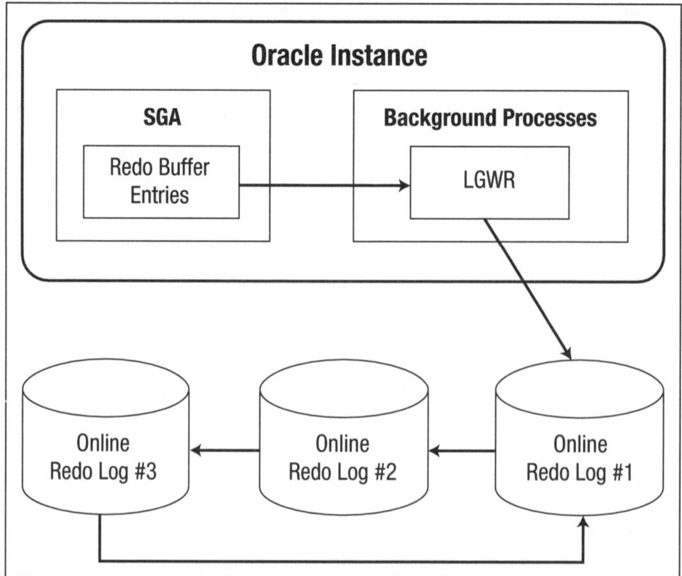

Figure 3.2 The online redo log writing process.

Each redo log entry is assigned a System Change Number (SCN) to uniquely identify the committed transactions.

The contents of an online redo log file should never be modified.

The mode in which the database runs dictates the existence of archived redo logs. An archived redo log is essentially a copy of its online redo log group. Archived logs are essential in the backup and recovery process, because along with a valid database backup, they guarantee that all committed data can be recovered in the event of a failure.

Oracle provides numerous data dictionary views to get information on the redo log files:

- *V$LOG*—Provides information on the number of members in each log group, the group number, log sequence number, size of the group, number of mirrors, status (**CURRENT** or **INACTIVE**), checkpoint change numbers, and other details.

```
SQL> desc V$LOG
 Name                           Null?    Type
 ------------------------------ -------- ----
 GROUP#                                  NUMBER
 THREAD#                                 NUMBER
 SEQUENCE#                               NUMBER
 BYTES                                   NUMBER
 MEMBERS                                 NUMBER
 ARCHIVED                                VARCHAR2(3)
 STATUS                                  VARCHAR2(16)
 FIRST_CHANGE#                           NUMBER
 FIRST_TIME                              DATE
```

- *V$LOGFILE*—Provides information on the names, status (**STALE** or **INVALID**), and group of each log file member.

```
SQL> desc V$LOGFILE
 Name                           Null?    Type
 ------------------------------ -------- ----
 GROUP#                                  NUMBER
 STATUS                                  VARCHAR2(7)
 MEMBER                                  VARCHAR2(513)
```

- *V$LOG_HISTORY*—Provides information on log history from the control file.

```
SQL> desc V$LOG_HISTORY
 Name                           Null?    Type
 ------------------------------ -------- ----
 RECID                                   NUMBER
 STAMP                                   NUMBER
 THREAD#                                 NUMBER
 SEQUENCE#                               NUMBER
 FIRST_CHANGE#                           NUMBER
 FIRST_TIME                              DATE
 NEXT_CHANGE#                            NUMBER
```

- *V$ARCHIVE_DEST*—Provides information on the location of the archived redo log destinations, status, and whether archiving success must be achieved.

```
SQL> desc V$ARCHIVE_DEST
 Name                           Null?    Type
 ------------------------------ -------- ----
 ARCMODE                                 VARCHAR2(12)
 STATUS                                  VARCHAR2(8)
 DESTINATION                             VARCHAR2(256)
```

Logical Database Structure

The logical database structure is comprised of two main constructs:

- One or more tablespaces
- Schema objects

Tablespaces

A *tablespace* is a logical storage structure that contains one or more data files. The logical storage structures, including tablespaces, segments, and extents, affect how the physical space is utilized. Tablespaces should be created judiciously, with the backup and recovery strategy kept in mind. The following are some guidelines for creating tablespaces:

- System and user data should be stored separately under different tablespaces to simplify backup and recovery operations.
- Temporary segments should exist in a dedicated tablespace so they can be recreated instead of recovered if the tablespace is lost. Temporary segments are used by Oracle for temporary storage such as sorting result

sets. Temporary segments don't contain business data. In the practical DBA world, temporary segments are typically recreated instead of recovered.

- Index data should be stored in a dedicated tablespace so it can be recreated rather than recovered.
- Data subject to frequent changes should be stored in a dedicated tablespace so that backups can be performed more frequently, which results in reduced recovery time.
- Read-only data should be stored in a dedicated tablespace to reduce overall backup time, because a backup is needed only when the tablespace is made read-only. When read-only data is centralized in a dedicated tablespace and the tablespace is designated as READONLY, a backup of this tablespace will be taken. Subsequent backups are not needed for the READONLY tablespace because the data doesn't change and the initial tablespace backup can be used to recover the read-only data. When read-only data is interspersed with data subject to change in a tablespace, the read-only data is backed up each time the tablespace is backed up. Centralizing read-only data in a dedicated tablespace reduces overall backup time because the read-only data is backed up less frequently.
- Rollback segments should exist in a dedicated tablespace to simplify backup and recovery operations.

Schema Objects

A *schema* is a set of database objects that inherits the name of its creator. Schema objects are logical structures such as tables, views, indexes, sequences, synonyms, stored procedures, and so on.

You will need to be familiar with the following **V$ VIEW**s: **VSGA, VINSTANCE, V$PROCESS, V$DATABASE, V$DATAFILE**, and **V$CONTROLFILE**. Familiarize yourself with these views by querying the data they contain.

Dynamic Performance Views

Oracle provides numerous data dictionary views to get information on the database and instance:

- *V$SGA*—Provides information on the memory sizes for the shared pool, log buffer, data buffer cache, and fixed memory sizes.

```
SQL> desc V$SGA
Name                           Null?    Type
------------------------------ -------- ----
 NAME                                   VARCHAR2(20)
 VALUE                                  NUMBER
```

- *V$INSTANCE*—Provides information on the status of the instance. Information available includes the following: instance name, instance mode, startup time, and host name.

```
SQL> desc V$INSTANCE
 Name                           Null?    Type
 ------------------------------ -------- ----
 INSTANCE_NUMBER                         NUMBER
 INSTANCE_NAME                           VARCHAR2(16)
 HOST_NAME                               VARCHAR2(64)
 VERSION                                 VARCHAR2(17)
 STARTUP_TIME                            DATE
 STATUS                                  VARCHAR2(7)
 PARALLEL                                VARCHAR2(3)
 THREAD#                                 NUMBER
 ARCHIVER                                VARCHAR2(7)
 LOG_SWITCH_WAIT                         VARCHAR2(11)
 LOGINS                                  VARCHAR2(10)
 SHUTDOWN_PENDING                        VARCHAR2(3)
```

- *V$PROCESS*—Provides information on the background and server processes for the instance.

```
SQL> desc V$PROCESS
 Name                           Null?    Type
 ------------------------------ -------- ----
 ADDR                                    RAW(4)
 PID                                     NUMBER
 SPID                                    VARCHAR2(9)
 USERNAME                                VARCHAR2(15)
 SERIAL#                                 NUMBER
 TERMINAL                                VARCHAR2(16)
 PROGRAM                                 VARCHAR2(64)
 BACKGROUND                              VARCHAR2(1)
 LATCHWAIT                               VARCHAR2(8)
 LATCHSPIN                               VARCHAR2(8)
```

- *V$DATABASE*—Provides database status and recovery information. Information available includes: the unique database identifier, the database name, the database creation date, the control file creation date and time, the last database checkpoint, and other details.

```
SQL> desc V$DATABASE
 Name                            Null?    Type
 ------------------------------- -------- ----
 DBID                                     NUMBER
 NAME                                     VARCHAR2(9)
 CREATED                                  DATE
 RESETLOGS_CHANGE#                        NUMBER
 RESETLOGS_TIME                           DATE
 PRIOR_RESETLOGS_CHANGE#                  NUMBER
 PRIOR_RESETLOGS_TIME                     DATE
 LOG_MODE                                 VARCHAR2(12)
 CHECKPOINT_CHANGE#                       NUMBER
 ARCHIVE_CHANGE#                          NUMBER
 CONTROLFILE_TYPE                         VARCHAR2(7)
 CONTROLFILE_CREATED                      DATE
 CONTROLFILE_SEQUENCE#                    NUMBER
 CONTROLFILE_CHANGE#                      NUMBER
 CONTROLFILE_TIME                         DATE
 OPEN_RESETLOGS                           VARCHAR2(11)
 VERSION_TIME                             DATE
```

- *V$DATAFILE*—Provides the names and locations of the data files that comprise the database. Information available includes: file sequence number, file name, file size, creation date, online or offline status, read-write state, last data file checkpoint, and other details.

```
SQL> desc V$DATAFILE
 Name                            Null?    Type
 ------------------------------- -------- ----
 FILE#                                    NUMBER
 CREATION_CHANGE#                         NUMBER
 CREATION_TIME                            DATE
 TS#                                      NUMBER
 RFILE#                                   NUMBER
 STATUS                                   VARCHAR2(7)
 ENABLED                                  VARCHAR2(10)
 CHECKPOINT_CHANGE#                       NUMBER
 CHECKPOINT_TIME                          DATE
 UNRECOVERABLE_CHANGE#                    NUMBER
 UNRECOVERABLE_TIME                       DATE
```

```
 LAST_CHANGE#                               NUMBER
 LAST_TIME                                  DATE
 OFFLINE_CHANGE#                            NUMBER
 ONLINE_CHANGE#                             NUMBER
 ONLINE_TIME                                DATE
 BYTES                                      NUMBER
 BLOCKS                                     NUMBER
 CREATE_BYTES                               NUMBER
 BLOCK_SIZE                                 NUMBER
 NAME                                       VARCHAR2(513)
```

- *V$CONTROLFILE*—Provides the name and status of control files.

```
SQL> desc V$CONTROLFILE
 Name                                Null?    Type
 ----------------------------------- -------- ----
 STATUS                                       VARCHAR2(7)
 NAME                                         VARCHAR2(513)
```

Importance Of Redo Logs, Checkpoints, And Archives

Online redo log group archiving is performed by either the Archiver (ARCH) background process when automatic archiving is started, or by a user process that issues SQL statements to archive the online redo log group manually. The ARCH process archives a redo log group after the group becomes inactive and the log switch to the next online redo log group has completed. At this point, a record is created in the database's control file identifying the archived redo log file. The group of online redo log files being archived cannot be reused and written to by the LGWR process until the ARCH process has concluded and released a lock on the redo log files. This ARCH locking process guarantees that the LGWR process does not accidentally overwrite a redo log file that needs to be archived. When the ARCH process has completed archiving the redo log files, a second record is written to the database's control file identifying the success of the archiving process.

The ARCH process uses the **LOG_ARCHIVE_DEST** parameter to specify the destination of the archived redo log files. This destination is usually a storage device separate from the Oracle database. The ARCH process can write out two copies of an online redo log group—the duplexing feature. The initialization parameter **LOG_ARCHIVE_DUPLEX_DEST** specifies the second location to write the archived redo log. The initialization parameter **LOG_ARCHIVE_MIN_SUCCEED_DEST** specifies the number of archive log destinations to which a redo log group must be successfully archived. A missing archived redo log file renders all subsequent archived redo log files useless. The archiving of online redo logs has two key advantages during backup:

- A database backup, together with online and archived redo log files, guarantees that all committed transactions can be recovered in the event of an operating system or disk failure.
- A backup taken while the database is open and in normal use can be used if an archived redo log is kept permanently.

File Synchronization Process During Checkpoints

During a checkpoint, the DBWR process writes all modified buffers in the database buffer cache to disk and LGWR writes all log buffer entries to disk. The checkpoint event ensures that all modified data blocks since the last checkpoint have been written to disk and all entries can be committed or rolled back depending on the commit status of the transaction. The checkpoint event synchronizes the write operations of DBWR and LGWR. Checkpoints occur during the following database events:

- When an online redo log file fills (known as a log switch)
- When a specified number of seconds passed after the last checkpoint (specified in the **LOG_CHECKPOINT_TIMEOUT** *init.ora* parameter)
- When a specified number of OS blocks have been written to the redo log files since the last checkpoint (specified in the **LOG_CHECKPOINT_INTERVAL** init.ora parameter)
- When manually instructed by a DBA using the **ALTER SYSTEM CHECKPOINT** command
- When a tablespace is taken offline
- When an online backup is initiated
- When the instance shuts down using the Normal or Immediate option

At each checkpoint event, the checkpoint number is updated in every database file header and in the control file by the CKPT process. The checkpoint number serves as a synchronization indicator for the data, redo, and control files. The database is in a "consistent" state if all the database files contain the same checkpoint number. During database startup, the control file is used to confirm that all files are at the same checkpoint number. Any discrepancy in the checkpoint numbers in the file headers leads to failure and requires recovery operations.

Checkpoints minimize the time spent in performing instance recovery because at every checkpoint, all modified data is written to disk and the redo log entries before the last checkpoint are no longer needed during the "roll-forward" process of instance recovery. The init.ora parameter **LOG_CHECKPOINTS_TO_ALERT** can be specified to determine if the target checkpoint frequency has been achieved.

Multiplexing Control Files And Redo Logs

To protect against single-point media failures, Oracle provides the capability to multiplex or mirror an instance's online redo logs and control files. When multiplexing online redo log files, the LGWR process simultaneously writes the same redo log information to multiple identically sized online redo log files. Figure 3.3 illustrates this process. The prerequisites for multiplexing online redo log files are as follows:

- Each group should have at least two redo log members per group, with each member on a different disk.
- All members of a group should hold identical information and be the same size.
- Each group should have the same number of members.
- Group members should be updated concurrently.

Oracle also supports multiplexing of control files. This functionality protects the control files against a single point of failure. An instance cannot start with a corrupted control file. The secondary control file ensures the Oracle instance always has a valid and current control file available, in case the primary control file gets corrupted. The recommended configuration consists of at least two control files on different disks.

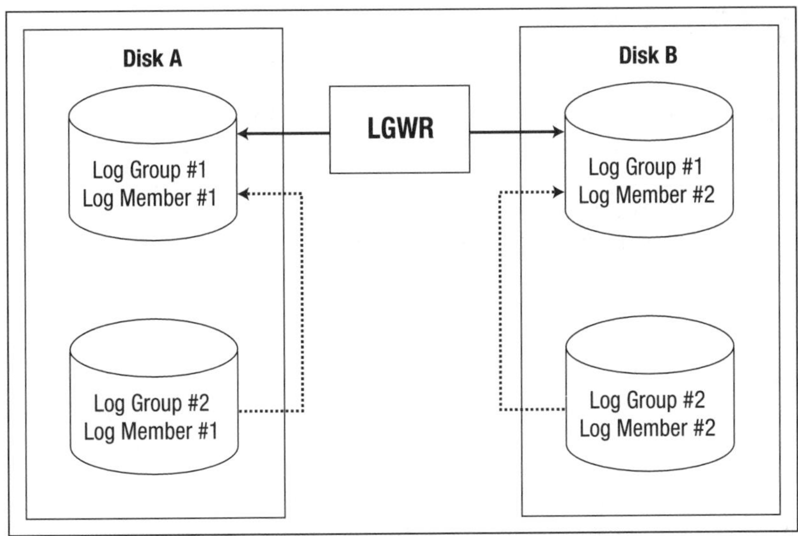

Figure 3.3 The multiplexing of online redo logs.

Practice Questions

Question 1

Which of the following architectural components is made up of background processes and memory buffers?

❍ a. The SGA

❍ b. The Oracle instance

❍ c. The Oracle database

❍ d. The PGA

The correct answer is b. An Oracle instance is comprised of memory structures and background processes. Answer a is incorrect because the SGA is the shared memory area that contains memory buffers. Answer c is incorrect because the Oracle database is made up of the physical database files and the logical storage structures. Answer d is incorrect because the PGA is a memory area reserved for a user process.

Question 2

What three main types of database files constitute an Oracle database?

❍ a. Data files, redo log files, and alert log file

❍ b. Data files, parameter file, and control file

❍ c. Data files, redo log files, and parameter file

❍ d. Data files, redo log files, and control file

The correct answer is d. An Oracle database is composed of one or more control files, one or more data files, and two or more redo log files. Answers a, b, and c are incorrect because an alert log file or a parameter file are supplementary files in an Oracle database.

Question 3

The database initialization parameter file sets the characteristics of which Oracle architectural component? [Choose all correct answers.]

- ❑ a. Background processes
- ❑ b. Oracle instance
- ❑ c. SGA
- ❑ d. Oracle database

The correct answers are a, b, and c. DBAs can use database initialization parameters to set the characteristics of background processes such as designate the archival directory location. DBAs can use the initialization parameters to set instance-wide characteristics such as the default date format. DBAs can also use database initialization parameters to adjust memory structure settings in the SGA; for example, they can set the number of database buffers in memory, how much space is initially allocated for a context area when it is created, the maximum number of database users, and so on. Answer d is incorrect because the database initialization parameters cannot be used to set the physical and logical storage characteristics of the Oracle database.

Question 4

Which SGA component contains copies of data blocks read from disk?

- ❍ a. Shared pool
- ❍ b. Large pool
- ❍ c. Database buffer cache
- ❍ d. Redo log buffer

The correct answer is c. When user-requested data is not found in the database buffer cache of the SGA, an associated server process will read the pertinent data blocks from the data files into the database buffer cache. Answer a is incorrect because the Shared Pool holds the library cache and the data dictionary cache. Answer b is incorrect because the Large Pool is used to allocate sequential I/O buffers from shared memory. Answer d is incorrect because the Redo Log Buffers hold redo entries that contain the changes made to the database by database transactions.

Question 5

Which background process is responsible for freeing resources held up by a failed user process?

❍ a. SMON

❍ b. PMON

❍ c. CKPT

❍ d. ARCH

The correct answer is b. The PMON process performs process recovery for failed user processes. It frees the resources the failed process was holding up. Answer a is incorrect because the SMON process performs instance recovery and free space coalescing. Answer c is incorrect because the CKPT process is responsible for notifying the DBWn at checkpoints so all modified data blocks in the SGA from the last checkpoint are written out to the datafiles. Answer d is incorrect because the ARCH process is responsible for copying the online redo log files to a designated archival destination.

Question 6

What action should you perform if you have two disks and wish to multiplex your redo log files, which are configured as two redo log groups with two members each?

❍ a. Put both groups on one of the two disks.

❍ b. Put each group on both disks.

❍ c. Place each member of each group on different disks.

❍ d. Add another disk with two more groups.

The correct answer is c. Multiplexing the redo log files protects against media failures. The redo log group members should be placed on different disks. Answer a is incorrect because it exposes the system to a single point of failure for all redo log members. Answer b is incorrect because we have two redo log groups and it is not possible to put each group on both disks. Answer d is incorrect because adding another disk with two more groups also exposes the system to a single point of failure for all redo log members.

Question 7

What background process is responsible for managing the database buffer cache?

- ❍ a. DBWR
- ❍ b. PMON
- ❍ c. LGWR
- ❍ d. ARCH

The correct answer is a. The DBWR process manages the database buffer cache. It writes changed blocks from the database buffer cache to the data files in batch. Answer b is incorrect because the PMON process performs process recovery for failed user processes. Answer c is incorrect because the LGWR process writes the redo log entries from the redo log buffer to the online redo log files. Answer d is incorrect because the ARCH process is responsible for copying the online redo log files to a designated archival destination.

Question 8

Which five background processes will cause the instance to fail if one of them fails? [Choose all correct answers.]

- ❑ a. DBWR
- ❑ b. LGWR
- ❑ c. CKPT
- ❑ d. SMON
- ❑ e. ARCH
- ❑ f. PMON

The correct answers are a, b, c, d, and f. On instance startup, the background processes are started. If DBWR, or LGWR, CKPT, SMON, PMON processes fail, the instance will fail to start. Answer e is incorrect because a failed ARCH process does not cause the instance to fail.

Question 9

What transpires when a checkpoint occurs?

❍ a. SMON coalesces contiguous free extents into larger free chunks.

❍ b. DBWR writes all modified data blocks in the database buffer cache to disk.

❍ c. PMON frees resources held by failed user processes.

❍ d. LGWR writes all modified data blocks in the database buffer cache to disk.

The correct answer is b. During a checkpoint event, the DBWR process writes all modified data blocks in the database buffer cache of the SGA to the database files, and the LGWR process writes all redo log entries in the log buffer to disk. Answers a and c are incorrect because they are triggered independent of a checkpoint. Answer d is incorrect because the LGWR process writes the redo log entries from the redo log buffer to the online redo log files.

Question 10

When does a checkpoint occur?

❍ a. When a user commits a transaction.

❍ b. When the **SHUTDOWN ABORT** command is issued by the DBA.

❍ c. When the DBA adds a new data file.

❍ d. When a log switch is needed.

The correct answer is d. Checkpoints occur during the following database events:

- When an online redo log file fills (known as a log switch).
- When a specified number of seconds passed after the last checkpoint (specified in the LOG_CHECKPOINT_TIMEOUT init.ora parameter).
- When a specified number of OS blocks have been written to the redo log files since the last checkpoint (specified in the LOG_CHECKPOINT_INTERVAL init.ora parameter).
- When manually instructed by a DBA using the ALTER SYSTEM CHECKPOINT command.
- When a tablespace is taken offline.

- When an online backup is initiated.
- When the instance shuts down using the Normal or Immediate option.

Answers a, b, and c are incorrect because they don't trigger a checkpoint.

Question 11

What Oracle architectural component enables backups to be made while the database is online?

- ❍ a. Archived redo log files
- ❍ b. Redo log files
- ❍ c. Data files
- ❍ d. Control files

The correct answer is a. When a database is running in **ARCHIVELOG** mode, online backups can be made. Answers b, c, and d are incorrect because online backups can be made only when the database is archiving redo log files.

Question 12

What is the importance of synchronizing all the database files in an Oracle database?

- ❍ a. Database recoverability can be guaranteed.
- ❍ b. The database will fail to open if the database files are not consistent.
- ❍ c. Read-write consistency can be guaranteed.
- ❍ d. Exports would contain inconsistencies.

The correct answer is b. At each checkpoint, all the control files, data files, and redo log files are synchronized by having the same checkpoint number. At database start, Oracle verifies that all the files contain the same checkpoint number. If any of the files have an inconsistent checkpoint number, the database will fail to open and recovery operations will be needed. Answer a is incorrect because synchronizing database files does not guarantee recoverability. A valid backup will guarantee recoverability. Answer c is incorrect because synchronizing database files does not guarantee read-write consistency. Answer d is incorrect because exports are independent of database file synchronization.

Need To Know More?

Dialeris, Connie. *Oracle8 Backup and Recovery Guide Release 8.0*, Part No. A58396-01, Oracle Corporation, 1997.

Leverenz, Lefty. *Oracle8 Concepts Release 8.0*, Part No. A58227-01, Oracle Corporation, 1997.

Loney, Kevin. *DBA Handbook, 8.0 Edition*, Oracle Press, 1999. ISBN 0-07882-289-0.

Velpuri, Rama. *Oracle Backup and Recovery Handbook*, Oracle Press, 1998. ISBN: 0-07882-389-7.

Oracle Backup And Recovery Configuration

Terms you'll need to understand:

- √ **ARCHIVELOG** mode
- √ **NOARCHIVELOG** mode
- √ SCN
- √ Online backup
- √ Offline backup
- √ Dynamic performance views
- √ Manual archiving
- √ Automatic archiving
- √ ARCH background process
- √ Multiplexed archived redo log file

Techniques you'll need to master:

- √ Understanding the archive modes of a database
- √ Viewing the archive mode of a database
- √ Issuing the **ARCHIVE LOG LIST** command
- √ Changing the archive mode of a database
- √ Using the dynamic performance views relating to the archived redo log files
- √ Understanding recovery implications of **NOARCHIVELOG** mode
- √ Configuring a database for manual redo log archiving
- √ Configuring a database for automatic redo log archiving
- √ Multiplexing archived redo log files

After gaining an understanding of the Oracle backup and recovery structures and processes, a database administrator (DBA) can proceed to configure Oracle for backup and recovery. Effective Oracle backup and recovery configuration requires you to understand the following concepts:

- Archive modes of a database
- Recovery implications of NOARCHIVELOG mode
- Configuring a database for redo log archiving
- Multiplexing archived redo log files

Archive Modes Of A Database

An Oracle8 database instance can operate in two distinctive backup modes: ARCHIVELOG and NOARCHIVELOG. The information on the archive mode is stored in the control file associated with the database. Each mode determines the type of backup and recovery procedures that can be performed.

ARCHIVELOG Mode

ARCHIVELOG mode enables the archiving of the online redo log files so that a history of redo information is maintained. When the command to operate in ARCHIVELOG mode is issued, the control file is updated accordingly. Setting the database in ARCHIVELOG mode does not enable the ARCH background process. The ARCH background process must be explicitly started to support automatic archiving of the online redo log files.

A filled online redo log file cannot be overwritten until a checkpoint has taken place and the ARCH background process has archived it. The log sequence number of the archived redo log file is recorded in the control file. All changes to the database are stored in the archived redo log files.

Be aware that when the archiving destination runs out of space, the database will hang until sufficient free space is available for more archived redo log files.

When this mode is in effect, complete recovery up to the point of disk and instance failure can be accommodated, because the current redo information and the redo history are available. An Oracle8 database in the ARCHIVELOG mode enables online hot backups. *Online hot backups* are backups made while the database is open and in use.

A DBA should be aware of the following implications when configuring the database for **ARCHIVELOG** mode:

- The database is protected from media failures.
- Online hot backups can be made while the database is online.
- When a non-**SYSTEM** tablespace goes offline in the event of a media failure, other parts of the database remain available, because full database restore is not needed; the data needed to recover the offline tablespace is in the redo history, which is composed of archived redo log files.
- Increase the number of online redo log groups to ensure that the archiving of online redo log files is completed before the files are overwritten.

When the database is operating in **ARCHIVELOG** mode, the following options are available for performing media recovery:

- Incomplete recovery up to a particular point in time
- Incomplete recovery up to the end of a particular archived redo log file
- Incomplete recovery up to a particular system change number (SCN)
- Using the archived redo log files in conjunction with the backup copies of the damaged data files to bring the data files up-to-date irrespective of the database being online or offline

NOARCHIVELOG Mode

If the database is set up for **NOARCHIVELOG** mode, no redo history is maintained. The **NOARCHIVELOG** mode disables the archiving of the online redo log files. In this mode, an online redo log group becomes inactive once it fills up. As the checkpoint at the log switch completes, the group becomes available for reuse by the LGWR process. Recovery operations are limited, because only the most recent changes made to the database stored in the groups of the online redo log are available. Due to the recycling of online redo log files, a loss of transactions may result, because older redo log files needed for recovery are no longer available. When redo log files are overwritten, media recovery is limited to the last full backup. This mode only protects a database from instance failure. By default, an Oracle database is configured for **NOARCHIVELOG** mode.

A DBA should be aware of the following implications when configuring the database for **NOARCHIVELOG** mode:

- Online hot backups cannot be performed.
- Data will be lost since the most recent full backup.
- Each database backup must include the complete set of control, redo log, and data files.
- Operating system backups of the database can be performed only when the database is shut down.
- Complete offline database backups affect database availability.
- If a tablespace becomes unavailable in the event of a failure, the database is inoperative until the tablespace has been dropped or the whole database has been restored from backups.

Viewing The Archive Mode Of A Database

To view the archive mode of an Oracle8 database, a DBA can use tools including the Server Manager, the SQL*Worksheet, or the Instance Manager. Using the Server Manager, Oracle responds with the following information after the **ARCHIVE LOG LIST** command has been issued:

```
C:\>svrmgr30

Oracle Server Manager Release 3.0.5.0.0 - Production

(c) Copyright 1997, Oracle Corporation. All Rights Reserved.

Oracle8 Enterprise Edition Release 8.0.5.0.0 - Production
With the Partitioning and Objects options
PL/SQL Release 8.0.5.0.0 - Production

SVRMGR> connect internal
Password:
Connected.
SVRMGR> archive log list
Database log mode              No Archive Mode
Automatic archival             Disabled
Archive destination            %RDBMS80%\
Oldest online log sequence     232
Current log sequence           235
SVRMGR>
```

The **ARCHIVE LOG LIST** command provides information on the archive mode and the status of the archiving for the database. There are six **ARCHIVE LOG LIST** display elements:

- Database log mode indicates the current archiving mode.
- Automatic archival indicates the status of the ARCH background process.
- Archive destination indicates the target location where archived redo log files will reside.
- Oldest online log sequence indicates the oldest online redo log sequence number.
- Next log sequence to archive indicates the next redo log to archive (applicable for **ARCHIVELOG** mode).
- Current log sequence indicates the sequence number of the current redo log file.

Figure 4.1 illustrates the SQL*Worksheet with **NOARCHIVELOG** mode after the **ARCHIVE LOG LIST** command is issued. Figure 4.2 illustrates the Instance Manager with **NOARCHIVELOG** mode.

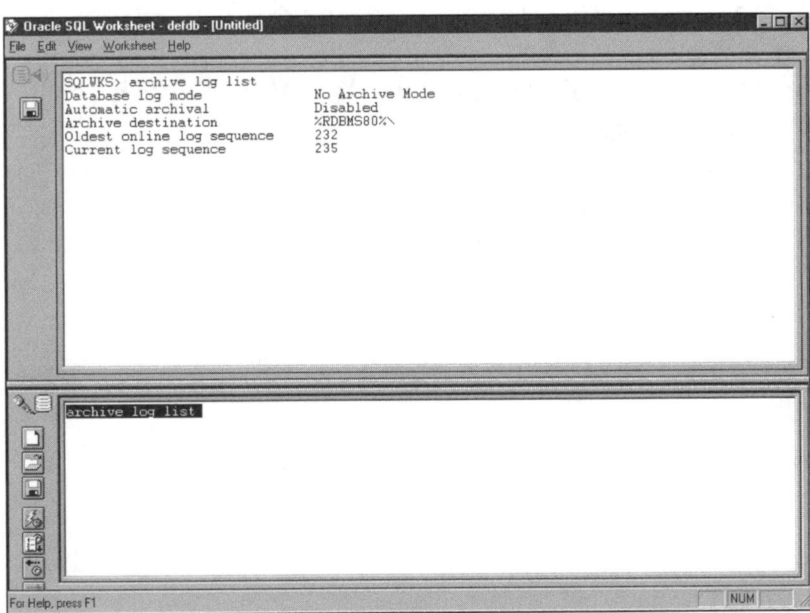

Figure 4.1 The SQL*Worksheet with **NOARCHIVELOG** mode after issuing the **ARCHIVE LOG LIST** command.

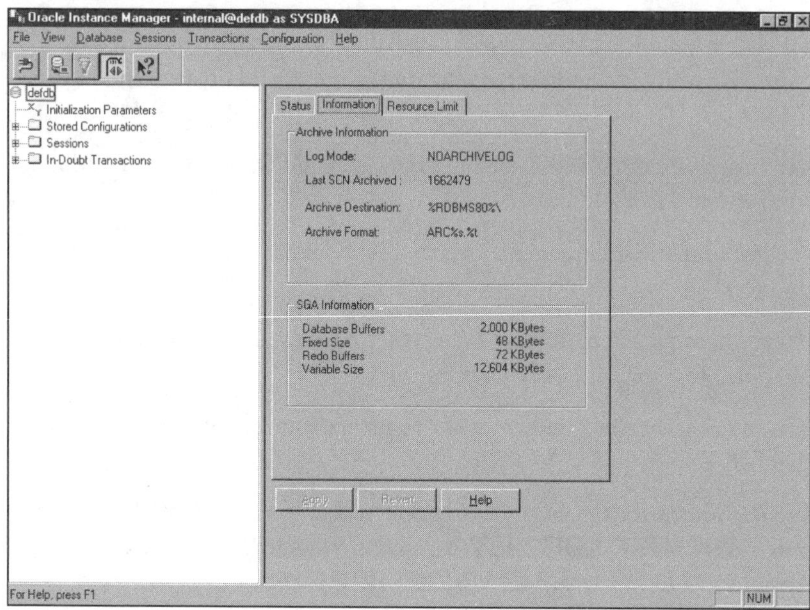

Figure 4.2 The Instance Manager with **NOARCHIVELOG** mode.

Changing The Archive Mode Of A Database

The **ALTER DATABASE** command is used to change the archiving mode while the database is in a **MOUNT** state. A user must have the **ALTER SYSTEM** privilege to change the archive mode of the database. To enable **ARCHIVELOG** mode for redo log files, issue the following command:

```
ALTER DATABASE ARCHIVELOG
```

To disable **ARCHIVELOG** mode for the redo log files, issue the following command:

```
ALTER DATABASE NOARCHIVELOG
```

Know the database states associated with various commands since they are likely to appear in the exam. For example, the **ALTER DATABASE** command is used to change the archiving mode while the database is in a **MOUNT** state.

If the database is in **NOARCHIVELOG** mode, you can change the archive mode by logging into Server Manager. Use the following Server Manager command line statements to change a database from **NOARCHIVELOG** mode to **ARCHIVELOG** mode:

```
SVRMGR> startup mount
ORACLE instance started.
Total System Global Area                          15077376 bytes
Fixed Size                                           49152 bytes
Variable Size                                     12906496 bytes
Database Buffers                                   2048000 bytes
Redo Buffers                                         73728 bytes
Database mounted.
SVRMGR>
SVRMGR> archive log list
Database log mode              No Archive Mode
Automatic archival             Disabled
Archive destination            %ORACLE_HOME%\database\archive
Oldest online log sequence     232
Current log sequence           235
SVRMGR>
SVRMGR> alter database archivelog;
Statement processed.
SVRMGR> alter database open;
Statement processed.
SVRMGR>
```

To verify that the archive mode change took place, use the Server Manager, the SQL*Worksheet, or the Instance Manager. In the Server Manager, Oracle displays the following information after the **ARCHIVE LOG LIST** command has been issued:

```
SVRMGR> archive log list;
Database log mode              Archive Mode
Automatic archival             Disabled
Archive destination            %RDBMS80%\
Oldest online log sequence     232
Next log sequence to archive   235
Current log sequence           235
SVRMGR>
Statement processed.
```

Figure 4.3 illustrates the enabled **ARCHIVELOG** mode from the Instance Manager.

After the database archive mode has been changed from **NOARCHIVELOG** to **ARCHIVELOG**, a full offline database backup must be made. This new backup will be the backup against which all future archived redo log files will apply. The previous backup is of no value, because it was taken when the database was in **NOARCHIVELOG** mode.

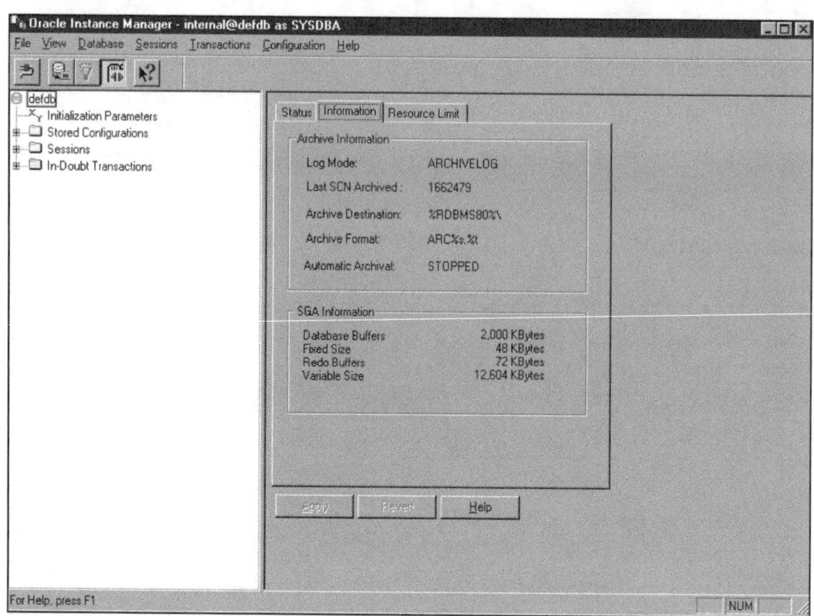

Figure 4.3 The enabled **ARCHIVELOG** mode from the Instance Manager.

If the database is in **ARCHIVELOG** mode, the archive mode can be changed via the Server Manager. The following Server Manager command line statements can be issued to change a database from **ARCHIVELOG** mode to **NOARCHIVELOG** mode:

```
SVRMGR> connect internal
Password:
Connected.
SVRMGR> startup mount;
ORACLE instance started.
Total System Global Area                          15077376 bytes
Fixed Size                                           49152 bytes
Variable Size                                     12906496 bytes
Database Buffers                                   2048000 bytes
Redo Buffers                                         73728 bytes
Database mounted.
SVRMGR> archive log list
Database log mode              Archive Mode
Automatic archival             Disabled
Archive destination            D:\ORANT\database\archive
Oldest online log sequence     232
Next log sequence to archive   235
Current log sequence           235
SVRMGR>
SVRMGR> alter database noarchivelog;
```

```
Statement processed.
SVRMGR> alter database open;
Statement processed.
SVRMGR>
```

To verify that the archive mode change took place, use the Server Manager, the SQL*Worksheet, or the Instance Manager. In the Server Manager, Oracle displays the following information after the **ARCHIVE LOG LIST** command has been issued:

```
SVRMGR> archive log list
Database log mode              No Archive Mode
Automatic archival             Disabled
Archive destination            %ORACLE_HOME%\database\archive
Oldest online log sequence     232
Current log sequence           235
SVRMGR>
```

Dynamic Performance Views

Oracle provides numerous data dictionary views to get information on the archived redo log files:

- *V$ARCHIVED_LOG*—Provides information on the archived redo log files from the control file.

```
SQL> desc V$ARCHIVED_LOG
 Name                            Null?    Type
 ------------------------------- -------- ----
 RECID                                    NUMBER
 STAMP                                    NUMBER
 NAME                                     VARCHAR2(513)
 THREAD#                                  NUMBER
 SEQUENCE#                                NUMBER
 RESETLOGS_CHANGE#                        NUMBER
 RESETLOGS_TIME                           DATE
 FIRST_CHANGE#                            NUMBER
 FIRST_TIME                               DATE
 NEXT_CHANGE#                             NUMBER
 NEXT_TIME                                DATE
 BLOCKS                                   NUMBER
 BLOCK_SIZE                               NUMBER
 ARCHIVED                                 VARCHAR2(3)
 DELETED                                  VARCHAR2(3)
 COMPLETION_TIME                          DATE

SQL>
```

- *V$ARCHIVE_DEST*—Provides information on all archived log destinations for the current instance. Information available includes: whether archiving success must be achieved (**MUST SUCCEED** or **BEST EFFORT**), status (**NORMAL** or **DISABLED**), and the destination specifications.

```
SQL> desc V$ARCHIVE_DEST
 Name                              Null?    Type
 -------------------------------  -------- ----
 ARCMODE                                    VARCHAR2(12)
 STATUS                                     VARCHAR2(8)
 DESTINATION                                VARCHAR2(256)

SQL>
```

- *V$DATABASE*—Provides information on the current state of archiving.

```
SQL> desc V$DATABASE
 Name                              Null?    Type
 -------------------------------  -------- ----
 DBID                                       NUMBER
 NAME                                       VARCHAR2(9)
 CREATED                                    DATE
 RESETLOGS_CHANGE#                          NUMBER
 RESETLOGS_TIME                             DATE
 PRIOR_RESETLOGS_CHANGE#                    NUMBER
 PRIOR_RESETLOGS_TIME                       DATE
 LOG_MODE                                   VARCHAR2(12)
 CHECKPOINT_CHANGE#                         NUMBER
 ARCHIVE_CHANGE#                            NUMBER
 CONTROLFILE_TYPE                           VARCHAR2(7)
 CONTROLFILE_CREATED                        DATE
 CONTROLFILE_SEQUENCE#                      NUMBER
 CONTROLFILE_CHANGE#                        NUMBER
 CONTROLFILE_TIME                           DATE
 OPEN_RESETLOGS                             VARCHAR2(11)
 VERSION_TIME                               DATE

SQL>
```

- *V$LOG_HISTORY*—Provides log file history information from the control file. Information available includes the thread number of the archived log file, the sequence number of the archived log file, the lowest SCN, the highest SCN, the control file record identifier, and the control file record stamp.

```
SQL> desc V$LOG_HISTORY
 Name                            Null?    Type
 ------------------------------- -------- ----
 RECID                                    NUMBER
 STAMP                                    NUMBER
 THREAD#                                  NUMBER
 SEQUENCE#                                NUMBER
 FIRST_CHANGE#                            NUMBER
 FIRST_TIME                               DATE
 NEXT_CHANGE#                             NUMBER

SQL>
```

Recovery Implications Of NOARCHIVELOG Mode

When the database is operating in **NOARCHIVELOG** mode, the following options are available for performing media recovery:

- The control files, data files, and redo log files from the most recent full database backup must be restored. This option performs media recovery using the physical operating system database files, whereas the user may choose to perform media recovery using the logical backups instead.
- If logical backups using the Export utility are available, the Import utility can be used to restore lost data. This technique results in an incomplete recovery that may include lost transactions.

Configuring A Database For Redo Log Archiving

Once the database is operating in **ARCHIVELOG** mode, the online redo log files can be archived manually or automatically. You can automate the archiving of the online redo log groups by setting the **LOG_ARCHIVE_START** initialization parameter to **TRUE**. This causes Oracle8 to start the ARCH background process, copy online redo log files when they are filled, and manage the archiving process. The ARCH process is disabled by default. The database should be shut down cleanly before you enable the archive process. For manual archiving, the DBA must use the Server Manager or the Backup Manager.

Oracle recommends enabling automatic archival of online redo log files.

To start the ARCH background process, issue the following SQL command in the Server Manager or the SQL*Worksheet:

```
ARCHIVE LOG START
```

This SQL command initiates automatic archiving using the archive destination specified in the **LOG_ARCHIVE_DEST** init.ora parameter. Invoke the **ARCHIVE LOG LIST** command to verify that automatic archiving has been started.

To stop automatic archiving, issue the following SQL statement in the Server Manager or the SQL*Worksheet:

```
ARCHIVE LOG STOP
```

Enabling The Archival Process (ARCH) In An Open Instance

There are five steps to take when enabling the ARCH process in an open instance:

1. Open the database.
2. Verify the database is operating in **ARCHIVELOG** mode, using the following code:

```
SVRMGR> archive log list
Database log mode              Archive Mode
Automatic archival             Disabled
Archive destination            %ORACLE_HOME%\database\archive
Oldest online log sequence     232
Next log sequence to archive   235
Current log sequence           235
SVRMGR>
```

3. Invoke the ARCH process to automatically archive redo log files:

```
SVRMGR> alter system archive log start to '/u02/oradata/TEST/
log'; (UNIX)
SVRMGR> alter system archive log start to
'd:\orant\database\TEST\log'; (NT)
```

4. Verify the ARCH process is enabled:

```
SVRMGR> archive log list
Database log mode              Archive Mode
```

```
Automatic archival              Enabled
Archive destination             D:\ORANT\database\archive
Oldest online log sequence      232
Next log sequence to archive    235
Current log sequence            235
SVRMGR>
```

5. The ARCH process automatically copies the redo log files to the archival destination when they are filled.

When the ARCH process is not initiated through the init.ora parameter file, it must be restarted at each instance startup.

Enabling Archival Process At Instance Startup

The ARCH process can be automatically started at instance startup by setting the **LOG_ARCHIVE_START** init.ora parameter. This will make manual archiving by the DBA unnecessary. When the **LOG_ARCHIVE_START** parameter is set to **TRUE**, the ARCH process is automatically invoked at instance startup. When the **LOG_ARCHIVE_START** parameter is set to **FALSE**, the ARCH process is disabled at instance startup.

Selectively Archiving Redo Log Files

To selectively archive redo log files, the **ALTER SYSTEM ARCHIVE LOG** command is used with the following options: thread, sequence, change, group, current, logfile, next, all, start, to, and stop. The **ALTER SYSTEM ARCHIVE LOG** command requires that the OSDBA or the OSOPER role be enabled.

Thread

Specifies the thread of the redo log file group to be archived. This parameter applies to the Oracle Parallel Server option in parallel mode.

Sequence

Specifies the log sequence number of the online redo log file group to manually archive.

Change

Specifies manual archiving based on the SCN. A log switch will be triggered if the SCN is in the current redo log file group.

If an SCN is specified with the **CHANGE** option and earlier unarchived redo log file groups exist, then all unarchived redo log groups up to and including the specified group will be archived by Oracle.

Group

Specifies the online redo log group to manually archive. The **DBA_LOG_FILES** data dictionary view can be used to retrieve the group number for the redo log file groups.

Current

Specifies the thread of the current redo log file group to be manually archived. This parameter will trigger a log switch.

If a thread of the current redo log file group is specified with the **CURRENT** option and earlier unarchived redo log file groups exist, then all unarchived redo log groups up to and including the specified group will be archived by Oracle.

Logfile

Identifies the redo log file group member to be manually archived.

If a redo log file group is specified for the **LOGFILE** option and earlier unarchived redo log file groups exist, then an error will be returned.

Next

Archives the oldest unarchived online redo log file group.

All

Specifies that all online redo log file groups are to be archived.

Start

Enables automatic archiving of redo log file groups.

To

Specifies the archival destination for the copies of the online redo log group.

Stop

Disables automatic archiving of redo log file groups.

Manually Disable Archiving

Regardless of how the ARCH process is started, use the Backup Manager or the **ALTER SYSTEM** command in the Server Manager to disable the archival process. The following steps detail how to manually disable the archival process:

1. Issue the following command to stop the ARCH background process:

   ```
   SVRMGR> alter system archive log stop;
   ```

2. Modify the init.ora parameter file by setting the following parameter to disable automatic archiving:

   ```
   LOG_ARCHIVE_START=FALSE
   ```

3. Make sure the database is operating in **NOARCHIVELOG** mode after the ARCH process is disabled. Stopping the ARCH process has no effect on the archive mode of the database. When all redo log file groups are filled and not archived, the database will hang if it is in **ARCHIVELOG** mode.

The following code snippet shows how to stop automatic archiving from the Server Manager or the SQL*Worksheet:

```
SVRMGR> archive log stop;
Statement processed.
SVRMGR> archive log list
Database log mode              Archive Mode
Automatic archival             Disabled
Archive destination            D:\ORANT\database\archive
Oldest online log sequence     232
Next log sequence to archive   235
Current log sequence           235
SVRMGR>

SVRMGR> startup mount
ORACLE instance started.
Total System Global Area                        15077376 bytes
Fixed Size                                         49152 bytes
Variable Size                                   12906496 bytes
Database Buffers                                 2048000 bytes
Redo Buffers                                       73728 bytes
Database mounted.
SVRMGR> archive log list
Database log mode              No Archive Mode
Automatic archival             Disabled
Archive destination            %ORACLE_HOME%\database\archive
Oldest online log sequence     232
Current log sequence           235
```

Multiplexing Archived Redo Log Files

An Oracle8 new feature enables the DBA to multiplex or duplex the archived redo log files to protect them against media failure. There are two init.ora parameters to set: **LOG_ARCHIVE_DUPLEX_DEST** and **LOG_ ARCHIVE_ MIN_SUCCEED_DEST**. The **LOG_ARCHIVE_ DUPLEX_DEST** parameter specifies the location where copies of the archived log files will be stored. The location can be a file name or a device name. The file name may include %s or %S for the log sequence number and the default is operating system dependent. The device name may include a directory or path and is used to specify the default location where copies of the archived redo log files will be written to. The device name should not point to a raw device. The **ALTER SYSTEM** command can be used to dynamically set the **LOG_ ARCHIVE_DUPLEX_DEST** parameter.

When specifying the path names, ensure they are set in accordance with operating system conventions. Unix and NT path names are different.

The **LOG_ARCHIVE_MIN_SUCCEED_DEST** parameter specifies the number of archived redo log destinations to which the online redo log files must be successfully written. It can be set to 1 (the default) or 2.

Practice Questions

Question 1

Which archive mode is in effect for a default installation of the Oracle Server?

❍ a. **ARCHIVELOG** mode with automatic archiving.

❍ b. **NOARCHIVELOG** mode.

❍ c. **ARCHIVELOG** mode with manual archiving.

❍ d. None of the above.

The correct answer is b. The default Oracle Server installation sets the database for NOARCHIVELOG mode. Under this mode, no redo log history is maintained. Answers a, c, and d are incorrect because the default installation mode is the NOARCHIVELOG mode.

Question 2

Which command is used to manually disable archiving irrespective of the starting mode?

❍ a. **ALTER DATABASE**

❍ b. **ALTER TABLESPACE**

❍ c. **ALTER SYSTEM**

❍ d. **ALTER SESSION**

❍ e. **ALTER TABLE**

The correct answer is c. The ALTER SYSTEM ARCHIVE LOG STOP statement is issued to disable archiving. Answers a, b, d, and e are incorrect because they cannot be used to disable archiving.

Question 3

Which of the *init.ora* parameter should be set for duplexing the archived redo log files?

- ❍ a. **LOG_ARCHIVE_DUPLEX_DEST**
- ❍ b. **LOG_ARCHIVE_DUPLEX**
- ❍ c. **LOG_ARCHIVE_MIN_SUCCEED_DEST**
- ❍ d. **LOG_ARCHIVE_DEST**

The correct answer is a. The **LOG_ARCHIVE_DUPLEX_DEST** specifies the archived redo log file duplexing location. Answer b is incorrect because it is an invalid parameter. Answer c is incorrect because it specifies the number of archived redo log destinations to which the online redo log files must be successfully written. Answer d is incorrect because the **LOG_ARCHIVE_DEST** parameter specifies the primary archived redo log file location.

Question 4

Which command can be issued to get the current log sequence number?

- ❍ a. **ARCHIVE LOG ALL**
- ❍ b. **LIST ALL ARCHIVE**
- ❍ c. **ARCHIVE LIST**
- ❍ d. **ARCHIVE LOG LIST**

The correct answer is d. The **ARCHIVE LOG LIST** command provides information on the archive mode and the status of the archiving for the database. The **ARCHIVE LOG LIST** displayed elements include: database log mode, which indicates the current archiving mode; automatic archival, which indicates the status of the ARCH background process; archive destination, which indicates the target location where archived redo log files will reside; oldest online log sequence, which indicates the oldest online redo log sequence number; next log sequence to archive, which indicates the next redo log to archive (applicable for **ARCHIVELOG** mode); and the current log sequence, which indicates the sequence number of the current redo log file. Answers a, b, and c are invalid commands.

Question 5

Which backup method should you employ to enable complete recovery up to the point of media failure?

- ❍ a. Operating system backup without archiving.
- ❍ b. Logical backup using the conventional path of the Export Utility.
- ❍ c. Operating system backup with archiving.
- ❍ d. None of the backup methods enable complete recovery up to the point of media failure.

The correct answer is c. An operating system backup with archiving facilitates a complete recovery, because the redo log history is available for reapplying all database transactions. Answer a is incorrect because an operating system backup without archiving only enables restoration to the last full backup. Answer b is incorrect because logical backups using the Export utility only enables restoration to the point in time when the logical backups were made. Answer d is incorrect because an operating system backup with archiving will enable a complete recovery up to the point of media failure.

Question 6

What will happen if the **LOG_ARCHIVE_DEST** location runs out of space?

- ❍ a. The redo log files will be overwritten.
- ❍ b. The database will hang.
- ❍ c. Redo log file writing continues.
- ❍ d. Archiving will stop.

The correct answer is b. When archiving is enabled, redo log files are not overwritten until they have been archived. When the archival destination runs out of space, the ARCH background process will fail, which causes the database to hang. Answer a is incorrect because the redo log files will be overwritten when sufficient free space is available in the LOG_ARCHIVE_DEST location. Answer c is incorrect because the redo log file writing will not continue until sufficient space is available in the LOG_ARCHIVE_DEST location. Answer d is incorrect because the ARCH process will fail until sufficient free space is available in the LOG_ARCHIVE_DEST location.

Question 7

When a database is operating in **ARCHIVELOG** mode, when will the redo log files get overwritten due to the cyclical writing by the LGWR?

- ❍ a. At the start of the checkpoint, after the redo log file is archived.
- ❍ b. At the start of the checkpoint, before the redo log file is archived.
- ❍ c. After the checkpoint completes, before the redo log file is archived.
- ❍ d. After the checkpoint completes, after the redo log file is archived.

The correct answer is d. When operating in **ARCHIVELOG** mode, the redo log files cannot be reused until they have been archived. With automatic archiving, the ARCH background process copies the oldest unarchived redo log group to the archival location at a log switch. Each log switch triggers a checkpoint event. Answers a and b are incorrect because redo log files get overwritten after the checkpoint completes. Answer c is incorrect because redo log files get overwritten after the redo log file is archived.

Question 8

What command needs to be issued to change the database to **ARCHIVELOG** mode?

- ❍ a. **ALTER DATABASE**
- ❍ b. **ALTER TABLESPACE**
- ❍ c. **ALTER SYSTEM**
- ❍ d. **ALTER SESSION**

The correct answer is a. The **ALTER DATABASE ARCHIVELOG** command is used to put the database in **ARCHIVELOG** mode while the database is in the **MOUNT** state. Answers b, c, and d are incorrect because those commands cannot be used to change the database mode to **ARCHIVELOG**.

Question 9

Which init.ora parameter should be set to specify the minimum number of redo log file copies that needs to be successfully created when duplexing archived redo log files?

- ❍ a. **LOG_ARCHIVE_SUCCEED**
- ❍ b. **LOG_ARCHIVE_MIN_SUCCEED_DEST**
- ❍ c. **LOG_ARCHIVE_DUPLEX_DEST**
- ❍ d. **LOG_ARCHIVE_DEST**

The correct answer is b. The LOG_ARCHIVE_MIN_SUCCEED_DEST parameter specifies the minimum number of redo log file copies that must be successfully written. The parameter can be set to 1 or 2. Answer a is incorrect because it is an invalid parameter. Answers c and d are incorrect because they specify the primary and the duplex archived redo log file destinations.

Question 10

Which Server Manager command can be issued to check which archive mode is in effect for the database?

- ❍ a. **SELECT * FROM V$LOGFILE**
- ❍ b. **SELECT * FROM V$DATAFILE**
- ❍ c. **ARCHIVE LOG ALL**
- ❍ d. **ARCHIVE LOG LIST**

The correct answer is d. The ARCHIVE LOG LIST command displays information about the archive mode of the database. Answers a and b are incorrect because these V$VIEWs don't contain information about the archive mode for a database. Answer c is incorrect because it is an invalid command.

Question 11

Which of the following is a backup implication for a database operating in **NOARCHIVELOG**?

- ❍ a. A complete recovery up to the point of media failure can be performed.
- ❍ b. Backups using the Export utility cannot be used.
- ❍ c. A full database backup including the control files, the data files, and the redo log files must be performed during each backup.
- ❍ d. The data files must be individually backed up.

The correct answer is c. When a database is operating in **NOARCHIVELOG** mode, only offline full backups can be accommodated. Recovery will require a backup of the full database. Answer a is not correct because a complete recovery up to the point of media failure cannot be performed for **NOARCHIVELOG** databases. Answer b is incorrect because in **NOARCHIVELOG** mode, backups based on the Export utility can be used. Answer d is incorrect because the data files don't need to be individually backed up for a database operating in NOARCHIVELOG mode.

Question 12

In a **NOARCHIVELOG** database, which state should the database be in when performing recovery from media failure using data files and redo log files?

- ❍ a. **OPEN**
- ❍ b. **MOUNT**
- ❍ c. **CLOSED**
- ❍ d. **NOMOUNT**

The correct answer is c. The database must be offline to perform backup and recovery operations for a database in **NOARCHIVELOG** mode, because the full set of database backup files are restored using operating system commands. Answers a, b, and d are incorrect because these database states are not used to perform recovery from media failure when the database is in NOARCHIVELOG mode.

Need To Know More?

Dialeris, Connie. *Oracle8 Backup and Recovery Guide Release 8.0*, 1997, Part No. A58396-01, Oracle Corporation, 1997.

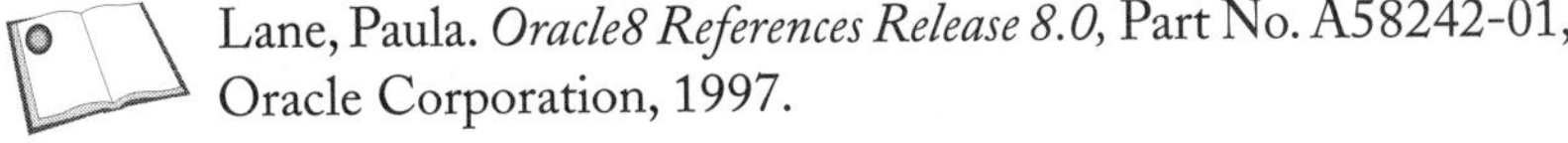

Lane, Paula. *Oracle8 References Release 8.0,* Part No. A58242-01, Oracle Corporation, 1997.

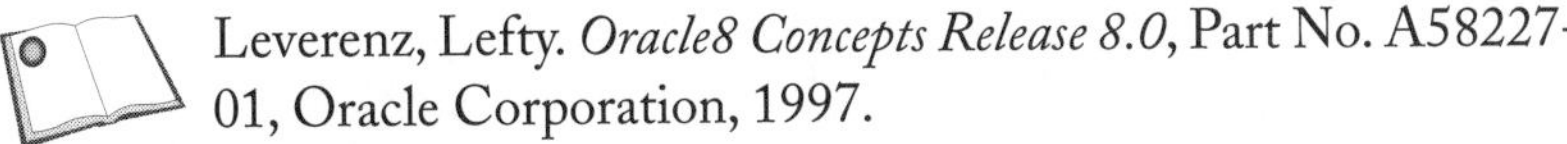

Leverenz, Lefty. *Oracle8 Concepts Release 8.0*, Part No. A58227-01, Oracle Corporation, 1997.

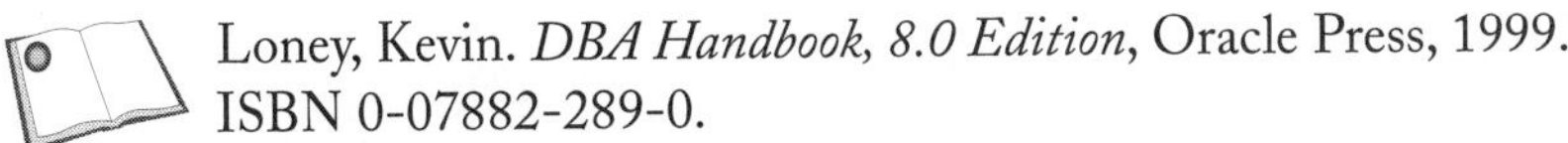

Loney, Kevin. *DBA Handbook, 8.0 Edition*, Oracle Press, 1999. ISBN 0-07882-289-0.

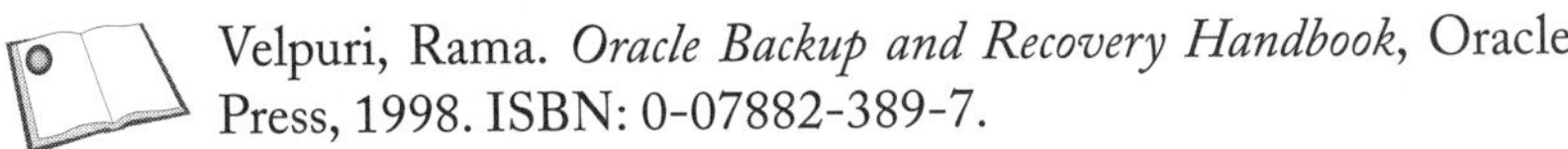

Velpuri, Rama. *Oracle Backup and Recovery Handbook*, Oracle Press, 1998. ISBN: 0-07882-389-7.

Oracle Recovery Manager Overview

Terms you'll need to understand:

- √ Recovery Manager (**RMAN**)
- √ Backup Manager
- √ Oracle Enterprise Manager (OEM)
- √ **V$BACKUP_CORRUPTION**
- √ **V$COPY_CORRUPTION**
- √ Recovery catalog
- √ Recovery catalog database
- √ Target database
- √ Channel
- √ Backup set
- √ Backup piece
- √ Incremental block level backup
- √ Unused block compression
- √ Snapshot control file
- √ **CONTROL_FILE_RECORD_KEEP_TIME**

Techniques you'll need to master:

- √ Understanding Recovery Manager (**RMAN**) characteristics
- √ Understanding **RMAN** components, packages, interfaces, and startup process
- √ Understanding additional issues when using **RMAN**
- √ Understanding when to use **RMAN**
- √ Understanding the Backup Manager tool
- √ Understanding the recovery catalog
- √ Understanding the recovery catalog creation process
- √ Understanding control files and the resynchronization process with respect to the **RMAN**
- √ Connecting to **RMAN** with or without a recovery catalog

This chapter provides information on a new feature in Oracle8—the Oracle Recovery Manager (RMAN) utility. Specific topics discussed include the following:

- Overview of the RMAN
- When to use RMAN
- Backup Manager overview
- Recovery catalog overview
- RMAN advantages and disadvantages, with the recovery catalog
- Recovery catalog creation
- Control file information with respect to RMAN
- Resynchronizing the control file
- Connecting to RMAN

Overview Of The Recovery Manager

The Recovery Manager (RMAN) is an Oracle-provided utility that enables DBAs to manage the backup, restore, and recovery processes for organizations. One of the key components of RMAN lies in the Oracle-proprietary operating system independent scripting language that will be covered in Chapter 6.

RMAN records all backup, restore, and recovery activities in the control file. The physical backup files are stored on a disk or tape. RMAN interfaces with the target Oracle server by creating server processes that provide connection, backup, restore, and recovery services through a PL/SQL interface. You can access RMAN features using the command line interface or the GUI interface via the Oracle Enterprise Manager's Backup Manager tool.

RMAN Characteristics

The characteristics of RMAN include the following:

- It enables the backup of the database, the tablespaces, the data files, the control files, and the archived redo log files.
- It supports database storage of frequently run operations that are specified in the form of scripts.
- It supports incremental block level backups. This capability enables DBAs to associate backup time to the number of changes made to the database instead of to the size of the database.

- It reduces the size of the backup by the compression of unused blocks.
- It allows the DBA to specify the number of open files and the size of backup pieces for each backup. This capability overcomes operating system (OS) limits on concurrent open files and enables a backup piece to reach the maximum file size supported by the OS or the Media Manager.
- It can be started from the Backup Manager or the operating system. The Unix **cron** utility or the Windows NT **at** utility are typical operating system utilities used in conjunction with **RMAN**.
- It can detect corrupted blocks during backup and restore operations. **RMAN** writes corruption information in the database alert log file, trace files, and the control file. You can also access the corruption information by querying the **V$BACKUP_CORRUPTION** and the **V$COPY_CORRUPTION** data dictionary views. The following code sample provides the view details:

```
SQL> desc v$backup_corruption
 Name                           Null?    Type
 ------------------------------ -------- ----
 RECID                                   NUMBER
 STAMP                                   NUMBER
 SET_STAMP                               NUMBER
 SET_COUNT                               NUMBER
 PIECE#                                  NUMBER
 FILE#                                   NUMBER
 BLOCK#                                  NUMBER
 BLOCKS                                  NUMBER
 CORRUPTION_CHANGE#                      NUMBER
 MARKED_CORRUPT                          VARCHAR2(3)

SQL> desc v$copy_corruption
 Name                           Null?    Type
 ------------------------------ -------- ----
 RECID                                   NUMBER
 STAMP                                   NUMBER
 COPY_RECID                              NUMBER
 COPY_STAMP                              NUMBER
 FILE#                                   NUMBER
 BLOCK#                                  NUMBER
 BLOCKS                                  NUMBER
 CORRUPTION_CHANGE#                      NUMBER
 MARKED_CORRUPT                          VARCHAR2(3)
```

- It supports distributed backup, restore, and recovery operations for the Oracle parallel server.
- It provides improved perfoRMANce through automatic utilization of parallel operations, reduction of the amount of redo information generated during online database backups, I/O restrictions on a read per file and per second basis, and tape streaming.
- It supports the use of third-party media management tools such as Legato and Veritas to interface with storage devices.

RMAN Components

The RMAN is comprised of the following components:

- RMAN *executable engine*—This translates RMAN commands into a sequence of steps that directly affect the physical files.
- RMAN *interface*—This enables the DBA to issue command to the executable engine via an interactive and a batch mode interface using command files.
- *Target database*—This is the database that requires the backup, restore, or recovery operations.
- *Recovery catalog*—A central repository of information about the target database that was extracted initially from the control file of the target database.
- *Channel*—An RMAN resource allocation that establishes a connection from RMAN to the target database for backup, restore, or recovery operations. For each channel, RMAN creates a server process on the target database.

RMAN Packages

Upon running the *catproc.sql* script located in the **$ORACLE_HOME/rdbms/admin** directory, two sets of RMAN packages are created. These packages support RMAN functionality such as querying information that RMAN needs from the recovery catalog or the target database control file or interface with the OS for creating, restoring, and recovering backups of data files and archive log files. The following code sample extracted from the *catproc.sql* file shows the addition of RMAN support:

```
Rem on-disk versions of RMAN support
@@dbmsRMAN.sql
@@prvtrmns.plb
```

```
@@dbmsbkrs.sql
@@prvtbkrs.plb
```

The *dbms*RMAN*.sql* and *prvtrmns.plb* files created the DBMS_RCVCAT and DBMS_RCVMAN packages. RMAN uses the DBMS_RCVCAT package to maintain information in the recovery catalog. The DBMS_RCVMAN file queries the recovery catalog or the control file.

The *dbmsbkrs.sql* and *prvtbkrs.plb* files created the DBMS_ BACKUP_ RESTORE package. The DBMS_BACKUP_RESTORE package provides the interface to the Oracle server for creating and restoring backups of data files and archived log files. The Oracle server will read and write backups.

RMAN Startup Process

The RMAN startup process follows these steps:

- The RMAN user process is created.
- The RMAN user process creates two server processes—a default process and a polling process—that connect to the target database. The default process is responsible for SQL command executions, control file resynchronizations, and redo log file roll-forward. The polling process is responsible for locating Remote Procedure Call (RPC) completions. There is only one polling process per Oracle instance.
- RMAN creates additional server processes for writing to disk or tape.
- When a recovery catalog is being used, RMAN creates a server process that connects to a recovery catalog database and facilitates recovery catalog information retrieval and maintenance.
- When a recovery catalog is not being used, RMAN retrieves the backup and recovery information from the database control file.

RMAN Interfaces

RMAN provides two ways to access its functionality:

- Command line interface
- GUI interface

Command Line Interface

In the RMAN command line interface, RMAN behaves as a command line interpreter (CLI) with its own proprietary command language. The CLI interprets user requests in the form of RMAN commands. The CLI supports commands in both an interactive mode and a batch mode using command files.

GUI Interface

The RMAN GUI interface is available through OEM's Backup Manager tool. It provides all the functionality available via the command line interface.

Things To Consider When Using RMAN

You should keep in mind the following issues when using RMAN:

- RMAN is not the only way to perform backup and recovery operations in Oracle8. You could choose to perform backup, restore, and recovery operations using only operating system mechanisms.
- RMAN will use a catalog if one is available, but it is not a catalog in itself.
- RMAN does not support backing up pre-Oracle8 databases.
- The Enterprise Backup Utility (EBU) is not compatible with RMAN. The EBU does not support Oracle8 databases—it provides backup and recovery functionality for Oracle7 databases only. The EBU is not compatible with Oracle running on Windows NT systems.
- A recovery catalog is required when there is a need to store frequently run scripts, to track backup and restore information for historical purposes, or to use RMAN features.
- When a recovery catalog is not used, the DBA should perform the following actions:
  - Multiplex control files and place them on different disks.
  - Maintain a detailed record of what was backed up, when the backup was performed, and all RMAN backup logs.
- Password files are needed to support remote administration and security needs.
- RMAN does not back up the following files:
  - the *init.ora* file
  - password files
  - online redo log files
  - operating system files

When To Use RMAN

Backups performed using OS mechanisms can also be performed by RMAN. A DBA should consider the advantages of using RMAN and site-specific requirements when determining when to use RMAN. The advantages of using RMAN include the following:

- It supports incremental block level backups. Backup time is proportional to the number of changes made to the database instead of the size of the database. Backups take less time, because only changed blocks are backed up.
- It supports backup, restore, and recovery operations for the Oracle parallel server.
- It offers improved performance by the use of parallel operations, reduction of the amount of redo information generated during online database backups, definition of I/O restrictions, and tape streaming.
- It offers tight integration with third-party media management tools such as Legato and Veritas to interface with storage devices. Check your documentation for specific supported platforms.
- It detects corrupted blocks during backup and restore operations. RMAN writes corruption information in the database alert log file, trace files, and the control file.
- Smaller backup files are required as a result of the compression of unused blocks.
- It enables the backup of the database, the tablespaces, the data files, the control files, and the archived redo log files.
- It supports database storage of frequently run operations that are specified in the form of scripts.

Backup Manager Overview

The Backup Manager is one of the DBA tools within the Oracle Enterprise Manager (OEM) administrative toolset. It provides a GUI interface that enables you to manage your database backup and recovery environment. Installation and configuration of OEM is required before you can use the Backup Manager.

The Backup Manager is a client application program that runs on Windows NT and interfaces with the RMAN server processes in the target database. The DBA should set up a password file to support remote database administration and SYSDBA access required by the Backup Manager. The Backup Manager can be used along with the RMAN command line interface.

The Backup Manager has two subsystems related to Oracle8:

- *Oracle8 Recovery Manager*—Provides an intuitive GUI interface for **RMAN**, the command line backup and recovery utility designed specifically for the Oracle8 database.
- *Operating system backup*—Provides automated control file backup and tablespace backup and recovery capabilities.

You must establish a connection to your target database that requires the backup, restore, or recovery operations before using the Backup Manager. To connect to the Backup Manager using a recovery catalog, perform the following steps:

1. Start OEM.
2. In the Navigator window, highlight and connect to the target database that requires backup.
3. Invoke the Backup Manager (Tools|Applications). Figure 5.1 shows an example Backup Manager interface.
4. Select the Oracle8 Recovery Manager subsystem when the Backup Manager Subsystem dialog box is displayed. Figure 5.2 shows the Backup Manager Subsystem Selection dialog box.

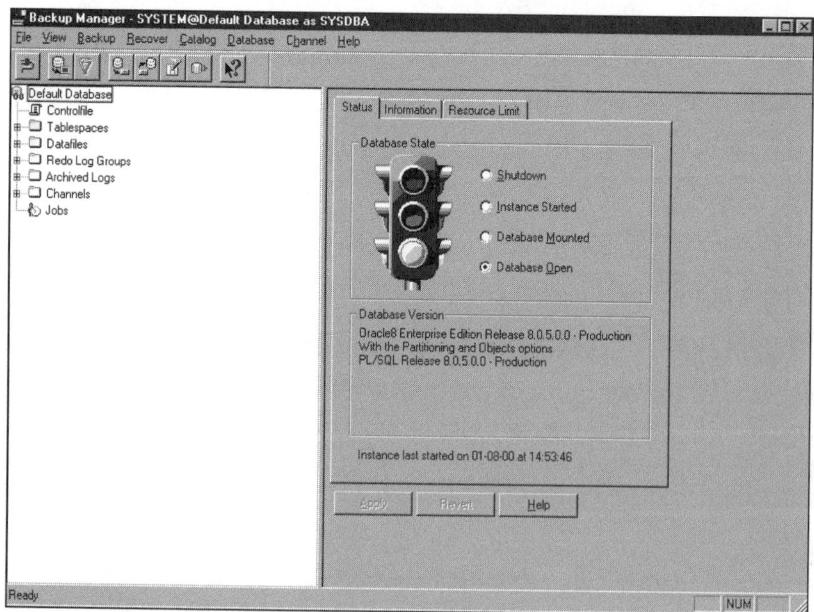

Figure 5.1 The Backup Manager interface.

5. Select the Use Recovery Catalog menu item from the Catalog menu.
6. Select the Connect String menu item from the Catalog menu. Enter the username, password, and connect string for the recovery catalog database when the Recovery Catalog Login dialog box is displayed. Figure 5.3 shows the Recovery Catalog Login dialog box.

When you're performing online backups, make sure the target database is in archivelog mode.

Figure 5.2 The Backup Manager Subsystem Selection dialog box.

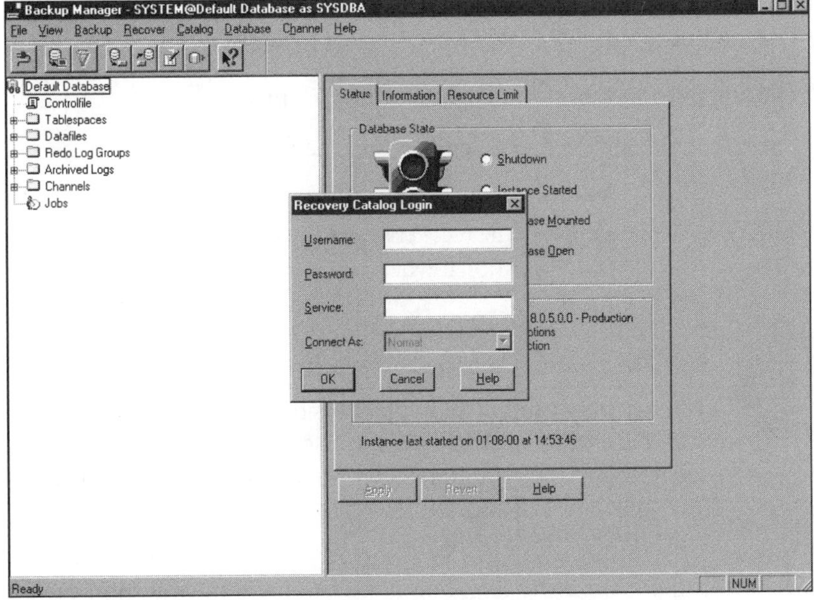

Figure 5.3 The Recovery Catalog Login dialog box.

Recovery Catalog Overview

The recovery catalog is a central repository of information residing on a remote system that contains information about the structure and previous backups of the target database. It is maintained by the **RMAN** utility. The recovery catalog enables DBAs to store historical information on backup, restore, and recovery operations. The information in a recovery catalog includes the following:

- The name and time of backup sets. A *backup set* is comprised of a backup of the data files or the archived redo log files. The physical files contained in a backup set are called *backup pieces*.
- The name of and timestamp on the backup data files.
- Which archived redo log files have been created by the database and backups made by **RMAN**.
- The physical structure of the database. The information is initially populated from the database control file.
- Stored scripts that facilitate frequently executed commands.

The actual backups of data are stored as files on storage devices such as disk or tape. The recovery catalog consists of a set of database objects in a specially created Oracle8 schema. The size of the recovery catalog schema depends on the following factors:

- The number of target databases that needs to be monitored.
- The number and size of the **RMAN** stored scripts.
- The number of archived redo log files and the data file backups for each target database.

The DBA needs to incorporate the recovery catalog into the enterprise's backup plan. The recovery catalog is optional when you're using the **RMAN** utility.

If a recovery catalog is used, essential information is stored in both the control file and in a separate database.

The recovery catalog should not reside in the target database (database to be backed up), because the database can't be recovered in the mounted state. Make sure enough resources are available. Oracle recommends placing the recovery catalog in a separate tablespace.

If there are many target databases to back up, you should consider creating multiple recovery catalog databases to support them.

RMAN Advantages And Disadvantages With The Recovery Catalog

Using the recovery catalog with the RMAN utility offers these advantages:

- It supports the preservation of historical information about backup, restore, and recovery actions.
- It supports database storage of frequently executed scripts for backup, restore, and recovery operations.
- It supports tablespace point-in-time recovery.
- It supports incremental block level backups.
- It provides RMAN with additional functionality.

The disadvantages of using the recovery catalog with the RMAN utility include the following:

- The maintenance overhead of the remote database in which the recovery catalog resides can exceed available resources or may not be cost-effective.
- Using the recovery catalog can result in duplication of effort when automated backup, restore, and recovery are not required, because existing procedures that are performed manually or through the OS are adequate.
- There is no requirement for RMAN features such as tablespace point-in-time recovery or automatic recovery when a current control file is not available.

Recovery Catalog Creation

You can create the recovery catalog using tools such as the OEM toolset, SQL*Plus, or Server Manager from the command line. The following recovery catalog creation steps use Server Manager:

- Choosing a remote database where the recovery catalog will reside.
- Determining the backup and resynchronization schedule for the recovery catalog.
- Creating a tablespace for the catalog:

```
SVRMGR> create tablespace RMAN_data
datafile '<file specification>'
     size 20M autoextend on next 20M maxsize 60M;
```

- Creating an **RMAN** user:

```
SVRMGR> create user RMAN identified by RMAN
     2> default tablespace RMAN_data temporary tablespace
temporary_data
     3> quota unlimited on RMAN_data;
```

- Granting the **RECOVER_CATALOG_OWNER** role to the **RMAN** user for maintaining and querying the recovery catalog:

```
SVRMGR> grant RECOVERY_CATALOG_OWNER to RMAN;
```

- Granting applicable DBA privileges to the **RMAN** user:

```
SVRMGR> connect internal as sysdba
Password:
Connected.
SVRMGR> grant dba, sysdba to RMAN;
Statement Processed.
SVRMGR>
```

The target database must be set up for remote SYSDBA access to use the **RMAN** against the target database.

A password file must exist for granting the SYSDBA role.

- Connecting as the **RMAN** user and running the *cat*RMAN.*sql* file to create the database objects for the recovery catalog:

```
SVRMGR> connect RMAN/RMAN
Connected.
SVRMGR> @%ORACLE_HOME%\rdbms80\admin\catRMAN.sql (for NT)
Or
SVRMGR> @$ORACLE_HOME/rdbms/admin/catRMAN.sql (for UNIX)
...
```

- Automating recovery catalog operations such as backup and resynchronization.

Control File Information

The *control file* contains information about the backup, restore, and recovery operations performed by the **RMAN** utility. The amount of information stored in the control file depends on the frequency of backups, the size of the target database, and the default or specified retention period. The init.ora parameter **CONTROL_FILE_RECORD_KEEP_TIME** is used to specify the number of days the **RMAN** information is stored in the control file before being overwritten. Setting a low value will cause the information to get overwritten more frequently and minimize control file growth. The default is seven days. If a recovery catalog is being used, it is recommended that you specify a lower value.

When you're using a recovery catalog, always ensure that the resynchronization process occurs more frequently than overwrites to the control file.

The control file will grow only when there is no free space in the control file and no available overwrite space for entries older than the time specified by CONTROL_FILE_RECORD_KEEP_TIME.

RMAN may create a snapshot control file when it needs a read-consistent image of the control file. A snapshot control file is needed when **RMAN** is querying the noncircular reuse records for data file, tablespace, online redo log file, and thread information. The default location in which the snapshot control file is created under Unix is **$ORACLE_HOME/dbs/snapcf_<dbname>.f**. You can specify a different location using the following command:

```
RMAN> set snapshot controlfile name to '<file specification>';
```

Because the recovery catalog contains information that is duplicated in the control file, the **RMAN** utility can use the recovery catalog to re-create control files in the event they are lost.

Resynchronizing The Control File

Information in the recovery catalog is initially extracted from the target database control file. Any structural changes such as adding tablespaces will cause the control file and the recovery catalog to get "out of synch," because the control file updates are not automatically reflected in the recovery catalog. It is highly recommended that you automate the recovery catalog resynchronization process. The frequency of the resynchronization process depends on the following factors:

- How fast the archive log files are created.
- How often the database structures change.
- The perfoRMANce requirement of the resynchronization process.

Some RMAN commands such as backup, copy, switch, and restore will perform automatic resynchronization.

Connecting To Oracle Recovery Manager

You have two options for connecting to the RMAN utility:

- Using a recovery catalog
- Without a recovery catalog

Connecting To RMAN Using A Recovery Catalog

To connect to RMAN using a recovery catalog, perform the following steps:

- Determine the target database that needs to be backed up.
- Determine the recovery catalog database for the target database.
- Use one of the following methods to connect to RMAN:
    - For local RMAN connections, specify the following code samples at the OS prompt:

```
Unix:
$ ORACLE_SID=your_local_target_database_instance
$export ORACLE_SID
$ RMAN rcvcat RMAN/RMAN@remote_recovery_catalog_instance
RMAN> connect target (password file not in use)
Or
RMAN> connect target username_at_target_db/password
(password file in use)

NT:
C:\> set ORACLE_SID=your_local_target_database_instance
C:\> RMAN80 rcvcat RMAN/
RMAN@remote_recovery_catalog_instance
```

```
Recovery Manager: Release 8.0.5.0.0 - Production

RMAN-06008: connected to recovery catalog database

RMAN> connect target (password file not in use)
Or
RMAN> connect target username_at_target_db/password
(password file in use)
```

- For RMAN connections initiated by a user with SYSDBA privileges, specify the following code samples at the OS prompt:

```
$ RMAN target username_with_sysdba_privileges/password
rcvcat RMAN/RMAN@remote_recovery_catalog_instance
```

- For remote RMAN connections, specify the following code samples at the OS prompt:

```
$ RMAN target username_at_remote_target_db/password rcvcat
RMAN/RMAN@remote_recovery_catalog_instance
```

The connect string for remote connections should be a valid Transparent Network Substrate (TNS) alias contained in the tnsnames.ora file.

Connecting To **RMAN** Without Using A Recovery Catalog

To connect to RMAN without using a recovery catalog, perform the following steps:

- Determine the target database that needs to be backed up.
- Use one of the following methods to connect to RMAN:
    - For local RMAN connections, specify the following code samples at the OS prompt:

```
Unix:
$ ORACLE_SID=your_local_target_database_instance; export
ORACLE_SID
$ RMAN nocatalog
RMAN> connect target (password file not in use)
```

```
Or
RMAN> connect target username_at_target_db/password
(password file in use)

NT:
C:\> set ORACLE_SID=your_local_target_database_instance
C:\> RMAN80 nocatalog

Recovery Manager: Release 8.0.5.0.0 - Production
RMAN-06009: using target database controlfile instead of
recovery catalog

RMAN> connect target (password file not in use)
Or
RMAN> connect target username_at_target_db/password
(password file in use)

RMAN-06005: connected to target database: ORCO
RMAN>
```

- For **RMAN** connections initiated by a user with SYSDBA privileges, specify the following code samples at the OS prompt:

```
$ RMAN target username_with_sysdba_privileges/password
nocatalog
```

- For remote **RMAN** connections, specify the following code samples at the OS prompt:

```
$ RMAN target username_at_remote_target_db/password
nocatalog
```

The target database must be mounted or open for **RMAN** to connect, and if a recovery catalog is used, the catalog must be open.

To access online help on **RMAN** command line arguments, you can type the following invalid **RMAN** command line specification and get useful descriptions of valid **RMAN** command line arguments and usages:

```
C:\>RMAN80 ?

Argument     Value          Description
-----------------------------------------------------------------
target       quoted-string  connect-string for target
                            database (required)
rcvcat       quoted-string  connect-string for recovery catalog
debug        none           if specified, activate debuggin mode
cmdfile      quoted-string  name of input command file
msglog       quoted-string  name of output message log file
trace        quoted-string  name of output debugging message
                            log file
append       none           if specified, msglog opened in append
                            mode
-----------------------------------------------------------------
Both single and double quotes (' or ") are accepted for a
quoted-string.
On some operating systems, you must escape quotes from the shell.

RMAN-00569: ================error message stack follows============
RMAN-00552: syntax error in command line arguments
RMAN-01006: error signalled during parse
RMAN-02001: unrecognized punctuation symbol "?"

C:\>
```

Practice Questions

Question 1

What utility can be used to interact with **RMAN** in a GUI interface?

❍ a. Software Manager

❍ b. Backup Manager

❍ c. Server Manager

❍ d. SQL*Worksheet

❍ e. Enterprise Backup Utility

The correct answer is b. The Backup Manager is a GUI client application program that runs on Windows NT and interfaces with the RMAN server processes in the target database. Answers a, c, d, and e are incorrect, because they don't provide the capability to interact with RMAN.

Question 2

What initialization parameter can be used to specify the number of days before **RMAN** information in the control file can be overwritten?

❍ a. **CONTROL_FILE_RECORD_REUSE_TIME**

❍ b. **CONTROL_FILE_RECORD_REUSE**

❍ c. **CONTROL_FILE_RECORD_KEEP_TIME**

❍ d. **CONTROL_FILE_RECORD_KEEP**

❍ e. **CONTROL_FILE_EXPIRE_TIME**

The correct answer is c. The CONTROL_FILE_RECORD_KEEP_TIME initialization parameter can be used to specify the number of days that RMAN keeps backup, restore, and recovery information in the control file. Answers a, b, d, and e are incorrect, because they are invalid initialization parameters.

Question 3

Which of the following are characteristics of **RMAN**? [Choose two]

- ❑ a. It is the only backup option available for an Oracle8 database.
- ❑ b. It generates more redo information.
- ❑ c. It provides detection of corrupted blocks.
- ❑ d. It is compatible with EBU.
- ❑ e. It supports incremental block level backups.

The correct answers are c and e. **RMAN** features include detection of corrupted blocks and support for incremental block level backups. Answer a is incorrect, because **RMAN** is not the only backup option for Oracle8 databases. Answer b is incorrect, because **RMAN** generates less redo information. Answer d is incorrect, because EBU is not compatible with **RMAN** and does not support Oracle8.

Question 4

What script file needs to be run to create database objects for the recovery catalog?

- ❍ a. **RMAN**.sql
- ❍ b. utl**RMAN**.sql
- ❍ c. dbms**RMAN**.sql
- ❍ d. cat**RMAN**.sql

The correct answer is d. Running the cat**RMAN**.sql script file is part of the recovery catalog creation process. Answers a, b, and c are incorrect, because they are invalid script files.

Question 5

Under which of the following circumstances should you use **RMAN** with a recovery catalog?

❍ a. When support for the execution of backup scripts is required.

❍ b. When you need to minimize the amount of required disk space.

❍ c. When the backup of archived redo log files requires the use of a recovery catalog.

❍ d. When historical information about backup, restore, and recovery actions are required.

The correct answer is d. A recovery catalog should be used with RMAN to store and maintain historical information about backup, restore, and recovery actions. Answer a is incorrect, because a recovery catalog only provides storage for the scripts. Answer b is incorrect, because additional storage space is required for the recovery catalog. Answer c is incorrect, because a recovery catalog is not required when you're performing backups of the archived redo log files.

Question 6

Which of the following needs to be created to support tablespace point-in-time recovery?

❍ a. An **RMAN** configuration file

❍ b. A complete offline database backup using OS mechanisms

❍ c. Backup scripts

❍ d. A recovery catalog

The correct answer is d. A recovery catalog is required to perform tablespace point-in-time recovery. Answer a is incorrect, because it is an invalid file. Answers b and c are incorrect, because they don't need to be created to perform tablespace point-in-time recovery.

Question 7

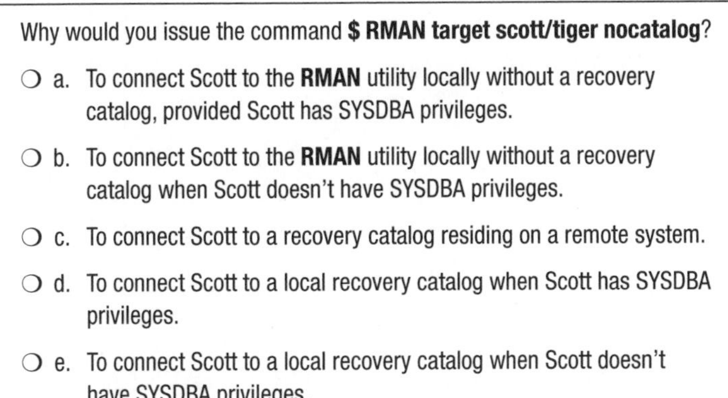

Why would you issue the command **$ RMAN target scott/tiger nocatalog**?

❍ a. To connect Scott to the **RMAN** utility locally without a recovery catalog, provided Scott has SYSDBA privileges.

❍ b. To connect Scott to the **RMAN** utility locally without a recovery catalog when Scott doesn't have SYSDBA privileges.

❍ c. To connect Scott to a recovery catalog residing on a remote system.

❍ d. To connect Scott to a local recovery catalog when Scott has SYSDBA privileges.

❍ e. To connect Scott to a local recovery catalog when Scott doesn't have SYSDBA privileges.

The correct answer is a. The given command can be used to connect a user with SYSDBA privileges to the RMAN utility locally without a recovery catalog. Answer b is incorrect, because Scott needs SYSDBA privileges to connect to the RMAN utility locally without a recovery catalog. Answers c, d, and e are incorrect, because the given command can't be used to connect to a recovery catalog.

Question 8

In a typical On-Line Transaction Processing (OLTP) database environment, what would be the minimum frequency for the resynchronization of the recovery catalog and its target database?

❍ a. Yearly

❍ b. Quarterly

❍ c. Monthly

❍ d. Weekly

❍ e. Daily

The correct answer is e. You should resynchronize the recovery catalog at least once a day with its target database, because updates in the control file are not automatically applied to the recovery catalog. The frequency of the resynchronization process depends on the following factors: How fast the archive log files are created, how often the database structures change, and the perfoRMANce requirement for the resynchronization process. Answers a, b, c, and d are incorrect, because they are inadequate for a typical OLTP database environment.

Question 9

Which database role contains privileges that enable the user with the granted role to query and maintain the recovery catalog?

- ❍ a. **CONNECT**
- ❍ b. **RESOURCE**
- ❍ c. **DBA**
- ❍ d. **SYSDBA**
- ❍ e. **RECOVERY_CATALOG_OWNER**

The correct answer is e. The RECOVERY_CATALOG_OWNER role contains privileges that enable the user to query and maintain the recovery catalog. Answers a, b, c, and d are incorrect, because these database roles don't contain privileges to query and maintain the recovery catalog.

Question 10

What **RMAN** command can be issued to enable **RMAN** to create a temporary backup copy of the control file?

- ❍ a. **RMAN> backup controlfile name to '/disk01/RMAN_backup/prod_ctrl_1.snp';**
- ❍ b. **RMAN> resync catalog from controlfilecopy '/disk01/RMAN_backup/prod_ctrl_1.snp';**
- ❍ c. **RMAN> reset database to incarnation '/disk01/RMAN_backup/prod_ctrl_1.snp';**
- ❍ d. **RMAN> set snapshot controlfile name to '/disk01/RMAN_backup/prod_ctrl_1.snp';**

The correct answer is d. The RMAN command SET SNAPSHOT CONTROLFILE NAME TO '<file specification>' is used to create a temporary backup of the control file. Answer a is incorrect, because it is an invalid RMAN command. Answers b and c are incorrect, because they perform other RMAN functions.

Need To Know More?

Dialeris, Connie. *Oracle8 Backup and Recovery Guide Release 8.0*, Part No. A58396-01, Oracle Corporation, 1997.

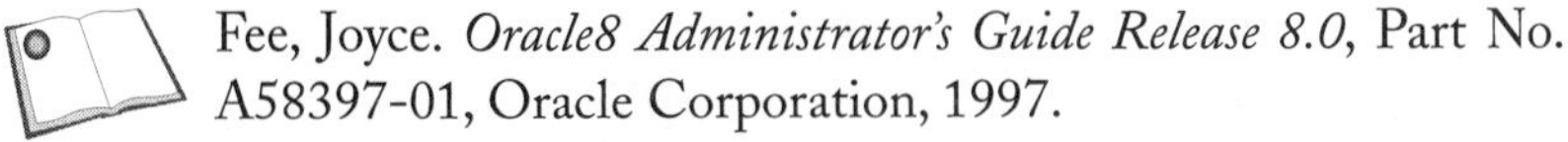

Fee, Joyce. *Oracle8 Administrator's Guide Release 8.0*, Part No. A58397-01, Oracle Corporation, 1997.

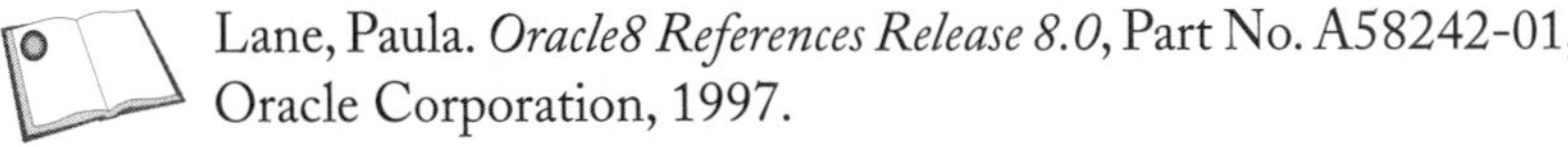

Lane, Paula. *Oracle8 References Release 8.0*, Part No. A58242-01, Oracle Corporation, 1997.

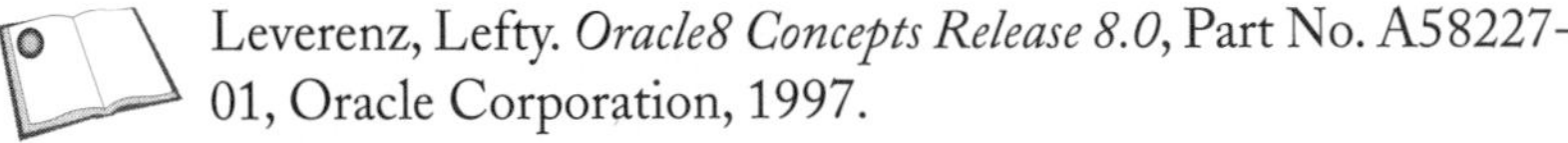

Leverenz, Lefty. *Oracle8 Concepts Release 8.0*, Part No. A58227-01, Oracle Corporation, 1997.

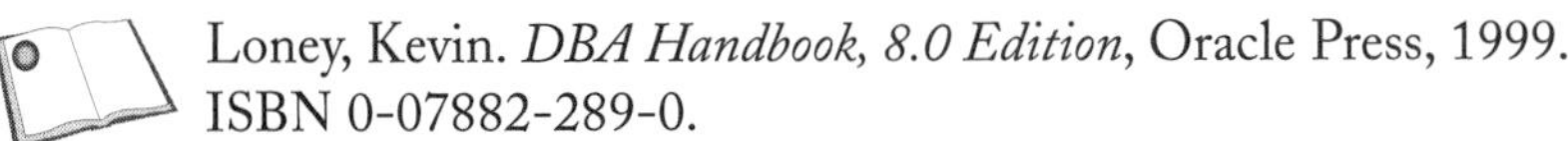

Loney, Kevin. *DBA Handbook, 8.0 Edition*, Oracle Press, 1999. ISBN 0-07882-289-0.

Velpuri, Rama. *Oracle Backup and Recovery Handbook*, Oracle Press, 1998. ISBN: 0-07882-389-7.

6

Oracle Recovery Catalog Maintenance

Terms you'll need to understand:

- √ **Register Database** command
- √ **Resync Catalog** command
- √ **Reset Database** command
- √ Incarnation
- √ Backup set
- √ Backup piece
- √ Data file copy
- √ Channel
- √ **Change** command
- √ **Catalog** command
- √ **Report** command
- √ **List** command
- √ Stored scripts
- √ **Run** command
- √ **RC_DATABASE**
- √ **RC_TABLESPACE**
- √ **RC_DATAFILE**
- √ **RC_STORED_SCRIPT**
- √ **RC_STORED_SCRIPT_LINE**

Techniques you'll need to master:

- √ Invoking Recovery Manager (**RMAN**) with a recovery catalog
- √ Registering a database
- √ Resynchronizing a database
- √ Resetting a database
- √ Understanding recovery catalog maintenance
- √ Re-creating the recovery catalog
- √ Understanding report and list generation
- √ Using **RMAN** scripts for backup and recovery operations
- √ Understanding useful data dictionary views for the recovery catalog

This chapter provides information on using the Oracle Recovery Manager (RMAN) with a recovery catalog. We'll focus on maintenance activities on the recovery catalog and introduce you to commands for registering, resynchronizing, and resetting the database. You will learn how to use the **Change** and **Catalog** commands to maintain the recovery catalog and learn how to rebuild a lost or damaged recovery catalog. You will also learn about **RMAN**'s report generation, list generation, and stored scripts. Lastly, you will learn about useful data dictionary views for the recovery catalog.

Invoking Recovery Manager

Several methods invoke the **RMAN** tool, including the following:

- Without a recovery catalog. Refer to Chapter 5 for details.
- With a recovery catalog using the **RCVCAT** option.
- Using an interactive mode interface.
- Using a batch mode interface via the **CMDFILE** option.
- Using the batch mode interface with a message log file via the **MSGLOG** option for recording **RMAN** actions and results. The message log file can be appended or overwritten. The **APPEND** option can be used to continue writing to an existing message log file.

When you're starting **RMAN**, all command options are optional except one: You must connect to a target database.

Registering A Database

To use **RMAN** against a target database, you must set up the target database for remote SYSDBA access. To configure a database for remote SYSDBA access, perform the following steps:

1. Login to your server as the Oracle user and set the **ORACLE_HOME** and the **ORACLE_SID** environment variables.
2. Change to the *dbs* or *database* directory in your **ORACLE_HOME** directory.
3. Rename your password file if one exists. The password file name format is orapw concatenated with the Oracle SID. An example password file name is orapwORCL.
4. Run the **ORAPWD** or **ORAPWD80** executable to create a new password file, as illustrated by the following sample code:

```
Unix:
$ORACLE_HOME/bin/orapwd file=orapwORCL password=mypassword
entries=10

NT:
D:\ORANT\BIN> orapwd80 file=orapwORCL password=mypassword
entries=10
```

5. Shut down your database.
6. Edit the *init<SID>.ora* file. Add the following parameter statement to the file:

```
REMOTE_LOGIN_PASSWORDFILE = EXCLUSIVE
```

You can use the Instance Manager to modify initialization parameters.

7. Start your database using tools like the Server Manager or the Instance Manager.
8. Login as internal or sys and create a user that will have remote SYSDBA privileges. The following sample code creates a username **REMOTEUSER** with password XXXXXXXX and the SYSDBA role:

```
SVRMGR> connect internal
Password:
Connected.
SVRMGR> create user REMOTEUSER identified by REMOTEPWD;
Statement processed.
SVRMGR> grant connect, resource to REMOTEUSER;
Statement processed.
SVRMGR> grant SYSDBA to REMOTEUSER;
Statement processed.
SVRMGR>
```

9. Download the *init<SID>.ora* file and the *config<SID>.ora* file from the server to the **$ORACLE_HOME\sysman\ifiles** directory in the client machine.
10. Edit the **IFILE** path in the *init<SID>.ora* file to match the location on the client machine.
11. Test the remote SYSDBA login account.

Before you can perform any backups against a target database using **RMAN** with a recovery catalog, you must register the target database in the recovery catalog. The target database must be in the mounted or open state, because information about the target database is extracted from the control file to the recovery catalog. The following steps describe how to register a target database with the recovery catalog using the **RMAN** command line interface:

1. Connect to the target database as **SYSDBAUSER** from the command line:

```
RMAN> RMAN80 Target SYSDBAUSER/PASSWORD@targetdb_loc RCVCAT
rman/rman@catalogdb_loc

Recovery Manager: Release 8.0.5.0.0 - Production

RMAN-06005: connected to target database: TARGETDB
RMAN-06008: connected to recovery catalog database

RMAN>
```

2. Issue the **REGISTER DATABASE** command. The **REGISTER DATABASE** command synchronizes the recovery catalog with the target database control file. The following sample code illustrates this command:

```
RMAN> register database;

RMAN-03022: compiling command: register
RMAN-03023: executing command: register
RMAN-08006: database registered in recovery catalog
RMAN-03023: executing command: full resync
RMAN-08029: snapshot controlfile name set to default value:
%ORACLE_HOME%\DATABASE\SNCF%ORACLE_SID%.ORASE\SN
RMAN-08002: starting full resync of recovery catalog
RMAN-08004: full resync complete
RMAN>
```

To register the target database using the Backup Manager, perform the following steps:

1. The target database must be a discovered service. The Oracle8 Intelligent Agent must be running on the target database to enable service discovery. Figure 6.1 illustrates two Oracle8 databases that have been registered in the OEM as discovered services.

If the target database has not been discovered, select the Navigator menu in the OEM console, then select Service Discovery|Discover New Services. Figure 6.2 illustrates the Service Discovery option.

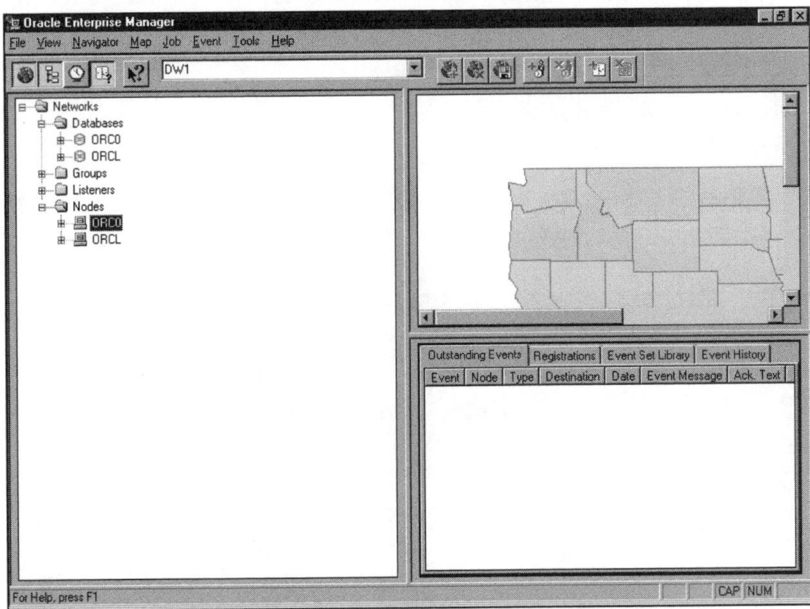

Figure 6.1 Discovered services in the OEM.

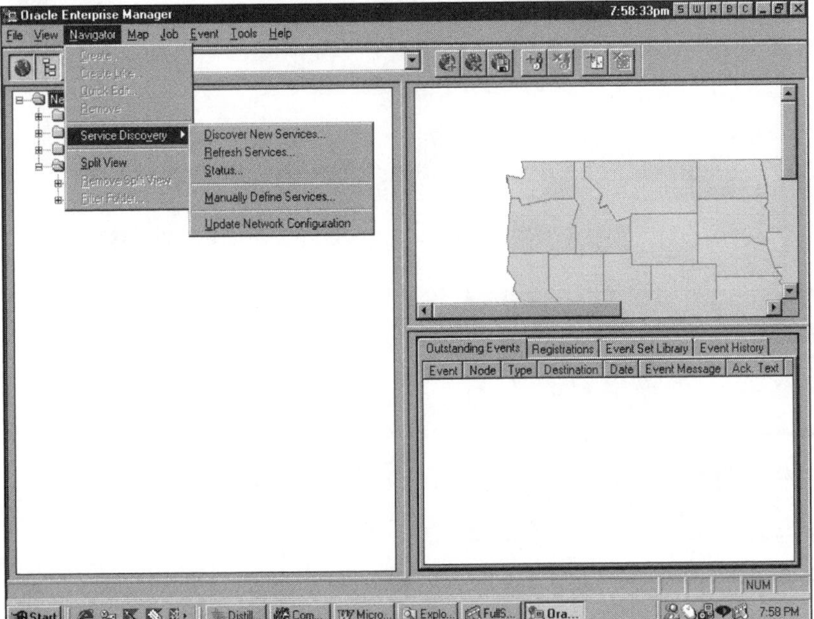

Figure 6.2 Service Discovery option in the OEM.

Once the target database has been discovered, check the preferred connection credentials under User Preferences. Make sure SYSDBA access is specified to any target database that needs to be backed up. Figure 6.3 illustrates the User Preferences dialog box with the Preferred Credentials tab.

2. Select the target database and start the Backup Manager. The Backup Manager Subsystem selection dialog box appears, as illustrated in Figure 6.4.

3. The Recovery Manager backup interface is displayed when you select the Oracle8 Recovery Manager option, as illustrated in Figure 6.5.

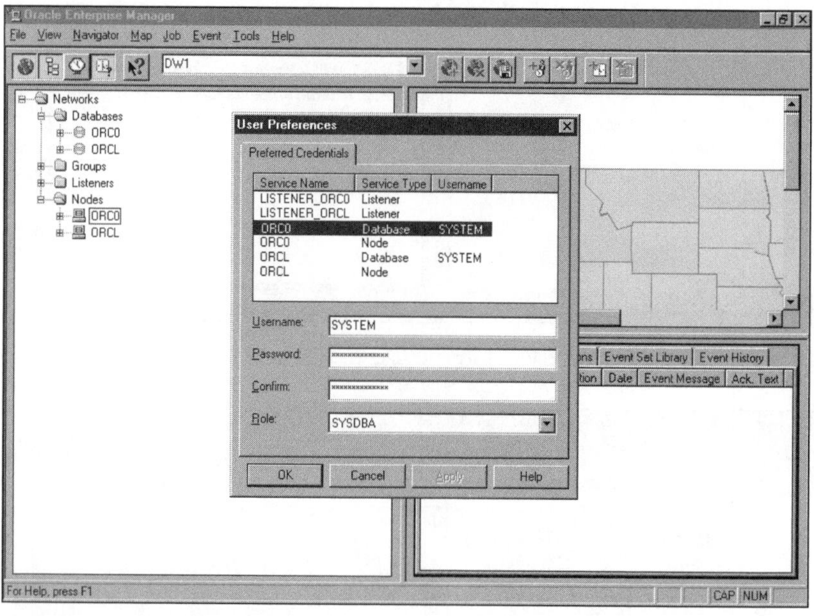

Figure 6.3 Preferred Credentials for connecting to the target database.

Figure 6.4 The Backup Manager Subsystem selection dialog box.

4. Connect to the recovery catalog. Choose Catalog|Connect String. Enter the **RMAN** connect information in the Recovery Catalog Login dialog box. Figure 6.6 illustrates the Recovery Catalog Login dialog box.

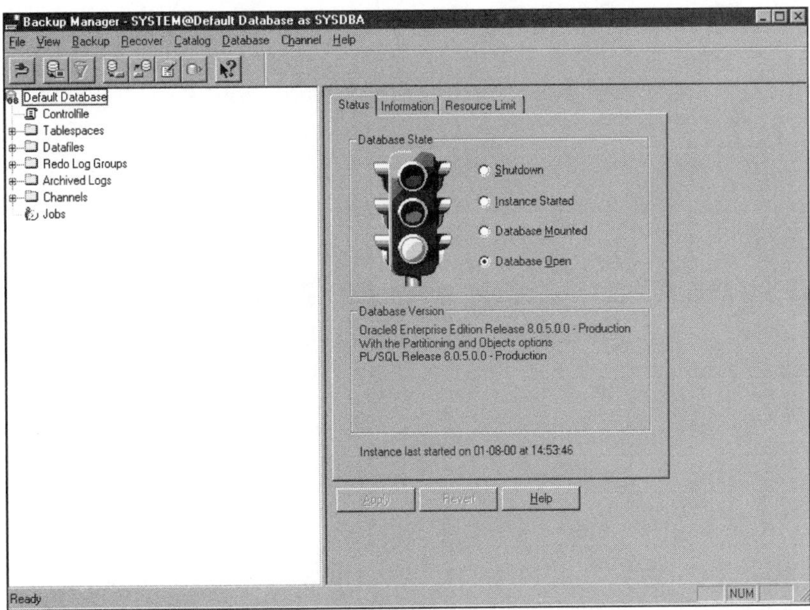

Figure 6.5 The Recovery Manager backup interface.

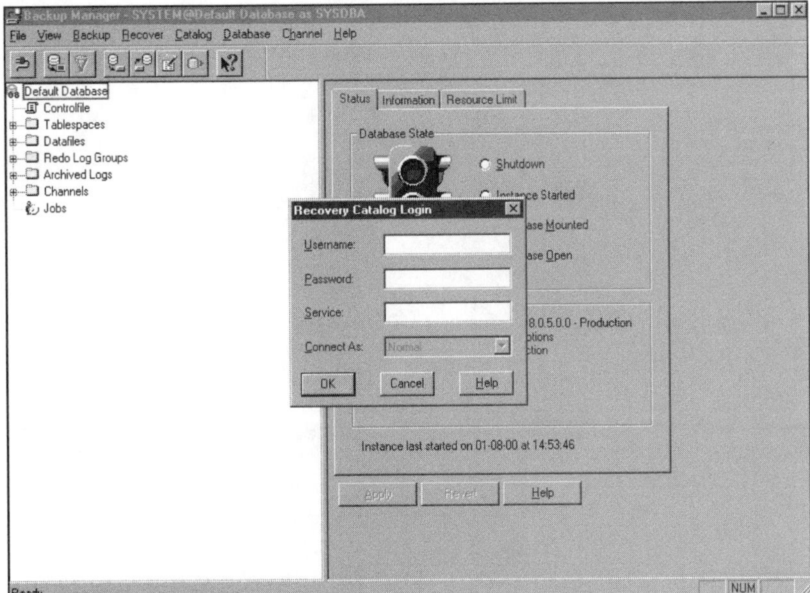

Figure 6.6 The Recovery Catalog Login dialog box.

5. Register the target database. Select Catalog|Use Recovery Catalog. The Resync, Reset, and Register options become available. Select the Register menu option. The Register target database dialog box appears, as illustrated in Figure 6.7.

The **REGISTER DATABASE** command has to be executed for all new target databases.

Resynchronizing A Database

The recovery catalog is not updated automatically when the following database events occur:

- A log switch takes place
- A redo log file is archived
- The database structure is changed

The **Resync Catalog** operation enables **RMAN** to compare the recovery catalog with the current control file of the target database and to update the recovery catalog with new or changed information. The **Resync Catalog** operation should

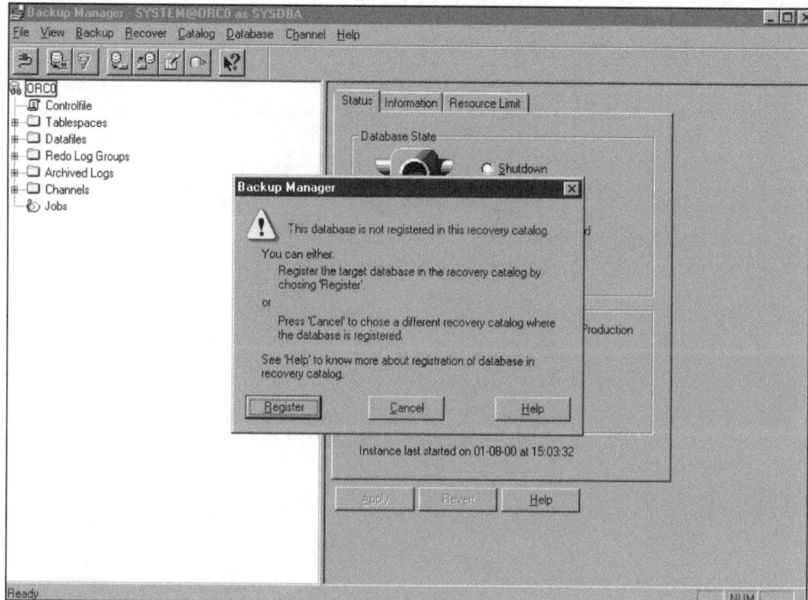

Figure 6.7 Register target database dialog box.

be performed frequently. For performance reasons, **RMAN** only resynchronizes the control file information that is inconsistent with the recovery catalog. The recovery catalog stores all pertinent information required for recovery.

Resync Catalog Command Syntax

The command syntax for the **Resync Catalog** command is as follows:

```
resync catalog [from controlfilecopy <control_file_name>];
```

Recovery Catalog Information Affected By The Resynchronization Process

When the **Resync Catalog** command is issued to **RMAN** and the target database is in the mounted state, the following information in the recovery catalog may be updated:

- Structural database information that is associated with data files and tablespaces. If the target database is in the open state, then the rollback segment information will also be updated.
- Log switch information. **RMAN** maintains log switch information so it knows what archived redo log files are available.
- Archived log copy information that is associated with archived redo log files.
- Backup history information relating to backup sets, backup pieces, backup set members, and file copies. This update will occur only when the recovery catalog database was unavailable and a backup or copy command was processed.

When To Perform The **Resync Catalog** Operation

The DBA is responsible for issuing a **Resync Catalog** command after making any structural database changes to the target database. A structural database change includes the following target database actions:

- Adding a rollback segment
- Dropping a rollback segment
- Adding a tablespace
- Dropping a tablespace
- Adding a data file to an existing tablespace

The DBA should be aware that if the target database has mounted a noncurrent control file such as a backup control file, a newly created control file, or an outdated control file, then the structural database information in the recovery catalog will not be updated.

RMAN will perform automatic resynchronization before and after a backup, restore, or recovery command if a connection to the recovery catalog database has been established. If a connection to the recovery catalog database can't be established, then the **Resync Catalog** command needs to be manually issued after the backup and copy commands. The following code sample shows the results of the **Resync Catalog** command, which by default is against the current target database control file:

```
RMAN> resync catalog;

RMAN-03022: compiling command: resync
RMAN-03023: executing command: resync
RMAN-08002: starting full resync of recovery catalog
RMAN-08004: full resync complete
RMAN>
```

To perform resynchronization against a backup control file, issue the following command:

```
RMAN> resync catalog from controlfilecopy
'<backup_control_file_specification>';
```

Alternatively, you can perform the following steps when using Backup Manager to resynchronize the recovery catalog database:

1. Select the target database from the OEM console and start the Backup Manager application.
2. Select the Oracle8 Recovery Manager Subsystem.
3. Connect to the recovery catalog. Choose Catalog|Connect String. Enter the **RMAN** connect information for the recovery catalog.
4. Resynchronize the recovery catalog. Select Catalog|Resync.

Resetting A Database

When an incomplete recovery has been performed for a target database, the target database will be opened with the **RESETLOGS** option, which resets the sequence number of the online redo log files to zero. Refer to Chapter 12 for detailed information on incomplete recovery.

The recovery catalog will not be accessible to **RMAN** until a **Reset Database** command has been issued. The **Reset Database** command directs **RMAN** to create a new incarnation or version of the target database information in the recovery catalog. An incarnation of a database is a sequence number used to identify a version of the target database prior to the reset of the log sequence number to zero. **RMAN** maintains database incarnations information so that applicable backups and archived redo log files are associated with the right incarnation. This prevents you from incorrectly applying redo log files to the wrong version of the database.

Reset Database Command Syntax

The command syntax for the **Reset Database** command is as follows:

```
Reset database [to incarnation <incarnation key identifier>];
```

The following code sample illustrates the result you'll get if you try to reset your database when the incarnation is already registered:

```
RMAN> reset database;
RMAN-03022: compiling command: reset
RMAN-03023: executing command: reset
RMAN-03026: error recovery releasing channel resources
RMAN-00569: ========error message stack follows==========
RMAN-03006: non-retryable error occurred during execution of com-
mand
RMAN-07004: unhandled exception during command execution on channel
RMAN-10032: unhandled exception during execution of job step 1:
RMAN-20009: database incarnation already registered
```

The **Reset Database To Incarnation** command is typically used to undo the **RESETLOGS** operation by restoring backups of prior incarnations/versions of the database. You can obtain the database incarnation key identifier by using the **List Incarnation Of Database** command, as illustrated by the following code sample:

```
RMAN> list incarnation of database;
RMAN-03022: compiling command: list
RMAN-06240: List of Database Incarnations
RMAN-06241: DB Key Inc Key DB Name DB ID  CUR Reset SCN Reset Time
RMAN-06242: ------ ------  ------- ------ --- ----- --- ----------
RMAN-06243: 1      2       ORCO    115732 YES 1         26-DEC-99
RMAN-06244: 1      7       ORCO    115732 NO  1075      22-DEC-99
RMAN> reset database to incarnation 7;
```

Alternatively, you can perform the following steps when using Backup Manager to reset the recovery catalog database:

1. Select the target database from the OEM console and start the Backup Manager application.
2. Select the Oracle8 Recovery Manager Subsystem.
3. Connect to the recovery catalog. Choose Catalog|Connect String. Enter the **RMAN** connect information for the recovery catalog.
4. Reset the recovery catalog. Select Catalog|Reset.

Recovery Catalog Maintenance

To effectively perform recovery catalog maintenance, a DBA should have an understanding of the following terminology:

- *Backup set*—A logical structure that is comprised of backup pieces.
- *Backup piece*—A physical file on a disk or tape that contains one or more data files or archived redo log files in **RMAN** format.
- *Data file copy*—A physical copy of a data file or control file on disk.
- *Archived logs*—Copies of redo log files for an archiving-enabled database.

The commands for performing recovery catalog maintenance include the following:

- **Allocate/Release Channel** command
- **Change** command
- **Catalog** command

Allocate/Release Channel Command

A *channel* is an **RMAN** resource allocation. Each allocated channel starts a new Oracle server process that performs backup, restore, and recovery operations. The number of channels allocated affects the degree of parallelism for backup, restore, and recovery. The type of channel specified determines whether the Oracle server process reads and writes to disk or through the Media Management Interface to a Media Manager. Any command that accesses the operating system must allocate a channel. Only one channel can be allocated at a time, so you should release the channel when all O/S commands have been completed. The following code sample illustrates the **Allocate Channel** and the **Release Channel** commands:

```
RMAN> allocate channel channel_a type disk;
RMAN> allocate channel for delete type 'SBT_TAPE';
RMAN> release channel channel_a;
```

The **for delete** option is used only for deleting files. It cannot be used as an input or output channel for a job. Refer to Chapter 8 for more information on the **Allocate Channel** command.

Change Command

The **Change** command is used on backup set, backup piece, data file copy, archive log, and control files. It performs the following actions.

- It updates the recovery catalog to mark files as **AVAILABLE** or **UNAVAILABLE** for restore and recovery. The following code sample illustrates using the **Change** command to mark an archived redo log file as unavailable:

  ```
  RMAN> change archivelog '/u1/archive/arch_999.rdo' unavailable;
  ```

- It removes references to nonexistent physical files from the control file and the recovery catalog. The following code sample illustrates removing a reference to an archived redo log file that no longer exists in the file system:

  ```
  RMAN> change archivelog '/u1/archive/arch_998.rdo' uncatalog;
  ```

- It determines files in the recovery catalog with corresponding physical files on storage devices and removes/deletes files from the recovery catalog without corresponding physical files. The following code sample illustrates using the **validate** option to remove a batch of files from the recovery catalog when they have been deleted from the physical storage media:

  ```
  RMAN> change archivelog all validate;
  ```

- It removes old files from the control file, recovery catalog, and from the physical media. The following code sample illustrates deleting a data file backup:

  ```
  RMAN> allocate channel for delete type disk;
  RMAN> change datafilecopy '/u1/oradata/appldata.bak' delete;
  RMAN> release channel;
  ```

Catalog Command

The **Catalog** command allows you to add data file copy information, archived redo log information, or control file copy information to the recovery catalog. The **Catalog** command records information for any of the following types of files:

- Files created before the installation of RMAN
- Files created using O/S backup mechanisms
- Files with the same database incarnation number
- Files that have Oracle8 or later file format
- Files that belong to the target database

When mirrored disk drives are broken, you can use the **Catalog** command to add the location of the file copies to the recovery catalog. When the disks are remirrored, you can use the **Change ... uncatalog** command to remove the file copies from the recovery catalog.

The following sample code illustrates adding data file copy and archived redo log file to the recovery catalog:

```
UNIX:
RMAN> catalog datafilecopy '/u1/backup/appldata.bak';
RMAN> catalog archivelog '/u1/archive/arch_102.log';

NT:
RMAN> catalog datafilecopy 'd:\orant\backup\appldata.bak';
RMAN> catalog archivelog 'd:\orant\archive\arch_102.log';
```

Re-Creating The Recovery Catalog

If the recovery catalog database is lost or damaged, the following actions will rebuild it:

1. Extract information from a backup control file by issuing the **Resync catalog from backup controlfile <file name>** command and rebuild the recovery catalog.
2. If an export dump file containing the data for the recovery catalog owner is available, then import the data and use the **Resync** command to synchronize with the target database.
3. After rebuilding the catalog database, issue **Catalog** commands to recatalog data file copies, control file copies, and archived redo log files.

You should be aware of the following issues when re-creating the recovery catalog:

- The **Catalog** command cannot be used to catalog backup sets or backup pieces. You must use the **Resync Catalog From Backup Controlfile** command to re-create information about backup sets.
- During resynchronization, **RMAN** may add records for files that no longer exist because no verification is performed. You can remove those records by using the **Change ... Delete** command.

Report And List Generation

The recovery catalog reporting commands enable DBAs to analyze and list information contained in the recovery catalog. Oracle8 supports two reporting commands:

- **Report** command
- **List** command

Report Command

The **Report** command is used to facilitate analysis of the backup, copy, restore, and recovery operations. This command provides more detailed analysis than the **List** command. You can produce reports using the **Report** command to meet requirements such as:

- Determining what files need to be backed up. You can use the **Report need backup...** command for this purpose.
- Determining which backups are no longer needed and can be deleted. You can use the **Report obsolete** command for this purpose.
- Determining which files are not recoverable due to unrecoverable operations. You can use the **Report unrecoverable...** command for this purpose.
- Determining the physical structure of the database at a point-in-time in the past. You can use the **Report schema** command for this purpose.

The **Report Need Backup** command is used to identify all data files needing a backup. This report assumes that the most recent backup would be used in the event of a restore. The options to the **Report Need Backup** command are as follows:

- *Incremental*—An integer value that specifies the maximum number of incremental backups that should be restored during recovery. A full backup is needed for a data file if it needs at least this number of incremental backups for recovery. The following code sample illustrates producing a report of files needing four or more incremental backups for recovery:

```
RMAN> report need backup incremental 4 database;
```

➤ *Days*—An integer value that specifies the maximum number of days since the last full or incremental backup of a file. A file will need a backup if the most recent backup occurred at least this number of days in the past. The following code sample illustrates producing a report showing files for the **appl1_data** tablespace that have not been backed up for four days:

```
RMAN> report need backup days 4 tablespace appl_data;
```

➤ *Redundancy*—An integer value that specifies the minimum level of redundancy needed. For example, a redundancy level of three requires a backup if there are not at least three backups available. The following code sample illustrates producing a report showing a redundancy level of two:

```
RMAN> report need backup redundancy 2;
```

Report Command Syntax

The **Report** command syntax relevant to this chapter is as follows:

```
Report need backup <options> = integer <object> <name>;
Report unrecoverable <object> <name>;
Report obsolete redundancy = integer;
Report schema <atClause>;
```

Table 6.1 describes command elements and their associated values.

You cannot specify both incremental and days as options.

Table 6.1 Elements of the Report Command.

Element	Value
Options	incremental; days; redundancy;
Object	datafile; tablespace; database;
Name	quoted_string;
AtClause	at time=<quoted_string>; at scn=integer; at logseq=integer;

List Command

The **List** command is used to display information on the database elements from the recovery catalog. Specifically, the **List** command can provide information on the following recovery catalog elements:

- Backup sets that contain a backup of a specified list of data files
- Copies of specified data files
- Backup sets containing a backup of a data file for a specified tablespace
- Copies of any data file for a specified tablespace
- Backup sets that include a backup of archived redo logs for a specified range
- Copies of archived redo logs with a specified range or name
- Database incarnations

List Command Syntax

The **List** command syntax relevant to this chapter is as follows:

```
List <Options> of <Object List> <values>;
List incarnation of database of <values>;
```

Table 6.2 decribes command elements and their associated values.

You cannot specify both incremental and days.

Table 6.2 Elements of the List Command.

Element	Value
Options	copy;
	backupset;
Object List	datafile <quoted_string>;
	tablespace <quoted_string>;
	database;
	archivelog all;
Values	tag=<quoted_string>;
	device type <quoted_string>;
	like <quoted_string>;
	from time=<quoted_string>;
	until Time=<quoted_string>;

You must connect to **RMAN** with a target database and a recovery catalog before using the **List** command.

The following code samples illustrate the use of the **List** command.

➤ List all file copies of data files in the **APP_DATA tablespace**:

```
RMAN> list copy of tablespace "APP_DATA";
```

➤ List incarnation for database **ORCL**:

```
RMAN> list incarnation of database ORCL;
```

➤ List all backup sets containing the data file **ecs01.ora**:

```
RMAN> list backupset of datafile "/u1/oradata/ecs01.ora";
```

Alternatively, you can perform the following steps when using Backup Manager to get a listing of backup sets and file copies:

1. Select the target database from the OEM console and start the Backup Manager application.
2. Select the Oracle8 Recovery Manager Subsystem.
3. Connect to the recovery catalog. Choose Catalog|Connect String. Enter the **RMAN** connect information for the recovery catalog.
4. Highlight a data file from the Navigator window.
5. Click on the Backups tab in the right-side window.

RMAN Scripts For Backup And Recovery Operations

An **RMAN** stored script is a set of **RMAN** commands that are stored in the recovery catalog. A **RMAN** stored script enables a DBA using **RMAN** on different platforms to access the scripts. A stored script can relate to a single database and can be executed only if you're using **RMAN** with the recovery catalog option. **RMAN** scripts enable DBAs to perform the following tasks:

➤ Plan, develop, and test backup, restore, and recovery command procedures.

- Specify and store frequently used backup, restore, and recovery operations in the recovery catalog database.
- Automate the backup, restore, and recovery process so user errors are minimized.

Script Commands

Four stored script commands enable DBAs to maintain scripts:

- CREATE—Creates a stored script in the recovery catalog:

```
Create script <quoted_string> {<commands-allocate, backup,
recover, sql> ; }
```

- REPLACE—Replaces and creates a stored script in the recovery catalog:

```
Replace script <quoted_string> {<commands-allocate, backup,
recover, sql> ; }
```

- DELETE—Deletes a stored script from the recovery catalog:

```
Delete script <quoted_string>;
```

- PRINT—Prints a stored script to the **RMAN** message log:

```
Print script <quoted_string>;
```

The following code samples illustrate the **Create Script**, **Replace Script**, and **Delete Script** commands:

```
RMAN> create script DailyBackup {
      Allocate channel c1 type disk;
      Backup
            Incremental level 0
            Format 'df_%d_%s_%p'
            Fileperset 10
            (database include current controlfile);
      sql 'alter database archive log current';}

RMAN> replace script CtrlFileCopy {
      Allocate channel c1 type disk;
      Copy
            Current controlfile to '/u1/oradata/backup/
cur_ctrl.ora';
```

```
    Release channel c1;
    }

RMAN> delete script CtrlFileCopy;
```

Run Command

The **Run** command is used to execute a stored script. The **Run** command can execute O/S commands, SQL scripts, backup commands, stored scripts, and so on. The basic syntax for the **Run** command is as follows:

```
Run { <commands> ; }
```

Commands can be one of the following: **allocate, backup, execute_script <name>, recover, sql, host,** etc.

The **Run** command compiles the commands into PL/SQL code blocks called *steps*. The steps are not written to the recovery catalog, but are run immediately from memory after the compilation phase. The **Run** commands can be stored in a script on the file system or alternatively, **RMAN** can be used to create scripts.

The following code samples illustrate the use of the **Run** command.

- Run an O/S command:

  ```
  RMAN> run { host "ls -al"; }
  ```

- Run an SQL command:

  ```
  RMAN> run { sql "alter system switch logfile"; }
  ```

- Run a stored script:

  ```
  RMAN> run { execute script DailyBackup; }
  ```

Data Dictionary Views For The Recovery Catalog

Several data dictionary views for the recovery catalog were created as a result of running the *catrman.sql* script file. These data dictionary views include the following:

- RC_DATABASE—Provides information on currently registered databases and their current incarnations:

```
SQL> desc rc_database
 Name                                      Null?    Type
 ----------------------------------------- -------- ------
 DB_KEY                                    NOT NULL NUMBER
 DBINC_KEY                                           NUMBER
 DBID                                      NOT NULL NUMBER
 NAME                                      NOT NULL VARCHAR2(8)
 RESETLOGS_CHANGE#                         NOT NULL NUMBER
 RESETLOGS_TIME                            NOT NULL DATE
```

- **RC_TABLESPACE**—Provides information on the tablespaces from the target database that are currently stored in the recovery catalog. Information on dropped tablespaces and tablespaces that belong to older database incarnations are also provided:

```
SQL> desc rc_tablespace
 Name                                      Null?    Type
 ----------------------------------------- -------- -------
 DB_KEY                                    NOT NULL NUMBER
 DBINC_KEY                                 NOT NULL NUMBER
 DB_NAME                                   NOT NULL VARCHAR2(8)
 TS#                                       NOT NULL NUMBER
 NAME                                      NOT NULL VARCHAR2(30)
 CREATION_CHANGE#                          NOT NULL NUMBER
 CREATION_TIME                                      DATE
 DROP_CHANGE#                                       NUMBER
 DROP_TIME                                          DATE
```

- **RC_DATAFILE**—Provides information on the data files from the target database that are currently registered in the recovery catalog:

```
SQL> desc rc_datafile
 Name                                      Null?    Type
 ----------------------------------------- -------- --------
 DB_KEY                                    NOT NULL NUMBER
 DBINC_KEY                                 NOT NULL NUMBER
 DB_NAME                                   NOT NULL VARCHAR2(8)
 TS#                                       NOT NULL NUMBER
 TABLESPACE_NAME                           NOT NULL VARCHAR2(30)
 FILE#                                     NOT NULL NUMBER
 CREATION_CHANGE#                          NOT NULL NUMBER
 CREATION_TIME                                      DATE
 DROP_CHANGE#                                       NUMBER
 DROP_TIME                                          DATE
 BYTES                                              NUMBER
```

```
 BLOCKS                                           NUMBER
 BLOCK_SIZE                              NOT NULL NUMBER
 NAME                                             VARCHAR2(1024)
 STOP_CHANGE#                                     NUMBER
 READ_ONLY                               NOT NULL NUMBER
```

- **RC_STORED_SCRIPT**—Provides information on scripts that are currently stored in the recovery catalog for a target database:

```
SQL> desc rc_stored_script
 Name                                    Null?    Type
 --------------------------------------- -------- --------
 DB_KEY                                  NOT NULL NUMBER
 DB_NAME                                 NOT NULL VARCHAR2(8)
 SCRIPT_NAME                             NOT NULL VARCHAR2(100)
```

- **RC_STORED_SCRIPT_LINE**—Provides information on the commands that make up the stored scripts:

```
SQL> desc rc_stored_script_line
 Name                                    Null?    Type
 --------------------------------------- -------- --------
 DB_KEY                                  NOT NULL NUMBER
 SCRIPT_NAME                             NOT NULL VARCHAR2(100)
 LINE                                    NOT NULL NUMBER
 TEXT                                    NOT NULL VARCHAR2(1024)
```

Practice Questions

Question 1

A new tablespace has been added to the production database. After you are connected to **RMAN**, which of the following commands should you issue to update the recovery catalog?

- ❍ a. **CATALOG**
- ❍ b. **CHANGE**
- ❍ c. **REGISTER**
- ❍ d. **RESYNC CATALOG**
- ❍ e. **UPDATE CATALOG**

The correct answer is d. The **RESYNC CATALOG** command, when issued with the target database in the mounted or open state, will update the recovery catalog information for log switches, archived logs, backup history, and physical database structures. Answers a, b, and c are incorrect, because they serve other purposes. Answer e is incorrect, because it is an invalid command.

Question 2

Which of the following data dictionary views should be used to retrieve a list of tablespaces registered in the recovery catalog for the XYZ database?

- ❍ a. **RC_DATAFILE**
- ❍ b. **RC_TABLESPACE**
- ❍ c. **RC_DATABASE**
- ❍ d. **RC_TABLESPACES**
- ❍ e. **DBA_TABLESPACES**

The correct answer is b. The **RC_TABLESPACE** data dictionary view provides information on tablespaces registered in the recovery catalog for the target database. Answers a and c are incorrect, because these data dictionary views don't provide information on tablespaces registered in the recovery catalog. Answer d is incorrect, because it is an invalid view. Answer e is incorrect, because it provides information on the tablespaces for a database that may not be registered in the recovery catalog.

Question 3

Evaluate this **RMAN** command:

```
RMAN> delete script 'backup_c';
```

What will this command accomplish if it is issued?

❍ a. It will remove the **backup_c** script from the recovery catalog.

❍ b. It will remove the script object from the **backup_c** file.

❍ c. It will remove the script object from the **backup_c** recovery catalog.

❍ d. It will remove the **backup_c** script from the target database.

❍ e. It will drop the script object from the **backup_c** recovery catalog.

The correct answer is a. The DELETE SCRIPT command removes a script from the recovery catalog. Answers b, c, d, and e are incorrect, because the sample command doesn't support these invalid tasks.

Question 4

When connected to **RMAN**, which **RUN** command option enables you to execute an operating system command?

❍ a. **ALLOCATE**

❍ b. **BACKUP**

❍ c. **SQL**

❍ d. **HOST**

❍ e. **EXECUTE SCRIPT**

The correct answer is d. The HOST option of the RUN command enables you to issue O/S commands within RMAN. Answers a, b, c, and e are incorrect, because these options serve other purposes.

Question 5

Which RMAN command should you use to identify all the data files that haven't been backed up in the last three days?

- ❍ a. **RMAN> report need backup days 3**
- ❍ b. **RMAN> list need backup days 3**
- ❍ c. **RMAN> report need backup days 3 tablespace app_data**
- ❍ d. **RMAN> list need backup days 3 tablespace app_data**
- ❍ e. **RMAN> report need backup redundancy 3**
- ❍ f. **RMAN> report need backup 3 days**

The correct answer is a. The **REPORT NEED BACKUP DAYS 3** command will list all the data files that have not been backed up in the last three days. Answers b and d are incorrect, because they are invalid list commands. Answer c is incorrect, because it will only show data files for the **app_data tablespace** that have not been backed up in the last three days. Answer e is incorrect, because it will only list all data files that have less than three backups available. Answer f is incorrect, because it is an invalid report command.

Question 6

What action is typically performed by the DBA after he or she creates a recovery catalog and starts **RMAN** for the first time?

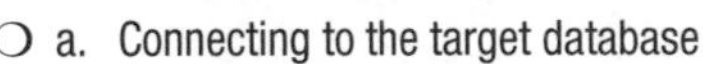

- ❍ a. Connecting to the target database
- ❍ b. Creating the **RMAN** user
- ❍ c. Registering the database
- ❍ d. Updating the recovery catalog
- ❍ e. Performing a backup against a target database

The correct answer is c. The DBA typically registers the target database after recovery catalog creation and initial invocation of **RMAN**. Answer a is incorrect, because the connection to the target database has already been established upon starting **RMAN**. Answer b is incorrect, because the **RMAN** user was created during recovery catalog initialization. Answers d and e are incorrect, because before a backup can be performed against a target database or updates applied to the recovery catalog, the target database must be registered in the recovery catalog.

Question 7

In **RMAN**, which of the following commands should you use to re-create the **DailyBackup** script?

- ❍ a. **RUN** command with the **REPLACE SCRIPT** option
- ❍ b. **CREATE SCRIPT** command with the **REPLACE** option
- ❍ c. **DELETE SCRIPT** command with the **REPLACE SCRIPT** command
- ❍ d. **REPLACE SCRIPT** command

The correct answer is d. The REPLACE SCRIPT command overwrites a stored script in the recovery catalog. Answers a, b, and c are incorrect, because they are invalid command specifications.

Question 8

The XYZ database is registered in a recovery catalog. Which of the following **RMAN** commands should be issued after a point-in-time recovery has been performed for the XYZ database?

- ❍ a. **RESTORE DATABASE**
- ❍ b. **RECOVER CATALOG**
- ❍ c. **RESTORE CATALOG**
- ❍ d. **RESET CATALOG**
- ❍ e. **RESET DATABASE**

The correct answer is e. After the XYZ database has been restored, recovered, and opened with the RESETLOGS option, the DBA needs to register the new version of the database in the recovery catalog using the RESET DATABASE command. Answers a, b, c, and d are incorrect, because they are invalid commands.

Question 9

Which **RMAN** command enables you to list the commands in the **DailyBackup** script?

❍ a. **print DailyBackup**

❍ b. **run print DailyBackup**

❍ c. **execute print DailyBackup**

❍ d. **print script DailyBackup**

The correct answer is d. The **PRINT SCRIPT** command sends the script to the **RMAN** message log, which lists the commands in the script. Answers a, b, and c are invalid command specifications.

Question 10

Evaluate this command:

```
RMAN> list backupset of datafile '/u1/oradata/
      app103.ora';
```

What task is accomplished after this command is issued?

❍ a. A list of all the data files in the same backup set as **app103.ora** is displayed.

❍ b. A list of all backups sets containing **app103.ora** is displayed.

❍ c. The location of the backup for **app103.ora** is displayed.

❍ d. The **app103.ora** file is added to the backup set.

The correct answer is b. The **LIST** command with the **BACKUPSET** option displays all the backup sets that contain the user-specified data file, tablespace, or all the archived redo logs. Answers a, c, and d are incorrect, because the sample command doesn't accomplish these tasks.

Need To Know More?

Dialeris, Connie. *Oracle8 Backup and Recovery Guide Release 8.0*, Part No. A58396-01, Oracle Corporation, 1997.

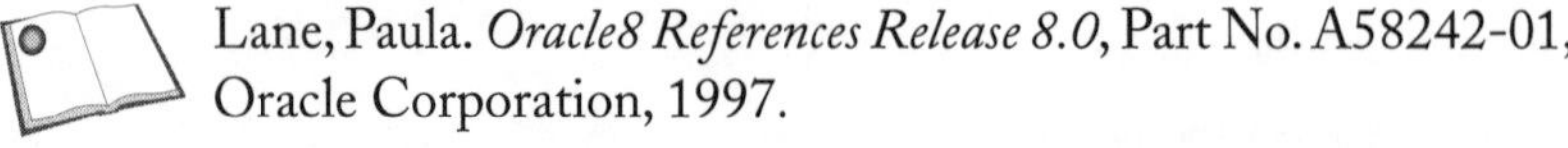

Lane, Paula. *Oracle8 References Release 8.0*, Part No. A58242-01, Oracle Corporation, 1997.

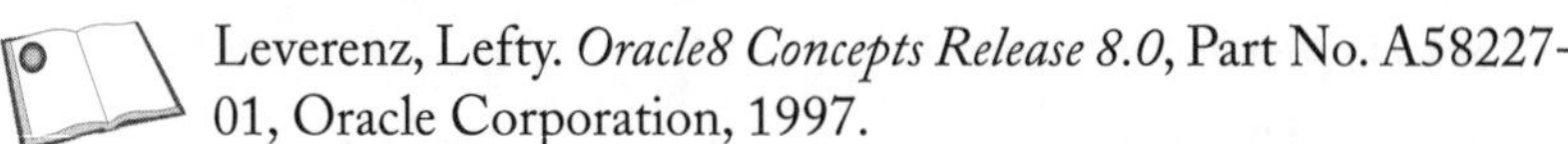

Leverenz, Lefty. *Oracle8 Concepts Release 8.0*, Part No. A58227-01, Oracle Corporation, 1997.

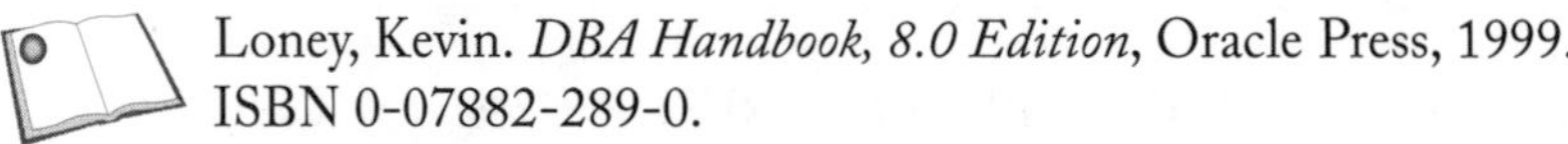

Loney, Kevin. *DBA Handbook, 8.0 Edition*, Oracle Press, 1999. ISBN 0-07882-289-0.

Velpuri, Rama. *Oracle Backup and Recovery Handbook*, Oracle Press, 1998. ISBN 0-07882-389-7.

7

Physical Backups Without Oracle Recovery Manager

Terms you'll need to understand:

- √ Physical database backup
- √ Closed (offline) database backup
- √ Open (online) database backup
- √ Backup mode
- √ **Logging** mode
- √ **Nologging** mode
- √ Read-only tablespace
- √ **V$DATAFILE**
- √ **V$CONTROLFILE**
- √ **V$LOGFILE**
- √ **V$TABLESPACE**
- √ **V$BACKUP**
- √ **V$DATAFILE_HEADER**

Techniques you'll need to master:

- √ Understanding physical backup methods
- √ Understanding recovery implications of closed and open database backups
- √ Understanding backup implications of **Logging** and **Nologging** modes
- √ Backing up control files
- √ Backing up read-only tablespaces
- √ Understanding useful data dictionary views for database backups

Oracle provides a variety of backup methods that help protect an Oracle database. There are three standard methods of backing up an Oracle database: exports, open (online) database backups, and closed (offline) database backups. An export is a logical backup of the database and is described in Chapter 13. A logical backup involves making a copy of the logical database structures with or without the associated business data. A logical backup does not involve the physical database files. The other two backup methods are physical backups of the database files. This chapter describes how to perform physical backups without using the Oracle Recovery Manager (RMAN) utility. Refer to Chapters 5, 6, and 8 for detailed information on the RMAN utility.

Physical Backup Methods

A physical database backup is a backup of the database files that is performed using operating system facilities while the database is open or closed. There are two types of physical backups:

- Closed (offline) database backup
- Open (online) database backup

Each physical backup method provides a different level of data recoverability. Selecting the most effective backup method for your database environment will help to minimize data loss from media failures and maximize data recovery.

You may also use third-party products for your database backups. If you do use a third-party product, you will need to understand how it works, either standalone or with Oracle. For some third-party backup products such as Legato, Oracle offers interfaces between the RMAN utility and the third-party backup product.

Closed Database Backups

A *closed* database backup is an operating system backup of the database files that is made after the database has been shut down cleanly using either SHUTDOWN NORMAL, SHUTDOWN IMMEDIATE, or SHUTDOWN TRANSACTIONAL. This backup method provides a complete snapshot of the database at the time of the database shutdown.

Closed database backups performed using **SHUTDOWN ABORT** are not reliable. DBAs typically restart the database and perform a normal shutdown prior to starting a closed database backup.

Typically, the files in a closed database backup include the following:

- Data files
- Control files
- Online redo log files
- Parameter files
- The password file

If the database has been shut down cleanly, it is not necessary to include the online redo log files as part of a closed full database backup. However, having the backup online redo log files does help in full database restore situations.

Use the closed database backup method to recover to the point of the last backup after a media failure.

Full pathnames of database files should be maintained and used in backups. In multiple database environments, you should give special consideration to setting up standard naming conventions so the appropriate database files are associated with the corresponding databases.

Taking A Closed Database Backup

Performing a full closed database backup when the Oracle server instance is shut down involves the following steps:

1. Generate an up-to-date listing of all pertinent files to back up.
2. Cleanly shut down the Oracle instance using the **SHUTDOWN NORMAL**, **SHUTDOWN IMMEDIATE**, or **SHUTDOWN TRANSACTIONAL** command.
3. Copy all data files, control files, redo log files, parameter files, and the password file to the designated backup location using the applicable operating system backup utility.
4. Restart the Oracle instance and open the database for general use.

You should consider the following when taking a closed database backup:

- If users might still be accessing the database at the time of database shutdown, the **SHUTDOWN IMMEDIATE** or the **SHUTDOWN**

TRANSACTIONAL command is more appropriate than the default **SHUTDOWN NORMAL** command.

- Consider fully automating the closed database backup process to minimize operator errors and to ensure pertinent files are consistently backed up.
- Files associated with read-only tablespaces don't need to be included in the full database backups.
- The parameter file and the password file should be included in the full database backup even though they are not physically part of the database.

Open Database Backups

Organizations that operate 24 hours a day, seven days a week have special needs for backup and recovery. If the business cannot afford to shut down the database to perform backups, then it should have the option to perform backups of the database while it is open and in use. An *open* database backup is a physical file backup of the database while the database is open and running in **ARCHIVELOG** mode, and the online redo log files are archived manually using the **ALTER SYSTEM ARCHIVE LOG SEQUENCE** command or automatic archiving (ARCH background process) has been enabled. DBAs can take backups of one or more tablespaces on a tablespace-by-tablespace basis or individual data files while the database is open and available for use.

Use the open database backup method to recover to the point of failure after a media failure.

Taking An Open Database Backup

Performing an open database backup when the Oracle server instance is online and in use involves the following steps:

1. Issue the **ALTER TABLESPACE BEGIN BACKUP** command (see the code sample below). This command will freeze the sequence number in the data file header so that if subsequent recovery is needed, the redo log files can be applied from the backup start time:

```
SVRMGR> alter tablespace appl_data begin backup;
```

2. Use an operating system backup utility to copy all the data files that make up the tablespace to the designated backup storage location (see

the code sample below). When the tablespaces are sequentially backed up, the log sequence numbers in the file headers of the backup files may not be the same:

```
For Unix:
$ cp /u01/oradata/appl1TEST.ora /u04/backup/oradata/appl1TEST.ora

For NT:
C:> copy d:\orant\database\appl1TEST.ora
f:\backup\oradata\appl1TEST.ora
```

3. Issue the **ALTER TABLESPACE END BACKUP** command to set the data files that make up the tablespace backed up in the previous step into normal mode. See the code sample below:

```
SVRMGR> alter tablespace appl_data end backup;
```

4. Issue the **ALTER SYSTEM SWITCH LOGFILE** command to trigger a log switch. The log switch will in turn trigger a database checkpoint that will synchronize all the file headers:

```
SVRMGR> alter system switch logfile;
```

The above steps should be repeated for all tablespaces, including the **SYSTEM** tablespace, rollback segment tablespace, temporary tablespace, and so on.

Automated scripts that have passed testing are highly recommended for performing open database backups.

Alternatively, you can use the Backup Manager tool to perform online tablespace backups. Follow these steps to back up a designated tablespace:

1. Invoke the Backup Manager tool from the Oracle Enterprise Manager (OEM) console and select the Operating System Backup subsystem. Refer to Figure 7.1 for the subsystem selection window.
2. Expand the Tablespaces node. Refer to Figure 7.2 for a display of tablespaces in the Backup Manager.
3. Click on the **USER_DATA** tablespace node.

Figure 7.1 Backup Manager subsystem selection window.

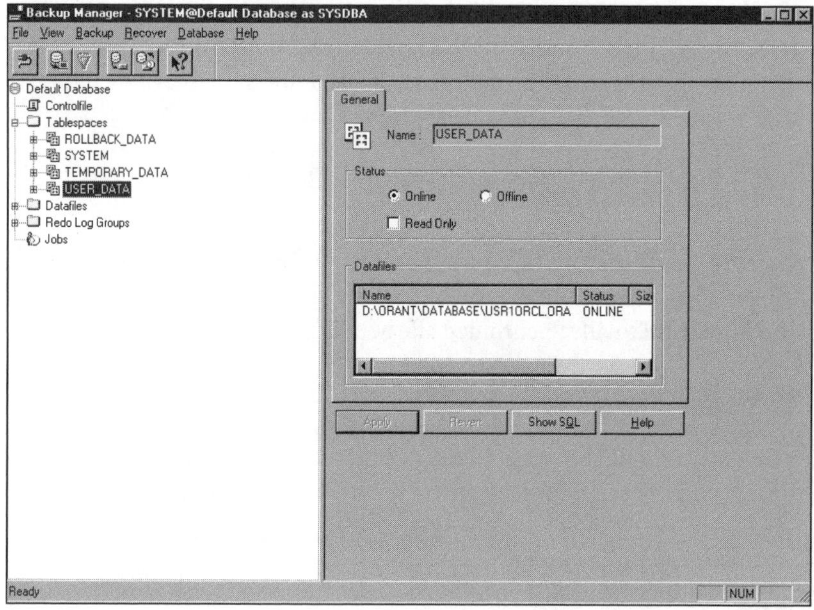

Figure 7.2 Listing of tablespaces from the Backup Manager.

4. Select Begin Online Backup option from the Backup menu. Refer to Figure 7.3 for this menu option.
5. Back up all the data files that make up the tablespace using the operating system's backup utility.
6. Select End Online Backup option from the Backup menu. Figure 7.4 shows this menu option.

If the Backup Manager is invoked outside of the OEM console, an error window will appear. Refer to Figure 7.5 for the Back Manager error window.

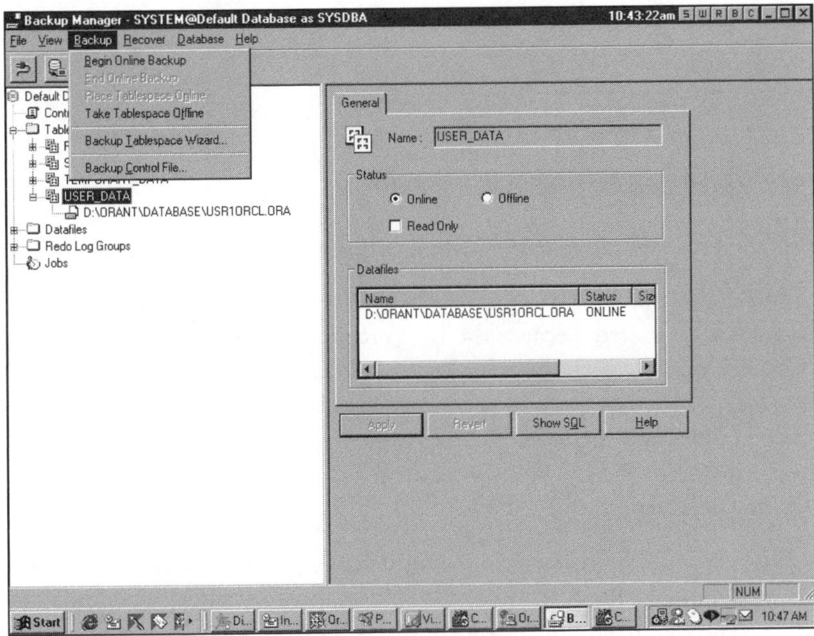

Figure 7.3 Begin Online Backup option in the Backup Manager's Backup menu.

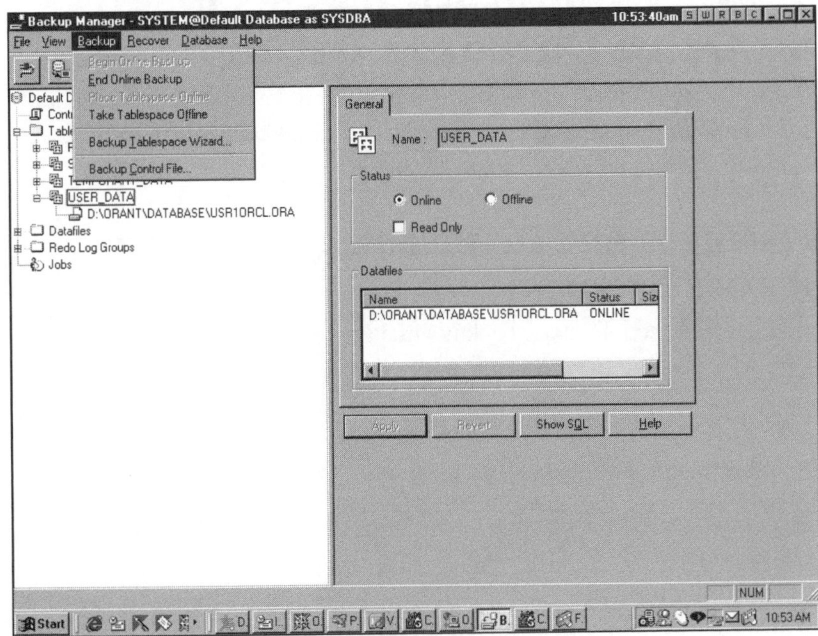

Figure 7.4 End Online Backup option in the Backup Manager's Backup menu.

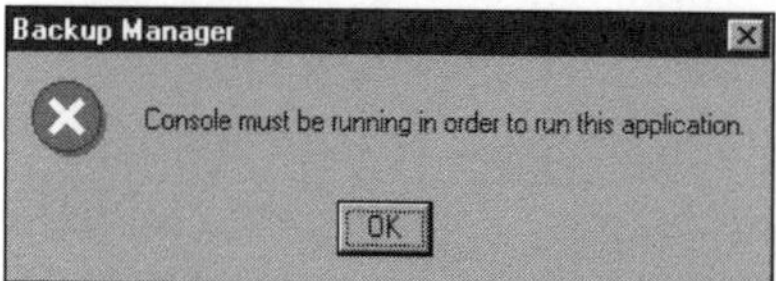

Figure 7.5 Backup Manager error window.

You should consider the following when taking an open database backup:

- When a data file has been put into backup mode, more redo log information is generated, because the LGWR process will write the entire Oracle block in which the changed transaction record resides to the redo log files, versus just the row information. This may affect the size of the redo log files and therefore increase storage space requirements. The performance of the LGWR process will be affected, because more writing will be performed.
- DBAs should try to minimize the time the data files for a tablespace are in backup mode, because more redo information is written while in backup mode. It is highly recommended that you take open database backups on a tablespace-by-tablespace basis.

Recovery Implications Of Closed And Open Database Backups

Closed and open database backups provide different levels of data recoverability. DBAs should consider the advantages and disadvantages of each backup method to derive an effective backup strategy.

Advantages And Disadvantages Of Closed Database Backups

Advantages of closed database backups include the following:

- A closed database backup is easy to understand and manage because it involves only three simple steps:
  - Shutting down the database cleanly
  - Copying all pertinent database files to the designated backup location
  - Starting up and opening the database
- Closed database backups require minimal operator intervention—DBAs typically automate the closed database backup process by running scripts that perform the three simple steps.

- A closed database backup may be an especially reliable backup method, because all database files are closed before the copy operation and they are consistent to a point-in-time.

Disadvantages of closed database backups include the following:

- They are unacceptable to organizations that require 24×7 continuous database availability, because the database is unavailable during the backup operation.
- Several factors (such as the database size, the number of data files, and the speed of the operating system copy process) affect the amount of downtime needed for taking closed database backups. The amount of downtime required may not meet site-specific operational needs.
- The closed database backup method supports recovery to the point of the last full closed database backup after a media failure. Business users may experience lost transactions and may need to re-enter data if their database transactions occurred after the last full closed database backup.

Advantages And Disadvantages Of Open Database Backups

Advantages of open database backups include the following:

- The database is available for normal use during the backup.
- Backups can be performed at a more granular level—tablespace or data file level.
- They meet backup requirements of 24×7 organizations.
- They support recovery to the point of failure after a media failure.

Disadvantages of open database backups include the following:

- They are conceptually more complex to understand and manage. The complexity increases the number of potential failure points.
- For database environments with high transaction volume, the free storage space on disk may run out quickly due to the accelerated rate at which redo log files are archived.
- They increase the level of effort from DBAs.
- They require additional DBA training.

Backup Implications Of Logging And Nologging Modes

Oracle provides two logging modes—**Logging** and **Nologging**—to support direct-load and some DDL operations that can be performed with or without logging of redo or undo information.

Logging Mode

In the **Logging** mode, full redo or undo data logging is performed for instance and media recovery. Full recovery is supported from the last backup. **Logging** mode is the default mode.

Nologging Mode

In the **Nologging** mode, full redo or undo data logging is bypassed. Some minimal logging is performed for data dictionary changes and new extent invalidations. During media recovery, the extent invalidations mark a range of data blocks as logically corrupt, because the redo data is not available. The **Nologging** mode can be specified for the table, index, or partition into which data will be inserted by using commands such as **ALTER TABLE, ALTER INDEX,** or **ALTER TABLESPACE.**

The **Nologging** mode improves the performance of direct-load operations, because the amount of redo or undo logging has been reduced significantly. Upon completion of the operation in **Nologging** mode, the pertinent database object should be reset to **Logging** mode so that subsequent modifications will be logged. A backup should be taken of the data after a **Nologging** operation, so that media recovery can be performed when the need arises.

The following code samples show how to set the **Nologging** attribute for a table, index, partition, or tablespace:

```
ALTER TABLE mytab NOLOGGING;

ALTER INDEX myindex NOLOGGING;

ALTER TABLE myparttab MODIFY PARTITION parta NOLOGGING;

ALTER TABLESPACE appl_ts NOLOGGING;
```

When the **Nologging** attribute is set for a table, partition, tablespace, or index, only selective operations performed on the schema object will make use of the **Nologging** mode. The **Nologging** attribute of the schema object will have no effect on operations such as **UPDATE, DELETE**, or conventional path **INSERT**. The **Nologging** mode is only applicable for the following operations:

- SQL*Loader direct path load
- Direct-load insert
- CREATE TABLE AS SELECT
- CREATE INDEX
- ALTER TABLE MOVE/SPLIT PARTITION
- ALTER INDEX SPLIT/REBUILD PARTITION
- ALTER INDEX REBUILD

Backing Up Control Files

Every Oracle database has at least one control file. A control file is the most important database file—it contains information on the physical structure of the database, database consistency, database synchronization, and database backup (when using the **RMAN** utility).

Every time an instance of an Oracle database is mounted, its control file is used to identify the data files and redo log files that must be opened for database operation to proceed. If the physical makeup of the database is altered (for example, a new data file or redo log file is created), the database's control file is automatically modified by Oracle to reflect the change. You should back up the control file any time structural changes are made to the database. Commands that make structural changes to the database configuration include the following:

- ALTER DATABASE ADD LOGFILE
- ALTER DATABASE DROP LOGFILE
- ALTER DATABASE ADD LOGFILE MEMBER
- ALTER DATABASE DROP LOGFILE MEMBER
- ALTER DATABASE ADD LOGFILE GROUP
- ALTER DATABASE DROP LOGFILE GROUP
- ALTER DATABASE NOARCHIVELOG
- ALTER DATABASE ARCHIVELOG
- ALTER DATABASE RENAME FILE

- CREATE TABLESPACE
- ALTER TABLESPACE ADD DATAFILE
- ALTER TABLESPACE RENAME DATAFILE
- ALTER TABLESPACE READ WRITE
- ALTER TABLESPACE READ ONLY
- DROP TABLESPACE

When backing up a control file, you can create a binary copy of the control file or a text script trace file that can be modified and subsequently run to create the copy. The **ALTER DATABASE BACKUP CONTROLFILE TO TRACE** command can be used to provide a text script trace file. The following code sample shows the content of a text script trace file:

```
CONTENT OF TEXT SCRIPT TRACE FILE:

Dump file D:\ORANT\RDBMS80\trace\ORA00414.TRC
Thu Dec 23 13:10:46 1999
ORACLE V8.0.5.0.0 - Production vsnsta=0
vsnsql=c vsnxtr=3
Windows NT V4.0, OS V5.101, CPU type 586
Oracle8 Enterprise Edition Release 8.0.5.0.0 - Production
With the Partitioning and Objects options
PL/SQL Release 8.0.5.0.0 - Production
Windows NT V4.0, OS V5.101, CPU type 586
Instance name: orcl

Redo thread mounted by this instance: 1

Oracle process number: 12

pid: 19e


*** SESSION ID:(10.705) 1999.12.23.13.10.46.074
*** 1999.12.23.13.10.46.074
# The following commands will create a new control file and use it
# to open the database.
# Data used by the recovery manager will be lost.
# Additional logs may
# be required for media recovery of offline data files. Use this
# only if the current version of all online logs are available.
STARTUP NOMOUNT
CREATE CONTROLFILE REUSE DATABASE "ORCL" NORESETLOGS NOARCHIVELOG
    MAXLOGFILES 32
```

```
    MAXLOGMEMBERS 2
    MAXDATAFILES 32
    MAXINSTANCES 16
    MAXLOGHISTORY 1630
LOGFILE
  GROUP 1 'D:\ORANT\DATABASE\LOG4ORCL.ORA'  SIZE 1M,
  GROUP 2 'D:\ORANT\DATABASE\LOG3ORCL.ORA'  SIZE 1M,
  GROUP 3 'D:\ORANT\DATABASE\LOG2ORCL.ORA'  SIZE 1M,
  GROUP 4 'D:\ORANT\DATABASE\LOG1ORCL.ORA'  SIZE 1M
DATAFILE
  'D:\ORANT\DATABASE\SYS1ORCL.ORA',
  'D:\ORANT\DATABASE\USR1ORCL.ORA',
  'D:\ORANT\DATABASE\RBS1ORCL.ORA',
  'D:\ORANT\DATABASE\TMP1ORCL.ORA'
;
# Recovery is required if any of the datafiles are restored
# backups, or if the last shutdown was not normal or immediate.
RECOVER DATABASE
# Database can now be opened normally.
ALTER DATABASE OPEN;
```

The **ALTER DATABASE BACKUP CONTROLFILE TO filespec** command will create a binary copy of the control file. Similar to the redo log files, Oracle supports mirroring/multiplexing of the control file to protect the control file from media failures. The init.ora parameter **CONTROL_FILES** can be used for multiplexing and naming the control files. The control files should be copied to the designated backup location during full backups.

Backing Up Read-Only Tablespaces

Read-only tablespaces are designed to hold infrequently changed database objects such as lookup tables. Data in read-only tablespaces require minimal backup and maintenance. When the status of a tablespace has been changed to read-only, the DBA needs to back up the read-only tablespace only once while the tablespace is in read-only status. The operations of read-only tablespaces include the following:

- The status of a tablespace is changed from read-write to read-only using the **ALTER TABLESPACE** command, as illustrated by the following code sample:

  ```
  SVRMGR> ALTER TABLESPACE lookup_data READ ONLY;
  ```

- Upon issuance of the **ALTER TABLESPACE** command, a database checkpoint is triggered for all the data files associated with the tablespace. The data file headers are set with the current System Change Number (SCN) and will not change while the status of the tablespace is read-only.

- Upon specifying a tablespace as read-only, you should take a backup of all data files for the tablespace to support subsequent recovery operations if needed.
- The DBWR background process will not perform any operations on the data files that comprise the read-only tablespaces. The DBWR background process will write only to data files whose tablespaces are in read-write state. Normal checkpoints will occur for data files whose tablespaces are in read-write state.

Things To Remember About Read-Only Tablespaces

When the database supports read-only tablespaces, the DBA should consider the following issues:

- Because writes are not performed on the data files for a read-only tablespace, the only case when the data files need to be recovered is when they are damaged.
- When the tablespace status has been changed from read-only to read-write, the DBWR background process will resume writing to the data files for the tablespace, and normal checkpoints will occur. The DBA should resume the normal backup schedule for all data files for this tablespace.
- The **ALTER TABLESPACE READ ONLY** command updates the control file. During recovery operations, the control file must accurately identify read-only tablespaces to avoid the recovery of the control file.

Useful Data Dictionary Views For Database Backups

You can use the following data dictionary views to obtain information about the files of a database that could be incorporated into the backup plan. You will need to be familiar with the data dictionary views associated with the different aspects of backup and recovery. As the views are introduced throughout this book, you should familiarize yourself with these views by querying the data they contain.

- **V$DATAFILE** provides the names and status of all data files:

```
SQL> desc V$DATAFILE
 Name                            Null?    Type
 ------------------------------- -------- ----
 FILE#                                    NUMBER
 CREATION_CHANGE#                         NUMBER
 CREATION_TIME                            DATE
 TS#                                      NUMBER
 RFILE#                                   NUMBER
 STATUS                                   VARCHAR2(7)
 ENABLED                                  VARCHAR2(10)
 CHECKPOINT_CHANGE#                       NUMBER
 CHECKPOINT_TIME                          DATE
 UNRECOVERABLE_CHANGE#                    NUMBER
 UNRECOVERABLE_TIME                       DATE
 LAST_CHANGE#                             NUMBER
 LAST_TIME                                DATE
 OFFLINE_CHANGE#                          NUMBER
 ONLINE_CHANGE#                           NUMBER
 ONLINE_TIME                              DATE
 BYTES                                    NUMBER
 BLOCKS                                   NUMBER
 CREATE_BYTES                             NUMBER
 BLOCK_SIZE                               NUMBER
 NAME                                     VARCHAR2(513)

SQL> select name datafile_name, status from v$datafile;

DATAFILE_NAME                                       STATUS
--------------------------------------------------- ------
D:\ORANT\DATABASE\SYS1ORCL.ORA                      SYSTEM
D:\ORANT\DATABASE\USR1ORCL.ORA                      ONLINE
D:\ORANT\DATABASE\RBS1ORCL.ORA                      ONLINE
D:\ORANT\DATABASE\TMP1ORCL.ORA                      ONLINE
```

- **V$CONTROLFILE** provides the names of all control files:

```
SQL> desc V$CONTROLFILE
 Name                            Null?    Type
 ------------------------------- -------- ----
 STATUS                                   VARCHAR2(7)
 NAME                                     VARCHAR2(513)

SQL> select name controlfile_name from v$controlfile;
```

```
CONTROLFILE_NAME
--------------------------------------------------------
D:\ORANT\DATABASE\CTL1ORCL.ORA
D:\ORANT\DATABASE\CTL2ORCL.ORA
```

- **V$LOGFILE** provides the names of all redo log files:

```
SQL> desc v$logfile
 Name                           Null?    Type
 ------------------------------ -------- ----
 GROUP#                                  NUMBER
 STATUS                                  VARCHAR2 (7)
 MEMBER                                  VARCHAR2 (513)

SQL> select member log_member from v$logfile;

LOG_MEMBER
------------------------------------------------------------
D:\ORANT\DATABASE\LOG4ORCL.ORA
D:\ORANT\DATABASE\LOG3ORCL.ORA
D:\ORANT\DATABASE\LOG2ORCL.ORA
D:\ORANT\DATABASE\LOG1ORCL.ORA
```

- **V$TABLESPACE** provides the names of all tablespaces:

```
SQL> desc v$tablespace;
 Name                           Null?    Type
 ------------------------------ -------- ----
 TS#                                     NUMBER
 NAME                                    VARCHAR2(30)

SQL> select name tablespace_name from v$tablespace;

TABLESPACE_NAME
------------------------------
SYSTEM
TEMPORARY_DATA
ROLLBACK_DATA
USER_DATA
```

When you're setting up scripts to perform open database backups, it is helpful to obtain the listing of all data files with their respective tablespaces to ensure that all pertinent files are included in the operating system copy procedure. As shown in the following code sample, the **V$TABLESPACE** and the

V$DATAFILE data dictionary views can be used together to obtain the listing of all data files with their respective tablespaces:

```
SQL> select t.name TABLESPACE_NAME,
  2         d.name FILENAME
  3    from v$tablespace t, v$datafile d
  4   where t.ts# = d.ts#
  5  order by 1;

TABLESPACE_NAME                FILENAME
------------------------------ ----------------------------------
ROLLBACK_DATA                  D:\ORANT\DATABASE\RBS1ORCL.ORA
SYSTEM                         D:\ORANT\DATABASE\SYS1ORCL.ORA
TEMPORARY_DATA                 D:\ORANT\DATABASE\TMP1ORCL.ORA
USER_DATA                      D:\ORANT\DATABASE\USR1ORCL.ORA
```

Alternatively, you can use the Backup Manager to identify the data files for a particular tablespace. Invoke the Backup Manager tool and log on as SYSDBA. Expand the Tablespaces node in the navigator window. Click on the name of the tablespace. Figure 7.6 shows the data files for a particular tablespace.

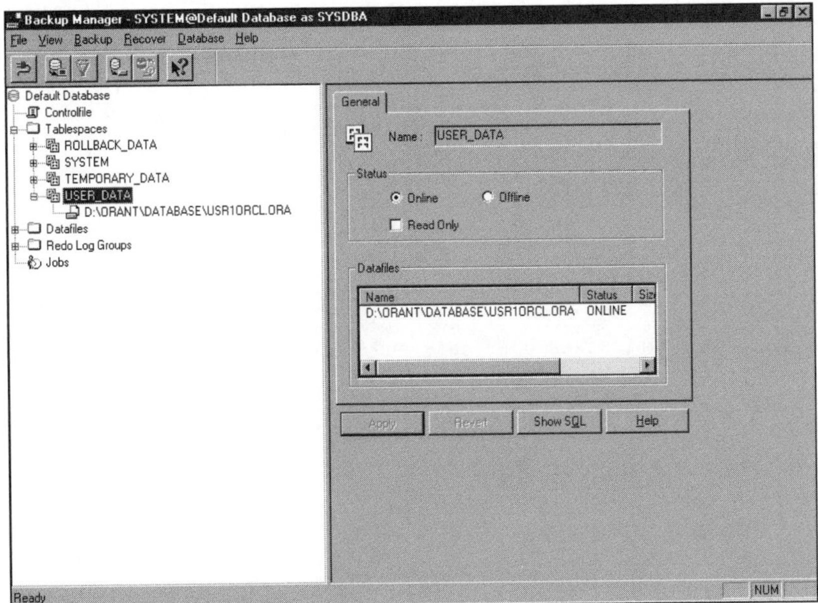

Figure 7.6 Using Backup Manager to identify data files for a particular tablespace.

You can use the following data dictionary views to obtain information about the status of data files during open database backups:

- **V$BACKUP** provides information on which data files are in backup mode. The status column value changes from **NOT ACTIVE** to **ACTIVE** when the **ALTER TABLESPACE BEGIN BACKUP** command is issued. The status column value changes to **NOT ACTIVE** when the file is backed up. The following code sample shows the column descriptions for the **V$BACKUP** data dictionary view and the changes to the status column values:

```
SQL> desc v$backup;
 Name                            Null?    Type
 ------------------------------  -------- ----
 FILE#                                    NUMBER
 STATUS                                   VARCHAR2(18)
 CHANGE#                                  NUMBER
 TIME                                     DATE

SQL> alter tablespace user_data begin backup;

Tablespace altered.

SQL> select * from v$backup;

    FILE# STATUS             CHANGE# TIME
--------- ------------------ ------- --------
        1 NOT ACTIVE               0
        2 ACTIVE             1748313 17-DEC-99
        3 NOT ACTIVE               0
        4 NOT ACTIVE               0

SQL> alter tablespace user_data end backup;

Tablespace altered.

SQL> select * from v$backup;

    FILE# STATUS             CHANGE# TIME
--------- ------------------ ------- --------
        1 NOT ACTIVE               0
        2 NOT ACTIVE         1748313 17-DEC-99
        3 NOT ACTIVE               0
        4 NOT ACTIVE               0
```

- **V$DATAFILE_HEADER** provides information about data files that are in backup mode. As shown by the following code sample, the **FUZZY** column value for the tablespace's data files changes to **YES** when the files are in backup mode, and the **FUZZY** column value changes to **NULL** when the files are out of backup mode:

```
SQL> desc v$datafile_header;
 Name                            Null?    Type
 ------------------------------- -------- ----
 FILE#                                    NUMBER
 STATUS                                   VARCHAR2(7)
 ERROR                                    VARCHAR2(18)
 FORMAT                                   NUMBER
 RECOVER                                  VARCHAR2(3)
 FUZZY                                    VARCHAR2(3)
 CREATION_CHANGE#                         NUMBER
 CREATION_TIME                            DATE
 TABLESPACE_NAME                          VARCHAR2(30)
 TS#                                      NUMBER
 RFILE#                                   NUMBER
 RESETLOGS_CHANGE#                        NUMBER
 RESETLOGS_TIME                           DATE
 CHECKPOINT_CHANGE#                       NUMBER
 CHECKPOINT_TIME                          DATE
 CHECKPOINT_COUNT                         NUMBER
 BYTES                                    NUMBER
 BLOCKS                                   NUMBER
 NAME                                     VARCHAR2(513)

SQL> alter tablespace user_data begin backup;

Tablespace altered.

SQL> select name, status, fuzzy from v$datafile_header;

NAME                                     STATUS  FUZ
---------------------------------------- ------ --
D:\ORANT\DATABASE\SYS1ORCL.ORA           ONLINE
D:\ORANT\DATABASE\USR1ORCL.ORA           ONLINE  YES
D:\ORANT\DATABASE\RBS1ORCL.ORA           ONLINE
D:\ORANT\DATABASE\TMP1ORCL.ORA           ONLINE

SQL> alter tablespace user_data end backup;

Tablespace altered.
```

```
SQL> select name, status, fuzzy from v$datafile_header;

NAME                                      STATUS  FUZ
----------------------------------------- ------ --
D:\ORANT\DATABASE\SYS1ORCL.ORA           ONLINE
D:\ORANT\DATABASE\USR1ORCL.ORA           ONLINE
D:\ORANT\DATABASE\RBS1ORCL.ORA           ONLINE
D:\ORANT\DATABASE\TMP1ORCL.ORA           ONLINE

SQL>
```

Practice Questions

Question 1

Which of the following sequence of steps is correct for performing an online backup of a tablespace without using the Recovery Manager utility?

- ❍ a. Shut down the database, copy the data files for the tablespace using operating system commands, start up the instance, and force a checkpoint.
- ❍ b. Place the tablespace in backup mode, copy the data files for the tablespace using operating system commands, place the tablespace in normal mode, and force a checkpoint.
- ❍ c. Place the tablespace in backup mode, copy the data files for the tablespace using operating system commands, and force a checkpoint.
- ❍ d. Copy the data files for the tablespace using operating system commands, place the tablespace in backup mode, force a checkpoint, and place the tablespace in normal mode.

The correct answer is b. The steps to performing an online backup are as follows: (1) Place the database in backup mode using the **ALTER TABLESPACE BEGIN BACKUP** command, (2) Use operating system commands to copy all the data files for the tablespace, (3) Use **ALTER TABLESPACE END BACKUP** command to place the tablespace in normal mode, and (4) Force a checkpoint to ensure file headers are synchronized. Answer a is incorrect, because the database remains online when you're performing online backups. Answer c is incorrect, because the step to return the tablespace to normal mode has been omitted. Answer d is incorrect, because the sequence of steps are not in the correct order.

Question 2

Which of the following commands should cause you to back up the control file? [Choose two]

- ❑ a. **CREATE INDEX**
- ❑ b. **CREATE TABLE**
- ❑ c. **ALTER DATABASE RENAME FILE**
- ❑ d. **CREATE SNAPSHOT**
- ❑ e. **ALTER TABLESPACE ADD DATAFILE**

The correct answers are c and e. The control file should be backed up when structural changes are made to the database. Answers c and e add and rename data files, which cause structural changes to the database. Answers a, b, and d are incorrect, because those commands do not cause structural changes to the database.

Question 3

Which files are not part of the physical database files, but should be backed up when you're performing a closed database backup? [Choose two]

- ❑ a. Archived log files
- ❑ b. Database parameter file
- ❑ c. Password file
- ❑ d. Control files
- ❑ e. Online redo log files

The correct answers are b and c. A closed database backup should include database files such as control files, data files, and online redo log files. If the database was shut down cleanly, it is not necessary to include the online redo log files. It is advisable to back up auxiliary files such as the database parameter file and the password file. Answer a is incorrect, because archived log files are not relevant for performing a closed database backup. Answers d and e are incorrect, because they are part of the physical database files that are included in a closed database backup.

Question 4

Which of the following views can be used to ensure that all the data files for a tablespace are in backup mode?

- ❍ a. **V$CONTROLFILE**
- ❍ b. **V$TABLESPACE**
- ❍ c. **V$DATABASE**
- ❍ d. **V$DATAFILE**
- ❍ e. **V$LOGFILE**
- ❍ f. **V$BACKUP**

The correct answer is f. The **V$BACKUP** view provides information on data files that are in backup mode. Answers a, b, c, d, and e are incorrect, because they don't contain information on the backup mode of data files.

Question 5

When you're performing online backups, the database must be in which mode?

- ❍ a. **MOUNT EXCLUSIVE**
- ❍ b. **NOARCHIVELOG**
- ❍ c. **NOMOUNT**
- ❍ d. **ARCHIVELOG**

The correct answer is d. The database must be in **ARCHIVELOG** mode to perform online backups. Answers a, b, and c are incorrect, because online backups require a database to be in **ARCHIVELOG** mode.

Question 6

Which data dictionary view can you use to get a listing of all the data files in the database for preparing an online backup procedure?

- ❍ a. **DBA_DATAFILES**
- ❍ b. **DBA_TABLESPACES**
- ❍ c. **DBA_TABLES**
- ❍ d. **DBA_DATA_FILES**

The correct answer is d. The **DBA_DATA_FILES** data dictionary view provides information on all the data files for a database. Answer a is incorrect, because it is an invalid view. Answers b and c are incorrect, because they don't contain information about the data files in a database.

Question 7

Which backup strategy is appropriate for a 24×7 organization?

- ❍ a. Perform frequent online backups in **NOARCHIVELOG** mode.
- ❍ b. Perform frequent offline backups in **NOARCHIVELOG** mode.
- ❍ c. Perform frequent offline backups in **ARCHIVELOG** mode.
- ❍ d. Perform frequent online backups in **ARCHIVELOG** mode.

The correct answer is d. If continuous database availability is required, then the online backup method should be selected, and the database should always be in **ARCHIVELOG** mode when you're performing online backups. Answer a is incorrect, because online backups requires **ARCHIVELOG** mode. Answers b and c are incorrect, because a 24×7 organization requires continuous database availability and cannot tolerate the downtime associated with offline backups.

Question 8

Why should a backup of a table be performed after the data is loaded using a direct load operation with the **Nologging** mode?

- ❍ a. The table needs to be included in the incremental backup set.
- ❍ b. The table needs to be included in the current backup set.
- ❍ c. The table structure has changed.
- ❍ d. The insert statements were not recorded in the redo log files.

The correct answer is d. When data is loaded using a direct load operation with the **Nologging** mode, the insertions are not recorded in the redo log files; therefore, the table should be backed up after the data load to ensure the recoverability of the inserted data. Answers a and b are incorrect, because a backup of a table is required due to the unavailability of the full redo or undo logging information. Answer c is incorrect, because a direct load operation in **Nologging** mode does not cause the table structure to change.

Question 9

What is the recommended action after a tablespace has been placed in read-only mode?

❍ a. Force a checkpoint.

❍ b. Force a log switch.

❍ c. Resync the control file.

❍ d. Perform a backup of the tablespace.

The correct answer is d. You need to back up the tablespace immediately after it has been placed in read-only mode. Answers a, b, and c are incorrect, because they are neither required nor recommended.

Question 10

Which of the following commands should you use to perform an online backup of the control file?

❍ a. **ALTER DATABASE BACKUP CONTROLFILE TO <filename>**

❍ b. **ALTER SYSTEM BACKUP CONTROLFILE TO <filename>**

❍ c. **ALTER DATABASE BACKUP CONTROLFILE TO TRACE**

❍ d. **ALTER SYSTEM BACKUP CONTROLFILE TO TRACE**

❍ e. **ALTER SESSION BACKUP CONTROLFILE TO <filename>**

The correct answer is a. The **ALTER DATABASE BACKUP CONTROLFILE TO <filename>** command is used to take an online backup of the control file. Answer c is incorrect, because it only creates a text script trace file that may subsequently be modified and executed to create the binary control file. Answers b, d, and e are incorrect, because they are invalid commands.

Need To Know More?

Dialeris, Connie. *Oracle8 Backup and Recovery Guide Release 8.0*, Part No. A58396-01, Oracle Corporation, 1997.

Lane, Paula. *Oracle8 References Release 8.0*, Part No. A58242-01, Oracle Corporation, 1997.

Leverenz, Lefty. *Oracle8 Concepts Release 8.0*, Part No. A58227-01, Oracle Corporation, 1997.

Loney, Kevin. *DBA Handbook, 8.0 Edition*, Oracle Press, 1999. ISBN 0-07882-289-0.

Velpuri, Rama. *Oracle Backup and Recovery Handbook*, Oracle Press, 1998. ISBN: 0-07882-389-7.

8

Physical Backups Using Oracle Recovery Manager

Terms you'll need to understand:

- ✓ Whole backup
- ✓ Full backup
- ✓ Incremental backup
- ✓ Operating system backup
- ✓ Closed database backup
- ✓ Open database backup
- ✓ Tag
- ✓ **ALLOCATE CHANNEL** command
- ✓ Image copy
- ✓ Backup set
- ✓ **COPY** command
- ✓ **BACKUP** command
- ✓ Backup piece
- ✓ **V$ARCHIVED_LOG**
- ✓ **V$COPY_CORRUPTION**
- ✓ **V$BACKUP_CORRUPTION**
- ✓ **V$BACKUP_SET**
- ✓ **V$BACKUP_PIECE**
- ✓ **V$BACKUP_DATAFILE**
- ✓ **V$BACKUP_REDOLOG**

Techniques you'll need to master:

- ✓ Understanding **RMAN** backup terms and concepts
- ✓ Using the **ALLOCATE CHANNEL** command
- ✓ Understanding the types of **RMAN** backups
- ✓ Using the **COPY** command
- ✓ Using the **BACKUP** command
- ✓ Using scripts to create backup sets
- ✓ Understanding incremental and cumulative backups
- ✓ Troubleshooting backup problems
- ✓ Understanding **RMAN**-centric data dictionary views

Oracle DBAs have two options when performing physical backups: They can take backups either with or without the Oracle Recovery Manager (RMAN). This chapter focuses on performing physical backups using RMAN. Refer to Chapter 7 for detailed information on taking physical backups without using RMAN.

Oracle recommends a flexible backup strategy that includes RMAN backups and operating system backups.

RMAN Backup Terms And Concepts

When using RMAN as part of a backup strategy, it is important for the DBA to gain an understanding of key RMAN terms and backup concepts, including the following:

- *Whole backup*—A backup comprised of the control file and all data files.
- *Full backup*—A backup of one or more user-specified files. This is not necessary in an incremental backup strategy. Only blocks that contain data are backed up.
- *Incremental backup*—A backup of data files that contain blocks that have changed since the last incremental backup. Incremental backups require a base-level or incremental level 0 backup. A base-level backup backs up all blocks containing data for the specified files.

Although incremental level 0 backups and full backups copy all blocks containing data in the specified data files, full backups can't be used in an incremental backup strategy.

- *Operating system backup*—A backup of database files such as a data file using OS utilities, rather than RMAN mechanisms.
- *Open database backup*—A backup of all or a portion of the database while it is open (online). DBAs should not put tablespaces in hot backup mode using the ALTER TABLESPACE BEGIN BACKUP command, because RMAN uses a different mechanism that significantly reduces the amount of redo required.
- *Closed database backup*—A backup of all or a portion of the database while it is closed (offline). The target database must be mounted but not

open during a closed database backup. When you're using a recovery catalog, the recovery catalog database must be in the open state.

RMAN supports backups of the following database components:

- The entire database
- The control file
- All data files in a tablespace
- A single data file
- All archived redo log files
- User-specified archived log files

When **RMAN** is being used, the online redo log files are not backed up.

Channel Allocation

A *channel* is an **RMAN** resource allocation. It is the method **RMAN** uses to interface with the Oracle server and the OS of the target database. A channel has the following characteristics:

- Every **RMAN** backup, restore, or recover command requires at least one channel.
- Each allocated channel starts a new Oracle server process for the target database, which performs backup, restore, and recovery procedures.
- The number of channels allocated affects the degree of parallelism for backup, restore, and recovery. This number determines the maximum degree of parallelization.
- The specified channel type determines whether the Oracle server process will read and write to disk or use the Media Management Interface. If the channel is of type disk, the Oracle server process will read and write backups to disk. If the channel is of type **SBT_TAPE**, the Oracle server process will read and write backups through a Media Manager. You can use the **V$BACKUP_DEVICE** view to determine supported device types for your OS or media manager.
- The following parameters in the **ALLOCATE CHANNEL** command can impose limits for the **COPY** and **BACKUP** commands:

- *Read Rate*—Limits the number of buffers read per second, per file. It reduces online performance via excessive disk IO. The syntax for this parameter is as follows:

```
SET LIMIT CHANNEL <channel name> READ RATE = <integer>
```

- *Kbytes*—Places a limit on the backup piece file size. This parameter is useful when an OS or device type has a restriction on the maximum file size. The syntax is as follows:

```
SET LIMIT CHANNEL <channel name> KBYTES = <integer>
```

- *Maxopenfiles*—Limits the number of concurrently open files for a large backup. The default value is 32. The parameter is useful in preventing the "too many files open" OS error. The syntax is as follows:

```
SET LIMIT CHANNEL <channel name> MAXOPENFILES = <integer>
```

ALLOCATE CHANNEL Syntax

The **ALLOCATE CHANNEL** command can be issued in a script or via the **RUN** command. Four output buffers are created by each allocated channel. Each output buffer has a size of **DB_BLOCK_SIZE*DB _FILE_ DIRECT_IO_COUNT**. The syntax for the **CHANGE...DELETE** command is as follows:

```
ALLOCATE CHANNEL FOR DELETE <device type> <options>;
```

The syntax for backup, restore, and recovery is as follows:

```
ALLOCATE CHANNEL <channel name> <device type> <options>;
```

The device type can be specified as **type=disk** for reading and writing from disk, **type=<quoted string>** for identifying a type of sequential IO device that is platform-specific, or **name=<quoted_string>** for identifying a port-specific IO device.

The options for the **ALLOCATE CHANNEL** command are parms, connect, and format. The parms option is a port-specific string and is not applicable when **type=disk**. The connect option specifies a connect string for the target database and is applicable for the Oracle Parallel Server. The format option specifies the default naming convention for backup pieces.

The Backup Manager can also be used to allocate a channel. The following steps describe using Backup Manager for this purpose:

1. Connect to the target database using the Oracle8 Recovery Manager subsystem.
2. Select the Channel|Create menu option.
3. Enter the channel name, channel limits, and other details in the Create Channel dialog box.
4. Click on the OK button to create the channel. The channel is displayed in the Navigator window.

Examples Using **ALLOCATE CHANNEL**

The following code sample, in which a file is removed from the operating system, shows channel allocation for the **CHANGE...DELETE** command:

```
RMAN> allocate channel for delete type disk;
RMAN> change datafilecopy
   2> '/ul/oradata/appl1.bak' delete;
RMAN> release channel;
```

The following code sample shows the creation of a channel named **ctest1** of type disk. The files created through this channel will have the format **/u1/oradata/backup/df1.app**. The channel can open only one file at a time, which is not suitable for tape streaming:

```
RMAN> run {
   2> allocate channel ctest1 type disk
   3> format = '/ul/oradata/backup/df1.app';
   4> set limit channel ctest1 maxopenfiles = 1;
   5> backup datafile 'appl.ora', 'applx.ora';}
```

Types Of RMAN Backups

RMAN supports two types of backups:

- Image copies
- Backup sets

Each backup type can be used independently or together. DBAs typically determine the optimal combination of these backups to incorporate into their backup and recovery strategy.

Using Tags

RMAN enables the DBA to assign a descriptive name to a backup set or image copy. This descriptive name is called a *tag*. A tag is subject to the same naming restrictions as other database objects. Tags offer numerous benefits, including:

- They provide a meaningful way for DBAs to reference a group of file copies or a backup set.
- They enable DBAs to easily query backed up files by incorporating them with the **LIST** command.
- They can be used in the **RESTORE** and **SWITCH** commands.
- They enable DBAs to use the same tag for multiple file copies or backup sets.

When a tag resolves to multiple data files, then **RMAN** uses the most recent data file that is available.

Image Copies

An *image copy* is a copy of a single file on disk (data file, archived redo log file, or control file) produced by an Oracle server process similar to an OS-produced file copy. The syntax for the image copy is as follows:

```
Copy <input file> to <location> <options>;
```

The input file can be specified as **datafile, datafilecopy [tag], backuppiece [tag], archivelog, controlfilecopy [tag]**, or **current controlfile**. The options can be specified as **tag=<name>, level 0**, or **nochecksum**.

The **COPY** Command

The **COPY** command is used as part of the **RUN** command to create an image copy of a file. The following code sample illustrates using the **RUN** command to make image copies for two data files:

```
RMAN> run{
   2> allocate channel ctest2 type disk;
   3> copy level 0
   4> datafile 2 to '/ul/oradata/backup/app2.ora',
   5> datafile 1 to '/ul/oradata/backup/appl.ora';
   6> release channel ctest2;}
```

The **ALLOCATE CHANNEL** command is required to write data to an output device. The **COPY** command performs the image copy. The **level 0** in line 3 indicates that the image copy will be part of an incremental backup set. Lines 4 and 5 specify the data files needing image copies and the target locations. A **RELEASE CHANNEL** should be issued to release the process if not needed. Otherwise **RMAN** will automatically perform this function.

The **RUN** command works only when the target database is mounted, or the target database is open and in archivelog mode.

Using Backup Manager To Create Image Copies

Follow these steps to create an image copy using the Backup Manager:

1. Verify that the Intelligent Agent is enabled on the server on which the target database resides, because the OEM job scheduler will be used.
2. Connect to the target database using the Oracle8 Recovery Manager subsystem.
3. Highlight a data file or control file in the Navigator window for which an image copy is needed.
4. Select the Backup|Image Copy menu option.
5. Specify the name of the channel, the destination location of the copy, tag name, and job scheduling options.

A job will be created in the OEM console. The image copy will appear in the detail window.

Image Copy Process

RMAN uses the following steps when it copies a file:

1. A server process (channel) works on one file at a time.
2. All blocks are copied.
3. Block corruption check is performed.
4. Checksum is calculated for verifying the integrity of the image copy.
5. File header of image copy is updated.
6. The control file is updated with the image copy information.

RMAN executes each copy command sequentially by default. To take advantage of parallel operations for the execution of one command at a time, you can do the following:

- Use one copy command for multiple files.
- Allocate multiple channels.

The following example code creates three channels (two channels will be active and one channel will be idle); two files (1 and 3) will be copied in parallel, and the second copy command will execute after the first copy command has completed:

```
RMAN> run {
   2>     allocate channel c1 type disk;
   3>     allocate channel c2 type disk;
   4>     allocate channel c3 type disk;
   5>     copy
   6>          datafile 1 to '/u1/oradata/backup/app1.ora',
   7>          datafile 3 to '/u1/oradata/backup/app3.ora',
   8>     copy
   9>          datafile 2 to '/u1/oradata/backup/app2.ora';}
```

Parallelism requires more system resources, but it results in improved backup and recovery performance.

An OS file copy made outside of **RMAN** is a valid image copy, but it cannot be used by **RMAN** until a **CATALOG** command is issued. **RMAN** supports both open and closed OS backup files. The following sample code shows an OS file copy used by **RMAN**:

```
...
SVRMGR> alter tablespace app_data begin backup;
SVRMGR> !cp app01.ora app01.bak
SVRMGR> alter tablespace app_data end backup;
...
$ rman target dbauser/dbapwd@target_db rcvcat dbauser/
dbapwd@catalog_db
RMAN> catalog datafilecopy 'app01.bak'
...
```

Image copies also support data files that are stored on mirrored disk systems. When a mirror disk fails, you can break the mirror to temporarily suspend restore operations. When mirroring has been resumed, you can use the **CHANGE...DELETE** command to remove the image copies and then use the **CATALOG** command to add the new image copies to the recovery catalog.

Things To Remember About Image Copy

You should be aware of the following image copy characteristics:

- An image copy can only be written to disk. When files are stored on disk, you can use them immediately without having to perform a restore from other offline storage media.
- An image copy is a physical copy of a single data file, archived log file, or control file.
- An image copy, like the OS backups, will copy all blocks including unused blocks. Image copies differ from OS backups, because the Oracle server process performs the physical copy operation, checks for block corruptions, and registers the copy in the control file.
- An image copy can be part of a full or incremental level 0 backup, because a file copy always include all blocks. A level 0 backup is typically used with an incremental backup set.

Backup Sets

A *backup set* is a backup of one or more data files, archived log files, or control files stored in an Oracle proprietary format. There are two types of backup sets:

- *Data file backup set*—This backup set is created when you back up a control file or one or more data files. This type of backup contains only used data file blocks because of the compression mechanism.
- *Archivelog backup set*—This backup set is created when you back up archived log files.

Unlike image copies, which are typically available on disks, backup sets may require that you perform **RMAN** restore operations before performing recovery operations.

Each file in a backup set must have the same Oracle block size. Control files and data files have the same block size, but the block size for archived log files are platform-dependent. You can include a control file in a backup set by using the **INCLUDE CONTROL FILE** syntax or by backing up file number 1, which is the system data file. The control file is written to the last data file backup set.

BACKUP Command

The **BACKUP** command is used to create backup sets. It is typically issued through the **RUN** command or in a script. The syntax is as follows:

```
BACKUP <level> ( <backup type> <options> );
```

Table 8.1 describes command elements and their associated values.

The format option specifies a location and a unique name for each backup set. The valid format specifiers include the following:

- **%p**—Indicates the backup piece number within the backup set. This value starts with one for each backup set and is incremented when each backup piece is created.
- **%s**—Indicates the backup set number, which is a counter in the control file. This counter starts at one and is incremented for each backup set.
- **%d**—Indicates the target database name.
- **%t**—Indicates the backup set timestamp as the number of seconds since a fixed reference date and time. This is a 4-byte value.
- **%u**—Indicates an eight-character name that represents the backup set number and the backup set creation time.

The Delete Input option specifies that the archived log files are deleted from the OS, control file, and recovery catalog after they have been backed up. The Skip option specifies file types to exclude from the backup set.

Table 8.1 Elements of the BACKUP command.

ELEMENT	VALUE
Level	Full, Incremental=0, Incremental=1, Incremental=2, and Incremental=3.
Backup type	datafile <quoted string>, datafilecopy <tag> <quoted_string>, tablespace <quoted_string>, database, archivelog all, current controlfile, controlfilecopy <quoted_string>, or backupset <key>.
Options	include tag=<quoted_string>, format=<quoted_straing>, include current controlfile, filesperset=<integer>, channel <name>, delete input, skip offline, skip readonly, and skip inaccessible.

Using Backup Manager To Create A Backup Set

You can create a backup set using the Backup Manager. The steps are as follows:

1. Verify that the Intelligent Agent is enabled on the server on which the target database resides, because the OEM job scheduler will be used.
2. Connect to the target database using the Oracle8 Recovery Manager subsystem.
3. Highlight the database, a tablespace, a data file, or archived logs.
4. Select the Backup|Backup Set menu option.
5. Specify the incremental level, whether the control file is included, tag names for each backup piece, channels needed, and job scheduling options.

A job will be created in the OEM console. All files included in the backup set are listed in the detail window. This information is not available elsewhere in the Backup Manager.

Multiplexing Files Into Backup Sets

When multiple files are written to the same backup set or backup piece, **RMAN** automatically:

- Allocates files to available channels
- Multiplexes the files
- Bypasses empty blocks

When **RMAN** multiplexes multiple data files into one physical file (set) and stores it on tape, **RMAN** writes a number of blocks from the first file, then the second file, then the third file, and so on until all data files are backed up. The following example code shows four data files that will be multiplexed together via the **filesperset** option:

```
RMAN> run {
   2>     allocate channel mychannel type 'SBT_TAPE';
   3>     backup
   4>     (database filesperset = 4);}
```

Data File Backup Set Process

RMAN follows these steps when creating a data file backup set:

1. Four memory buffers are allocated for each file in the backup set. The size of each buffer can be calculated as **DB_BLOCK_SIZE*DB_FILE_DIRECT_IO_COUNT**.

2. For each channel, files are sorted in descending size order.
3. A checkpoint is triggered for each file in the backup set.
4. Each file header block is copied.
5. The files are multiplexed if there are multiple files per set.
6. For incremental backups, the SCN in the buffer block is checked to determine whether it should be processed. For full or level 0 backups, **RMAN** checks whether the buffer block has ever been used.
7. When corrupt blocks are encountered, they are stored in the control file. You can query the **V$BACKUP_CORRUPTION** view for the corrupted block information after the backup operation.
8. The checksum is calculated.
9. Filled output buffers are sent to the output device.

Archived Log Backup Sets

An archived log backup set can have only archived log files. It is always a full backup. Incremental backups are not supported, because the DBA can specify the range of archived log files to back up. The archived log file backup process is as follows:

1. Archived log files for the backup set are ordered by channel and size.
2. Blocks are read and copied similar to the data file backup process. No blocks are bypassed.
3. Sequence and thread numbers are replaced with the block offset in the backup piece.
4. The backup set process is terminated if any corruptions are encountered.

The following code sample shows archived logs 200 to 205 backed up to a backup set, where each backup piece contains six archived logs; the archived logs are deleted from disk:

```
RMAN> run {
   2>   allocate channel tc1 type 'SBT_TAPE';
   3>   backup filesperset 6
   4>      format '/u1/oradata/backup/ar_%t_%s_%p'
   5>      (archivelog from logseq=200 until logseq=205
   6>      thread=1 delete input); }
```

Using Scripts To Create Backup Sets

You can create a script file that contains the **CREATE SCRIPT** syntax and a list of **RMAN** commands, then run it in **RMAN**. The script is then stored in the recovery catalog and can be called to action via the **RUN** command whenever it is needed. The script syntax is as follows:

```
CREATE SCRIPT <script name> { <commands> ; }
```

The valid commands include **ALLOCATE, BACKUP, COPY, RECOVER, SQL,** and **HOST**.

The following code sample shows the contents of a script file that creates three sets in parallel for a database with eight files; each set contains three multiplexed files:

```
create script BackupTest {
allocate channel ct1 type 'SBT_TAPE';
allocate channel ct2 type 'SBT_TAPE';
backup
     filesperset 3
     format '/u1/oradata/backup/df_%d_%s_%p'
     tag=mytag
     (database include current controlfile);}
```

After this script is stored in the recovery catalog, you can run it by issuing the following **RUN** command:

```
RMAN> run { execute script BackupTest; }
```

You can use the **LIST** command to list all files in the backup set, as shown in the following example code:

```
RMAN> list backupset of database tag=mytag;
RMAN-03022: compiling command: list
RMAN-06230: List of Datafile Backups
RMAN-06231: Key  File Type         LV ...
RMAN-06232: ---- ---- ------------ -- ...
RMAN-06233: 1132    1 Incremental   0 ...
RMAN-06233: 1132    2 Incremental   0 ...
...
```

The following code sample checks for any block corruptions:

```
SQL> select * from v$backup_corruption where file# in (1,2,3,...);
```

When using Backup Manager, the Backup Wizard is the only way to create backup scripts. Once the backup scripts are created, they cannot be edited, deleted, or run from the Backup Manager.

Backup Piece

A *backup piece* is a physical file made up of one or more Oracle data files or archived log files. A backup piece can belong to only one backup set. A backup set is comprised of a group of backup pieces. The **SET LIMIT CHANNEL ... KBYTES** command creates multiple pieces for a backup set. In the Backup Manager, you need to set the backup piece size when creating or altering a channel. The following code sample shows the **APP_DATA** tablespace backed up to one tape drive; the maximum file size for the tape is 4GB:

```
RMAN> run {
   2> allocate channel ctest type 'SBT_TAPE';
   3> set limit channel ctest kbytes 4194304;
   4> backup
   5> format 'df_%t_%s_%p' filesperset 3
   6> (tablespace app_data); }
```

The number of backup pieces written depends on the size of the output file. If the output file is greater than 4GB, then multiple backup pieces are written. Each backup piece contains blocks from up to three data files.

Things To Remember About Backup Sets

You should be aware of the following backup set characteristics:

- A backup set is a logical structure.
- A backup set may contain one or more physical files (backup pieces).
- Backup sets are created by the **BACKUP** command.
- Backup sets support tape streaming. The **filesperset** option specifies the number of data files in a backup set.
- Backup sets support writing to disk or tape. The default tape output device is **SBT_TAPE**, which writes to a tape device when using a media manager.
- Before performing recovery operations, you need to extract files from the restored backup set.
- Archived log backup sets are full backups by default; incremental backups are not supported for them.

- Blocks that don't contain data are not written in the backup sets, because compression is performed.
- You can set maximum size limits for each backup set piece to support backup sets that exceed the maximum size for an OS file, disk, or tape.
- To take advantage of parallel operations for creating backup sets, you can do the following:
  - Back up multiple files.
  - Allocate multiple channels.
  - Use the **filesperset** option in the **BACKUP** command. When the **filesperset** option is not explicitly specified, then only one channel will be used to create one backup piece for all the files.
  - Parallel operations are only available within each backup or copy command.

When working with backup sets, you should consider the following factors:

- The number of files in the target database
- The number of available storage devices
- The number of files per set needed for tape streaming
- The number of backup sets needed
- The number of files multiplexed per set
- The number of channels needed

Performing Incremental And Cumulative Backups

A data file backup set may be full, cumulative, or incremental. A full backup consists of one or more data files, image copies, archived log files, or a control file that contains all blocks. An incremental backup (**level** >= **0**) consists of one or more data files or a control file that contains modified blocks since the previous incremental backup. A cumulative incremental backup (**level** >= **0**) contains all blocks modified since the previous backup at a lower level than the current backup level.

Incremental Backups

The characteristics of incremental backups are as follows:

- The default is set to noncumulative.

- An incremental level n backup contains all modified blocks since the previous incremental backup at the same or lower level.
- An incremental backup requires an existing level 0 backup set or image copy, because it is based on changes made to the level 0 backups.
- An incremental backup contains fewer blocks than level 0 backups.
- Backup performance is better than level 0 backups.
- There are five levels of incremental backup—level 0 through level 4. When using multilevel incremental backups, only incremental backups from any level since the last base level (level 0) backup need to be restored.
- A level 0 backup should be performed if many blocks are modified frequently. If the updates are concentrated on few blocks, then higher level backups (level > 0) are more appropriate.

A sample backup scheme may consist of a level 0 incremental backup performed every Saturday, and a level 1 incremental backup performed Sunday through Friday. If a failure occurs on Tuesday, then Sunday and Monday incremental backups need to be restored. The following code sample sets the incremental level to 1:

```
RMAN> run {
   2> allocate channel xyz type disk
   3>      format = '/ul/oradata/backup/inc_%s_%p.ora';
   4> backup incremental level = 1 (database); }
```

Cumulative Incremental Backups

A *cumulative incremental backup* copies all modified blocks since the previous incremental backup at a level lower than the current incremental level. A cumulative incremental backup copies all blocks previously backed up at the same level. This backup process is more time-intensive and results in larger backup files than normal incremental backups. Performing cumulative incremental backups improves recovery speed, because fewer backups at each level are needed during recovery.

Things To Consider When Performing Backups Using RMAN

You should consider the following issues when using RMAN to create backups:

- RMAN must be able to connect to the target database. When a recovery catalog is not used, the target database must be either mounted or open to perform either closed or open backups, respectively.

- **RMAN** does not support backing up online redo log files. **RMAN** does support backing up archived redo log files when the target database is in **ARCHIVELOG** mode.
- If the target database is in **NOARCHIVELOG** mode, **RMAN** supports clean database, tablespace, and data file backups.
- **RMAN** does not back up password files, parameter files, or other configuration files.
- When using a recovery catalog, the recovery catalog database must be open.
- When an **RMAN** job terminates abnormally, you need to manually delete incomplete files from the operating system. You can terminate an **RMAN** job by using the Ctrl+C key combination in the interactive mode or by killing the **RMAN** process in the batch mode.
- It is a good practice to back up the control file frequently along with any data file backup.
- When Oracle8 detects corrupt data blocks during a backup, it writes information in the control file and in the alert log. The corrupt blocks are still included in the backup. You can query information about corrupt blocks from the control file using the **V$BACKUP_CORRUPTION** view for backup sets or **V$COPY_CORRUPTION** for image copies. You can use the **SET MAXCORRUPT** command to limit the number of new block corruptions allowed for a data file backup.
- Whenever **RMAN** performs a copy or backup set, it allocates input and output buffers. If IO slaves are not used, then memory is allocated from the large pool. You may need to configure the **LARGE_POOL_SIZE** parameter.
- When asynchronous IO is supported by the OS, IO slaves can be configured using three parameters: **DISK_ASYNCH_IO = TRUE**, **TAPE_ASYNCH_IO = TRUE**, and **BACKUP_TAPE_IO_SLAVES = TRUE**.
- When asynchronous IO is not available from the OS, you can set up more disk IO slaves for each channel using two parameters: **BACKUP_TAPE_IO_SLAVES = TRUE** and **BACKUP_DISK_IO_SLAVES = n**. Having additional IO slaves requires more sessions.
- You can query the **V$SGASTAT** view where **name = 'KSFQ_buffers'** to get information on memory usage by **RMAN**.

Troubleshooting Backup Problems

In the course of creating backups using RMAN, you may encounter problems along the way. The following are representative problems:

- When RMAN returns RPC error messages such as "RPC call failed to start on channel," ignore these harmless messages because they simply indicate that the target database is running slowly. Subsequent "RPC call OK" messages indicate that the target database is running at normal speed.
- When RMAN returns error number **7004 unhandled exception...on channel..**, this translates to "No tape device is available for RMAN to use." Check that the tape device is working properly.
- You can query the **V$SESSION_LONGOPS** view to check the status of a backup. The following sample code can be used to calculate the percentage of work completed:

```
SVRMGR> select round(sofar/totalwork*100,2) PCT_COMP
     2> from v$session_longops
     3> where compnam = 'dbms_backup_restore';
```

- If the percent completion value has not changed for a while, query the **V$SESSION_WAIT** view for any outstanding wait events:

```
SVRMGR> select event, pltext, seconds_in_wait
     2> from v$session_wait
     3> where wait_time = 0;
```

- When you suspect that the backup appears to be "hung" because RMAN progress has stopped and the **V$SESSION_WAIT** view does not return any information for the criteria **compnam ='dbms_backup_restore'**, you need to check the media manager to make sure it is still running smoothly. You also need to check the *sbtio.log* file located in the **$ORACLE_HOME/rdbms/log** directory, because media managers write information to this file.

Useful Data Dictionary Views

The following RMAN-centric data dictionary views can be used to query information about the control file:

- **V$ARCHIVED_LOG**—Provides information on archived redo log files, including backup status:

```
SQL> desc v$archived_log
 Name                            Null?    Type
 ------------------------------ -------- ----
 RECID                                    NUMBER
 STAMP                                    NUMBER
 NAME                                     VARCHAR2(513)
 THREAD#                                  NUMBER
 SEQUENCE#                                NUMBER
 RESETLOGS_CHANGE#                        NUMBER
 RESETLOGS_TIME                           DATE
 FIRST_CHANGE#                            NUMBER
 FIRST_TIME                               DATE
 NEXT_CHANGE#                             NUMBER
 NEXT_TIME                                DATE
 BLOCKS                                   NUMBER
 BLOCK_SIZE                               NUMBER
 ARCHIVED                                 VARCHAR2(3)
 DELETED                                  VARCHAR2(3)
 COMPLETION_TIME                          DATE
```

- **V$COPY_CORRUPTION**—Provides information on corrupted blocks for image copies:

```
SQL> desc v$copy_corruption
 Name                            Null?    Type
 ------------------------------ -------- ----
 RECID                                    NUMBER
 STAMP                                    NUMBER
 COPY_RECID                               NUMBER
 COPY_STAMP                               NUMBER
 FILE#                                    NUMBER
 BLOCK#                                   NUMBER
 BLOCKS                                   NUMBER
 CORRUPTION_CHANGE#                       NUMBER
 MARKED_CORRUPT                           VARCHAR2(3)
```

- **V$BACKUP_CORRUPTION**—Provides information on corrupted blocks for backup sets:

```
SQL> desc v$backup_corruption
 Name                            Null?    Type
 ------------------------------ -------- ----
 RECID                                    NUMBER
 STAMP                                    NUMBER
 SET_STAMP                                NUMBER
```

```
 SET_COUNT                                  NUMBER
 PIECE#                                     NUMBER
 FILE#                                      NUMBER
 BLOCK#                                     NUMBER
 BLOCKS                                     NUMBER
 CORRUPTION_CHANGE#                         NUMBER
 MARKED_CORRUPT                             VARCHAR2(3)
```

- **V$BACKUP_SET**—Provides information on all backup sets:

```
SQL> desc v$backup_set
 Name                          Null?    Type
 ----------------------------- -------- ----
 RECID                                  NUMBER
 STAMP                                  NUMBER
 SET_STAMP                              NUMBER
 SET_COUNT                              NUMBER
 BACKUP_TYPE                            VARCHAR2(1)
 CONTROLFILE_INCLUDED                   VARCHAR2(3)
 INCREMENTAL_LEVEL                      NUMBER
 PIECES                                 NUMBER
 START_TIME                             DATE
 COMPLETION_TIME                        DATE
 ELAPSED_SECONDS                        NUMBER
 BLOCK_SIZE                             NUMBER
```

- **V$BACKUP_PIECE**—Provides information on all backup pieces in all backup sets:

```
SQL> desc v$backup_piece
 Name                          Null?    Type
 ----------------------------- -------- ----
 RECID                                  NUMBER
 STAMP                                  NUMBER
 SET_STAMP                              NUMBER
 SET_COUNT                              NUMBER
 PIECE#                                 NUMBER
 DEVICE_TYPE                            VARCHAR2(17)
 HANDLE                                 VARCHAR2(513)
 COMMENTS                               VARCHAR2(81)
 MEDIA                                  VARCHAR2(65)
 CONCUR                                 VARCHAR2(3)
 TAG                                    VARCHAR2(32)
 DELETED                                VARCHAR2(3)
 START_TIME                             DATE
```

```
COMPLETION_TIME                                   DATE
ELAPSED_SECONDS                                   NUMBER
```

- **V$BACKUP_DATAFILE**—Provides information on data files, including number of corrupt blocks and the total number of blocks in each data file. This is useful when you need to create equal-sized backup sets.

```
SQL> desc v$backup_datafile
 Name                          Null?    Type
 ----------------------------- -------- ----
 RECID                                  NUMBER
 STAMP                                  NUMBER
 SET_STAMP                              NUMBER
 SET_COUNT                              NUMBER
 FILE#                                  NUMBER
 CREATION_CHANGE#                       NUMBER
 CREATION_TIME                          DATE
 RESETLOGS_CHANGE#                      NUMBER
 RESETLOGS_TIME                         DATE
 INCREMENTAL_LEVEL                      NUMBER
 INCREMENTAL_CHANGE#                    NUMBER
 CHECKPOINT_CHANGE#                     NUMBER
 CHECKPOINT_TIME                        DATE
 ABSOLUTE_FUZZY_CHANGE#                 NUMBER
 MARKED_CORRUPT                         NUMBER
 MEDIA_CORRUPT                          NUMBER
 LOGICALLY_CORRUPT                      NUMBER
 DATAFILE_BLOCKS                        NUMBER
 BLOCKS                                 NUMBER
 BLOCK_SIZE                             NUMBER
 OLDEST_OFFLINE_RANGE                   NUMBER
 COMPLETION_TIME                        DATE
```

- **V$BACKUP_REDOLOG**—Provides information on archived redo logs in backup sets:

```
SQL> desc v$backup_redolog
 Name                          Null?    Type
 ----------------------------- -------- ----
 RECID                                  NUMBER
 STAMP                                  NUMBER
 SET_STAMP                              NUMBER
 SET_COUNT                              NUMBER
 THREAD#                                NUMBER
```

```
SEQUENCE#                                   NUMBER
RESETLOGS_CHANGE#                           NUMBER
RESETLOGS_TIME                              DATE
FIRST_CHANGE#                               NUMBER
FIRST_TIME                                  DATE
NEXT_CHANGE#                                NUMBER
NEXT_TIME                                   DATE
BLOCKS                                      NUMBER
BLOCK_SIZE                                  NUMBER
```

Practice Questions

Question 1

What backup-related information in the **V$SESSION_LONGOPS** view would be of interest to DBAs?

❍ a. Information about archives that have been backed up

❍ b. Block corruption information

❍ c. Database events that are in wait state

❍ d. Percentage completion of backups in progress

The correct answer is d. The **V$SESSION_LONGOPS** view provides information on the progress of a backup. Answers a, b, and c are incorrect, because the **V$SESSION_LONGOPS** view does not provide these types of information.

Question 2

Your production database has eight data files stored across two disk drives. You have a requirement to perform a full database backup with two files in each backup set. How many channels should be allocated to take advantage of parallel backup operation?

❍ a. 5

❍ b. 4

❍ c. 3

❍ d. 2

❍ e. 1

The correct answer is d. To take advantage of parallel backup operation, you should allocate two channels of type disk to concurrently read from the two disk drives where the eight data files needing backup reside. Answers a, b, and c are incorrect, because you only have two disk drives. Answer e is incorrect, because a single channel can open one file at a time, so parallel operations do not apply.

Question 3

Which three types of files are not included in **RMAN** backups? [Choose three answers]

- ❑ a. Archived log file
- ❑ b. Parameter file
- ❑ c. Password file
- ❑ d. Data file
- ❑ e. Control file
- ❑ f. OS file

The correct answers are b, c, and f. **RMAN** doesn't back up parameter files, password files, and operating system files. Answers a, d, and e are incorrect, because **RMAN** does back up archived log files, data files, and control files.

Question 4

Evaluate the following **RMAN** command:

```
RMAN> run {
   2> allocate channel c1 type disk;
   3> format = '/u1/backup/app1_%s_%p.bak';
   4> backup
   5> incremental level = 0
   6> (database); }
```

What does this command accomplish?

- ❍ a. It backs up blocks changed since the last full backup.
- ❍ b. It takes advantage of parallel backup operation.
- ❍ c. It creates an image copy of the database.
- ❍ d. It initiates an incremental backup plan.

The correct answer is d. This sample **RMAN** command allocates a single channel for the backup set, specifies the name and location of the backup set, and creates a level 0 backup set. A level 0 backup is the basis for incremental backups. Answer a is incorrect, because a level 0 (base-level) backup copies all blocks in the data files. Answer b is incorrect, because parallel backup operation is not applicable when only one channel is allocated. Answer c is incorrect, because image copies are created by the **COPY** command.

Question 5

What is an **RMAN** backup set?

❍ a. One or more files stored in proprietary **RMAN** format

❍ b. A single file stored in proprietary **RMAN** format

❍ c. Only one or more data files

❍ d. One or more operating system files

❍ e. Only one or more archived redo log files

The correct answer is a. A backup set is a backup of one or more Oracle files and is created by the **RMAN BACKUP** command. There are two types of backup sets—data file backup set and archived log backup set. Answer b is incorrect, because a backup set could contain multiple files. Answer c is incorrect, because it applies to the data file backup set. Answer d is incorrect, because it applies to image copy backups. Answer e is incorrect, because it applies to archived log backup sets.

Question 6

When using **RMAN** to back up the target database, what are the two supported states for the target database? [Choose two answers]

❑ a. **OPEN**

❑ b. **CLOSED**

❑ c. **MOUNT**

❑ d. **NOMOUNT**

The correct answers are a and c. When you're performing offline backups using **RMAN**, the target database should be mounted but not open. When performing online backups using **RMAN**, the target database should be open. If a recovery catalog is being utilized, the recovery catalog database should be open. Answer b is incorrect, because it is applicable to taking offline database backups when not using **RMAN**. Answer d is incorrect, because the control file is not available to **RMAN** when the target database is in the **NOMOUNT** state.

Question 7

What types of backups does **RMAN** create? [Choose two answers]

- ❑ a. Image copy
- ❑ b. Export file
- ❑ c. OS file copy
- ❑ d. Image log
- ❑ e. Backup set
- ❑ f. Backup log

The correct answers are a and e. **RMAN** supports image copy backups and backup sets. Answer b is incorrect, because export files are created by the **EXPORT** utility. Answer c is incorrect, because OS backups are not created by **RMAN** but are supported. Answers d and f are incorrect, because they are invalid backup types.

Question 8

Which format specifier would enable you to include the target database name in the backup file name?

- ❍ a. **%u**
- ❍ b. **%n**
- ❍ c. **%p**
- ❍ d. **%s**
- ❍ e. **%t**
- ❍ f. **%d**

The correct answer is f. The valid format specifiers for the format option of the **RMAN BACKUP** command are as follows: **%d**—target database name, **%t**—backup set timestamp, **%s**—backup set number, **%p**—backup piece number, **%n**—padded target database name, and **%u**—encoded backup set number the backup set create time. Answers a, b, c, d, and e are incorrect, because they specify other attributes.

Question 9

What **RMAN** command should you use to copy a single control file?

- ❍ a. **CATALOG**
- ❍ b. **BACKUP**
- ❍ c. **CHANGE**
- ❍ d. **COPY**

The correct answer is d. The **RMAN COPY** command creates an image copy of a file similar to an OS file copy. It can be used to copy a control file, data file, or archived redo log file. Answers a, b, and c are incorrect, because they serve other purposes.

Question 10

Which of the following data dictionary views should you use to list corrupt blocks found during an image copy?

- ❍ a. **V$BACKUP_CORRUPTION**
- ❍ b. **V$COPY_CORRUPTION**
- ❍ c. **V$BACKUP_DATA_FILE**
- ❍ d. **V$BLOCK_CORRUPTION**

The correct answer is b. The **V$COPY_CORRUPTION** view provides information on the number of corrupt blocks encountered during an image copy backup. Answer a is incorrect, because it provides information on the number of corrupt blocks encountered for a backup set. Answers c and d are incorrect, because they are invalid views.

Need To Know More?

Dialeris, Connie. *Oracle8 Backup and Recovery Guide Release 8.0*, Part No. A58396-01, Oracle Corporation, 1997.

Lane, Paula. *Oracle8 References Release 8.0*, Part No. A58242-01, Oracle Corporation, 1997.

Leverenz, Lefty. *Oracle8 Concepts Release 8.0*, Part No. A58227-01, Oracle Corporation, 1997.

Loney, Kevin. *DBA Handbook, 8.0 Edition*, Oracle Press, 1999. ISBN 0-07882-289-0

Velpuri, Rama. *Oracle Backup and Recovery Handbook*, Oracle Press, 1998. ISBN 0-07882-389-7

9

Types Of Failures And Troubleshooting

Terms you'll need to understand:

- ✓ Alert.log
- ✓ **BACKGROUND_DUMP_DEST**
- ✓ **DBVERIFY**
- ✓ **DB_BLOCK_CHECKSUM**
- ✓ **LOG_BLOCK_CHECKSUM**
- ✓ Statement failure
- ✓ User process failure
- ✓ User error failure
- ✓ Instance failure
- ✓ Media failure

Techniques you'll need to master:

- ✓ Understanding the types of failures
- ✓ Using the trace files to diagnose backup and recovery problems
- ✓ Using the alert.log file to troubleshoot backup and recovery problems
- ✓ Using the **DBVERIFY** utility
- ✓ Configuring redo log checksums
- ✓ Configuring data file checksums

An understanding of the common types of failures in an Oracle database environment will enable the database administrator (DBA) to choose and perform appropriate recovery operations. It's important to understand the significance of database synchronization for instance and media recovery, because an Oracle database cannot be opened if any data files, redo log files, and control files are out of synch. To help maintain high recoverability and prevent data corruption, the DBA should perform the following recommended actions:

- Use the **DBVERIFY** utility to verify the validity of a backup and to identify data corruptions in data files.
- Configure checksum operations to ensure that data block corruptions don't exist in archived redo log files.

When backup and recovery problems are encountered, the DBA can use available log files and trace files to help troubleshoot the problems so that effective resolutions can be found.

Types Of Failures In An Oracle Database

Every database system is susceptible to failure. Typical failures include the following:

- Statement failure
- User process failure
- User error failure
- Instance failure
- Media failure

Each type of failure requires a different level of effort from the DBA. Recovery methods depend on the type of failure that occurs, the parts of the database that are affected, and the site-specific backup strategy.

Statement Failure

Statement failure occurs when an SQL statement fails. Representative statement failures include the following:

- A logical error exists in the user application. The user application attempts to insert a child record before creating the parent record.

- The user issues a **SELECT** statement against a nonexistent database table.
- The user enters bad data into the database table that violates integrity constraints.
- The user does not have the proper privileges to perform a database operation. For example, the user tries to insert a row into a database table with only **SELECT** privileges.
- The user attempts to create a database table that exceeds the allotted database space usage limit.
- The user performs an **INSERT** or **UPDATE** on a database table, causing Oracle to perform dynamic extension, but the tablespace contains insufficient free space.

The Oracle server or the operating system will typically return an error code and a message when a statement failure has been encountered. An automatic rollback operation is performed by the Oracle server for the failed SQL statement. Program control is returned to the user application.

The Oracle error code and error message can be used to troubleshoot and help resolve the failure.

To resolve statement failures, the following activities are typically performed by the DBA and/or the application developer:

- Fix the user application to reflect correct logical flow. This activity is typically performed by the application developer.
- Ensure database table exists and is user accessible. Verify table reference is specified properly, then reissue the SQL statement. This activity is typically performed by the DBA and the application developer.
- Reconstruct and reissue the SQL statement with good data. This activity is typically performed by the application developer.
- Provide the required database privileges for the user to successfully issue the statement. This activity is typically performed by the DBA.
- Issue the **ALTER USER** command to change the user's quota limit. This activity is typically performed by the DBA.

- Issue the **ALTER TABLESPACE** command as shown by the code example below to add file space to the tablespace. Alternatively, the DBA can issue the **ALTER DATABASE DATAFILE** command with the **RESIZE** and the **AUTOEXTEND** options as shown by the following code example:

```
ALTER TABLESPACE test_ts ADD DATAFILE
'd:\oradata\test02.ora' SIZE 100M;

ALTER DATABASE DATAFILE 'd:\oradata\test02.ora' RESIZE 200M;

ALTER DATABASE DATAFILE 'd:\oradata\test02.ora' AUTOEXTEND ON
NEXT 50M MAXSIZE 200M;
```

The Storage Manager administrative tool that is part of the Oracle Enterprise Manager (OEM) can be used to add new data files to tablespaces and to enable automatic extension of data files.

User Process Failure

User process failure occurs when a user process that is connected to the Oracle instance ends abnormally. Typical causes of user process failures include the following:

- An abnormal disconnect requested by a user. For example, a user pressed Ctrl+Break keys in the text version of SQL*Plus while connected to an Oracle database in a client/server environment.
- The user's session was abnormally ended when the user rebooted the client workstation while connected to an Oracle database in a client/server environment.
- A memory exception was raised by the user's application program that terminated the session. The user's application program omitted critical exceptions handling.

The DBA will rarely need to be involved in resolving user process failures. User process failure is recovered automatically by the PMON background process. The PMON process wakes up periodically to clean up after an abnormally terminated user process. The PMON process performs the following actions in the cleanup of failed user processes:

- Detects abnormally terminated server processes.

- Rolls back database transactions of abnormally terminated processes.
- Frees resources and locks that failed user processes were using.

User Error Failure

User error failure occurs when a user makes a mistake. Typical user error failures include the following:

- The user accidentally drops a database table:

```
SQL> DROP TABLE app_info_tab;
```

- The user deletes data from a database table in error:

```
SQL> DELETE from app_info_tab;
```

- The user accidentally truncates a database table:

```
SQL> TRUNCATE TABLE app_info_tab;
```

- The user found an error in his or her committed data:

```
SQL> UPDATE app_info_tab SET status_code = '10';
```

To resolve user error failures, the following activities are typically performed by the DBA:

- Properly train the database users so they are aware of the ramifications of their database actions on database integrity and availability.
- Understand the business and applications operations that may lead to data loss caused by user errors.
- Understand recovery procedures such as recovery using a valid backup for data loss caused by user errors.
- Understand point-in-time recovery, which can recover the database to the point in time just before the error occurred.

Instance Failure

Instance failure occurs when an Oracle instance fails. Types of instance failures include the following:

- Power outages that cause the database server to become unavailable.

- Operating system crashes that make the database instance inoperative.
- Hardware problems such as CPU failure or memory corruption that cause the database server to become unavailable.
- Failure of one or more of the Oracle background processes (DBWR, LGWR, PMON, SMON).

To resolve instance failures, the following activities should typically be performed by the DBA:

- Use the **STARTUP** command to start the instance, as shown by the code example below. Instance recovery restores a database to its transaction consistent state immediately before the instance failure. The Oracle server will automatically perform instance recovery that includes the roll-forward and rollback phases when the database is opened if it is necessary:

```
SVRMGR> connect / as SYSDBA;
Connected.
SVRMGR> startup;
. . .
Database opened.
SVRMGR>
```

- Inform database users that uncommitted data will need to be re-entered.
- Use available trace files and the instance alert.log file to help diagnose the cause of the failure.

Instance recovery is composed of six phases:

- Unsynchronized data files
- Roll-forward
- Committed and uncommitted data in data files
- Rollback
- Committed data in data files
- Synchronized data files

Unsynchronized Data Files

Instance failure can lead to unsynchronized files. An example is when a **SHUTDOWN ABORT** action is performed by the DBA. In this scenario, uncommitted data is lost, because modified data in memory has not been written to disk, and files are not synchronized before the shutdown.

Roll-Forward

The DBWR background process writes both committed and uncommitted data to the data files. In the roll-forward phase, all changes recorded in the log files are applied to the data blocks. Because the redo log files contain both before and after images of data, rollback segment entries may get created if there are one or more uncommitted data blocks in the data file and no rollback entry exists. The recovery process uses redo log buffers when applying changes in the redo log files. With respect to read-only data file, the changes in the redo log files are applied only if the status in the file header does not match the status in the control file.

Commited And Uncommitted Data In Data Files

Upon roll-forward phase completion, the data files will reflect all committed data, although some uncommitted data may still exist.

Rollback

In the rollback phase, uncommitted data from the data files is eliminated using the rollback segment entries created during the roll-forward phase. Data blocks are rolled back when the Oracle server or the user submits data block requests.

Committed Data In Data Files

Upon completion of the roll-forward and the rollback phases, the data files will contain only committed data.

Synchronized Data Files

At this phase, data file synchronization is achieved.

Media Failure

Media failure occurs when files needed by the database can no longer be accessed. This is the most serious type of failure that typically requires active DBA involvement. Typical causes of media failures include the following:

- Disk drive controller malfunction
- Disk drive head crash
- Physical problem in performing database file read or write operations
- Accidental erasure of database file

The key to resolving media failures is the existence of a tested backup strategy. The extent to which a DBA can minimize data loss and downtime resulting from a media failure is dependent upon the availability of backups. An effective recovery strategy is dependent upon the following factors:

- The backup method chosen.
- The files affected.

If archiving has been enabled, archived redo log files can be used to recover committed data since the last backup.

In addition to exam preparation, you need to be familiar with the types of failures in an Oracle database, because each failure type requires a different level of effort from the DBA to achieve effective recovery.

Database Synchronization

The Oracle server will not open a database unless all data files, redo log files, and control files are synchronized. The exception is when the data files are offline or part of a read-only tablespace. The types of failures affect the state of database synchronization. For statement or user error failures, the state of database synchronization remains unchanged. For instance failures, the database files may not be synchronized and recovery is performed automatically by the Oracle server. For media failures, the database files are not synchronized and recovery will require significant DBA involvement.

Synchronization of all data files, redo log files, and control files is based on the current checkpoint number. Archived and online redo log files are used to recover committed transactions, roll back uncommitted transactions, and synchronize the database files. During the recovery phase, Oracle automatically requests the pertinent archived and online redo log files. The DBA should ensure the redo log files exist in the proper storage location.

Using The **DBVERIFY** Utility

The **DBVERIFY** utility enables DBAs to perform physical data structure integrity checks on the data files. The **DBVERIFY** utility can be used to perform the following functions:

- Verify online data files.
- Verify a portion of a data file.

- Verify offline data files.
- Specify an error log to receive the output from the **DBVERIFY** utility.

DBVERIFY's impact on database activities is minimal, because the utility is external to the database. The **DBVERIFY** utility is invoked via a command line interface. It is typically used to verify that backed up data files are valid before they are used to restore a database or as a diagnostic aid for resolving data corruption errors.

The name of **DBVERIFY** depends on your operating system. For Unix, the executable name is *dbv*. For Windows NT, the executable name is *dbverf80*. The executable can be found in the Bin directory of the applicable Oracle Home directory. Refer to your Oracle documentation for using **DBVERIFY** on your system.

Parameters used with the **DBVERIFY** utility include the following:

- *FILE*—The name of the database file to verify.
- *START*—The block at which **DBVERIFY** will start. The block specification is in Oracle blocks. The default is to start with the first block in the file.
- *END*—The last block address to verify. The default is the last block in the file.
- *BLOCKSIZE*—The Oracle block size; the default is 2K.
- *LOGFILE*—The name of the log file to receive screen output. The default is to send output to the terminal screen.
- *FEEDBACK*—Causes **DBVERIFY** to display a single period (.) for every n pages verified. The default is no feedback.
- *HELP*—Lists on-screen usage help.
- *PARFILE*—The name of the parameter file to use.

The following example code shows how to get online help:

```
D:\ORANT>dbverf80 help=y

DBVERIFY: Release 8.0.5.0.0 - Production on Tue Nov 23 11:35:38
1999

(c) Copyright 1998 Oracle Corporation.  All rights reserved.
```

```
Keyword   Description         (Default)
---------------------------------------------
FILE      File to Verify      (NONE)
START     Start Block         (First Block of File)
END       End Block           (Last Block of File)
BLOCKSIZE Logical Block Size  (2048)
LOGFILE   Output Log          (NONE)
FEEDBACK  Display Progress    (0)
```

To verify the integrity of a data file named **test01.ora** starting with block 1 and ending with block 100, invoke the **DBVERIFY** utility with the following specifications.

For Unix:

```
$ dbv /oradata/test01.ora start=1 end=100
```

For Windows NT:

```
C:> dbverf80 d:\oradata\test01.ora start=1 end=100
```

The following is a sample output from the **DBVERIFY** utility:

```
DBVERIFY: Release 8.0.5.0.0 - Production on Tue Nov 23 11:58:35
1999

(c) Copyright 1998 Oracle Corporation.  All rights reserved.


DBVERIFY - Verification starting : FILE = test01.ora

DBVERIFY - Verification complete

Total Pages Examined         : 10
Total Pages Processed (Data) : 1
Total Pages Failing   (Data) : 0
Total Pages Processed (Index): 1
Total Pages Failing   (Index): 0
Total Pages Empty            : 0
Total Pages Marked Corrupt   : 0
Total Pages Influx           : 0
```

The following sample output illustrates blocksize mismatch:

```
D:\ORANT\DATABASE>dbverf80 file=test99.ora
```

```
DBVERIFY: Release 8.0.5.0.0 - Production on Tue Nov 23 11:46:20
1999

(c) Copyright 1998 Oracle Corporation.  All rights reserved.


DBV-00103: Specified BLOCKSIZE (2048) differs from actual (4096)
```

The following sample output illustrates corruptions found in the user-specified file:

```
DBVERIFY: Release 8.0.5.0.0 - Production on Tue Nov 23 11:46:46
1999

(c) Copyright 1998 Oracle Corporation.  All rights reserved.


DBVERIFY - Verification starting : FILE = log4orcl.ora
Page 1 is marked corrupt
***
Corrupt block relative dba: 0x00000001 file=0. blocknum=1.
Bad header found during dbv:
Data in bad block - type:249. format:0. rdba:0x00000001
last change scn:0x0000.16c7e8af seq:0x6d flg:0x9f
consistancy value in tail 0x00000000
check value in block header: 0x0, calculated check value: 0x0
spare1:0x0, spare2:0x0, spare2:0x800

. . . ..
Page 2048 is marked corrupt
***
Corrupt block relative dba: 0x00000800 file=0. blocknum=2048.
Bad header found during dbv:
Data in bad block - type:249. format:0. rdba:0x00000800
last change scn:0x0010.16b7f299 seq:0x0 flg:0x00
consistancy value in tail 0x35203561
check value in block header: 0x70, check value not calculated
spare1:0x0, spare2:0x0, spare2:0x0


DBVERIFY - Verification complete

Total Pages Examined         : 2048
Total Pages Processed (Data) : 0
Total Pages Failing   (Data) : 0
Total Pages Processed (Index): 0
```

```
Total Pages Failing   (Index): 0
Total Pages Empty            : 0
Total Pages Marked Corrupt   : 2048
Total Pages Influx           : 0
```

The page in the output from the **DBVERIFY** utility is the number of the Oracle blocks processed.

Configuring Checksum Operations

When the DBA suspects that data files or online redo log files may be corrupt, he or she can use checksums to detect the corruptions. Different procedures are used to configure Oracle to use checksum to verify blocks in the data files and in the online redo log files.

Data File Checksum

To configure Oracle to perform data file block checking, set the **DB_BLOCK_CHECKSUM** initialization parameter to **TRUE**. The default value is **FALSE**. When data file block checking is enabled, Oracle computes a checksum for each data file block and writes that checksum in the header of the data file block. Oracle uses the checksum to detect corruption in the block. Oracle will try to verify the data block each time it reads the data block from disk. When Oracle detects a corruption, it will return error code ORA-01578 and include information about the corrupted block in a trace file. The DBA should be aware that performance overhead is associated with the activation of data file checksum operations. Oracle recommends setting **DB_BLOCK_CHECKSUM** to **TRUE** only when directed by the Oracle support personnel to troubleshoot data corruption errors.

Because of the performance overhead implications, DBAs should set initialization parameters prudently.

Log File Checksum

If an online redo log file has an undiscovered corruption before the archiver creates the archive copy, the corruption has been propagated to the archived log file. This corrupted archived log file is unusable for subsequent data file recovery operations. To configure Oracle to perform redo log block checking, set the **LOG_BLOCK_CHECKSUM** initialization parameter to **TRUE**. The default value is **FALSE**. When redo log block checking is enabled, Oracle computes a checksum for each redo log block written to the current log and writes that checksum in the header of the redo log block. Oracle uses the checksum to detect corruption in the redo log block. Oracle will attempt to verify the redo log block when it writes the block to an archive log file and when the block is read from an archived log file during recovery.

If a redo log block is corrupted while trying to write the archive log, Oracle will try to read the block from another member of the log file group. If all members have the corrupted block, archiving will stop and the database may hang because redo generation is no longer possible. If the database hangs because of irrecoverable checksum error, the DBA can issue the **ALTER DATABASE CLEAR LOGFILE** command to initialize the log files. This will be addressed in Chapter 14. If all members have the corrupted block, the redo log file cannot be used for recovery operations. The DBA should be aware that some performance overhead is associated with the activation of redo log file checksum operations. Checksums should be used only when corruption is suspected as a result of host I/O subsystem failure.

Using Log And Trace Files To Diagnose Problems

The alert log (alert<SID>.log) is a file written by the Oracle server that contains informational, warning, and error messages relating to the status of the instance and the database. The initialization parameter **BACKGROUND_ DUMP_ DEST** controls where the alert log is placed. Information in the alert log includes the following:

- Database instance startups.
- Database instance shutdowns.
- A history of any physical changes that have been made to the database, such as the addition or change in status of data files, redo logs, and rollback segments.
- Optional information concerning checkpoints.
- Database errors, such as a corrupted member of a mirrored redo log or the filling of the archive log destination.
- Informational messages helpful for tuning, such as excessive archive waits for a checkpoint or waits that occur while redo logs are being written to archive.
- Database events.

The alert log is usually the first item the DBA examines for information when a nontrivial system problem has been discovered. The alert log is continuously appended to by the Oracle server so the DBA should periodically copy it to an alternate storage location for historical purposes and purge it to minimize unnecessary disk usage.

Oracle recommends checking the alert log on a regular basis to determine whether problems exist.

The following sample code shows the partial contents of an Oracle alert log file:

```
Starting up ORACLE RDBMS Version: 8.0.5.0.0.
System parameters with non-default values:
  processes                      = 59
  shared_pool_size               = 11534336
  control_files                  = D:\ORANT\DATABASE\ctl1ORCL.ora
  db_block_buffers               = 1000
  db_block_size                  = 2048
  log_archive_start              = TRUE
  log_archive_dest               = %ORACLE_HOME%\database\archive
  log_archive_format             = %ORACLE_SID%%S.%T
  log_buffer                     = 8192
  log_checkpoint_interval        = 10000
  db_files                       = 1024
  db_file_multiblock_read_count = 8
  sequence_cache_entries         = 10
  sequence_cache_hash_buckets    = 10
  remote_login_passwordfile      = EXCLUSIVE
  global_names                   = TRUE
  distributed_lock_timeout       = 300
  distributed_transactions       = 5
  open_links                     = 4
  db_name                        = ORCL
  text_enable                    = TRUE
  job_queue_processes            = 2
  job_queue_interval             = 10
  job_queue_keep_connections     = FALSE
  parallel_max_servers           = 5
  background_dump_dest           = %RDBMS80%\trace
  user_dump_dest                 = %RDBMS80%\trace
  max_dump_file_size             = 10240
```

```
PMON started with pid=2
DBW0 started with pid=3
ARCH started with pid=4
LGWR started with pid=5
CKPT started with pid=6
SMON started with pid=7
RECO started with pid=8
SNP0 started with pid=9
SNP1 started with pid=10
Mon Nov 22 14:39:36 1999
alter database "orcl" mount exclusive
Mon Nov 22 14:39:40 1999
Successful mount of redo thread 1, with mount id 909956652.
Mon Nov 22 14:39:40 1999
Database mounted in Exclusive Mode.
Completed: alter database "orcl" mount exclusive
Mon Nov 22 14:39:40 1999
alter database "orcl" open
Beginning crash recovery of 1 threads
Recovery of Online Redo Log: Thread 1 Group 3 Seq 251 Reading mem 0
  Mem# 0 errs 0: D:\ORANT\DATABASE\LOG2ORCL.ORA
Crash recovery completed successfully
Mon Nov 22 14:39:43 1999
Thread 1 advanced to log sequence 252
Thread 1 opened at log sequence 252
  Current log# 4 seq# 252 mem# 0: D:\ORANT\DATABASE\LOG1ORCL.ORA
Successful open of redo thread 1.
Mon Nov 22 14:39:43 1999
SMON: enabling cache recovery
SMON: enabling tx recovery
Mon Nov 22 14:39:47 1999
Completed: alter database "orcl" open
```

In addition to the alert log file, the DBA can use trace files to help troubleshoot system problems, because they contain information about the error. The Oracle trace files are created by the Oracle background processes when errors are encountered, and are written to the location specified by the initialization parameter **BACKGROUND_DUMP_DEST**. The name of the background process that created the trace file is included in the trace file name. The following sample illustrates trace file names for a Windows NT system:

```
orclARCH.trc
orclSMON.trc
orclDBWR.trc
orclPMON.trc
```

The following sample output from a trace file created by LGWR shows a missing online redo log file:

```
. . .
ORA-00313: open failed for members of log group 2 of thread 1
ORA-00312: online log 2 thread 1: '/oradata/log2b.ora'
ORA-27037: unable to obtain file status
SVR4 Error: 2: No such file or directory
Additional information: 3
ORA-00321: log 2 of thread 1, cannot update log file header
ORA-00312: online log 2 thread 1: 'oradata/log2b.ora'
ORA-00313: open failed for members of log group 2 of thread 1
. . .
```

The DBA should monitor trace files on a regular basis to help detect database problems. Periodically purging trace files will also reduce unnecessary disk usage.

Practice Questions

Question 1

Your database files are spread across six disks. Which type of failure occurs when one of the disks suffers a head crash?

❍ a. Instance failure

❍ b. Statement failure

❍ c. User process failure

❍ d. Media failure

The correct answer is d. One of the causes of media failure is a disk drive head crash. Answers a, b, and c are not correct, because a disk head crash will not cause these types of failures.

Question 2

Which type of failure occurs when a user application raises an address exception that abnormally terminates a user session?

❍ a. User process failure

❍ b. User error failure

❍ c. Media failure

❍ d. Instance failure

❍ e. Statement failure

The correct answer is a. A user process failure occurs when a user process abnormally ends. The PMON background process will automatically recover a failed user process. Answers b, c, d, and e are not correct, because an abnormally terminated user process doesn't cause those types of failures.

Question 3

The Oracle server automatically handles which of the following recovery operations? [Choose two.]

- ❑ a. Backup file restorations
- ❑ b. Roll-forward operations
- ❑ c. Rollback operations
- ❑ d. Control file creation

The correct answers are b and c. The Oracle server automatically performs instance recovery at instance start when required. The recovery process involves two stages: the roll-forward phase and the rollback phase. In the roll-forward phase, the Oracle server applies changes in the redo log files to the data files. During the rollback phase, the Oracle server removes any uncommitted data from the data files. Answer a is not correct, because backup file restorations are typically handled by the DBA. Answer d is not correct, because control file creation is performed by the DBA.

Question 4

Which type of failure occurs when a user accidentally deletes all the rows from the *DEPT* table?

- ❍ a. User process failure
- ❍ b. Statement failure
- ❍ c. Instance failure
- ❍ d. Media failure
- ❍ e. User error failure

The correct answer is e. User errors are caused by database users and typically require DBA involvement. User education and training will help minimize user error failures. Typical user error failures include: committing data in error, accidentally deleting all rows in a table, and dropping a table that is still needed. Answers a, b, c, and d are not correct, because accidentally deleting all rows in a table will not cause these kinds of failures.

Question 5

Which type of failure occurs when a user attempts to enter data into a table that violates a data integrity constraint?

- ❍ a. User process failure
- ❍ b. User error failure
- ❍ c. Statement failure
- ❍ d. Media failure

The correct answer is c. A statement failure occurs when the Oracle server cannot execute a SQL statement. When bad data is entered into a database table that violates integrity constraints, the SQL statement fails and the Oracle server returns an error code and a message. An automatic rollback operation is performed by the Oracle server, and program control is returned to the user application. Answers a, b, and d are not correct, because entering bad data into a database table doesn't cause these kinds of failures.

Question 6

Which type of failure occurs when a power outage causes the database server to become unavailable?

- ❍ a. User error failure
- ❍ b. Instance failure
- ❍ c. Media failure
- ❍ d. User process failure
- ❍ e. Statement failure

The correct answer is b. An instance failure can be caused by a power outage. Recovery from an instance failure is automatic at database startup. Answers a, c, d, and e are incorrect, because a power outage doesn't cause those types of failures.

Question 7

Which files must be synchronized for recovery? [Choose all correct answers.]

- ❑ a. Redo log files
- ❑ b. Export files
- ❑ c. Trace files
- ❑ d. Control files
- ❑ e. Data files
- ❑ f. Rollback files

The correct answers are a, d, and e. The Oracle server will not open a database when the redo log files, control files, and data files are not synchronized. Database recovery is required to achieve database synchronization. Answer b is incorrect, because export files do not require synchronization. Answer c is incorrect, because trace files are not used in recovery. Answer f is incorrect, because rollback files don't exist.

Question 8

Which file shows the last time the database was started?

- ❍ a. *init.ora*
- ❍ b. *config.ora*
- ❍ c. *smon.trc*
- ❍ d. *alert.log*

The correct answer is d. The alert.log file shows every database startup and shutdown. Answers a, b, and c are incorrect, because they don't contain database startup and shutdown information.

Question 9

Which file do DBAs typically examine first when a problem has been encountered by a database instance?

- ❍ a. Configuration file
- ❍ b. Trace file
- ❍ c. Alert log file
- ❍ d. SGA file

The correct answer is c. DBAs typically first look in the alert log file when there is a nontrivial database problem. The alert log file is a historical view of what has happened to the database and records all background process errors and structural changes made to the database. Answer a is incorrect, because the configuration file doesn't contain any error information. Answer b is incorrect, because a trace file is typically examined after the alert log file. Answer d is incorrect, because there is no such thing as an SGA file.

Question 10

If the DBWR process fails and the database shuts down, which file will contain information about the error that caused the DBWR process to fail?

- ❍ a. Initialization file
- ❍ b. DBWR trace file
- ❍ c. Alert log file
- ❍ d. Control file

The correct answer is b. When a background process fails, it will generate a trace log file to record the information about the error. The name of the trace file will typically include the process name and have a .trc file extension. Answers a and d are incorrect, because they don't contain information on DBWR errors. Answer c is incorrect, because it contains references to the DBWR trace file where detailed error information can be found.

Question 11

Which Oracle utility enables the DBA to check for data corruption in data files?

❍ a. **DBVERIFY**

❍ b. **ANALYZE**

❍ c. **EXPORT**

❍ d. **TKPROF**

The correct answer is a. The **DBVERIFY** utility is used to verify the structural integrity of data blocks in the data files. It can be used to verify online and offline data files. Answer b is incorrect, because **ANALYZE** computes statistics for tables and indexes. Answer c is incorrect, because **EXPORT** is used to perform logical backups of the database. Answer d is incorrect, because **TKPROF** is used for SQL tuning and optimization.

Question 12

Which initialization parameter should be set to detect redo log file block corruptions before they are archived?

❍ a. **BACKGROUND_DUMP_DEST**

❍ b. **LOG_BLOCK_CHECKSUM**

❍ c. **DB_BLOCK_CHECKSUM**

❍ d. **CHECKSUM**

The correct answer is b. There are two initialization parameters that can be set to detect block corruptions: **DB_BLOCK_CHECKSUM** pertains to detection of data file corruptions and **LOG_BLOCK_CHECKSUM** allows redo log files to be checked for corruptions. Answer a is incorrect, because it sets the location where trace files written by the Oracle background processes will be placed. Answer c is incorrect, because it pertains to data files. Answer d is incorrect, because it is an invalid initialization parameter.

Need To Know More?

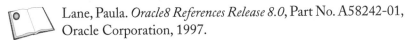

Dialeris, Connie. *Oracle8 Backup and Recovery Guide Release 8.0*, Part No. A58396-01, Oracle Corporation, 1997.

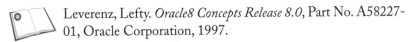

Lane, Paula. *Oracle8 References Release 8.0*, Part No. A58242-01, Oracle Corporation, 1997.

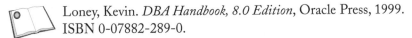

Leverenz, Lefty. *Oracle8 Concepts Release 8.0*, Part No. A58227-01, Oracle Corporation, 1997.

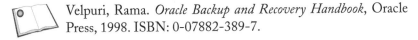

Loney, Kevin. *DBA Handbook, 8.0 Edition*, Oracle Press, 1999. ISBN 0-07882-289-0.

Velpuri, Rama. *Oracle Backup and Recovery Handbook*, Oracle Press, 1998. ISBN: 0-07882-389-7.

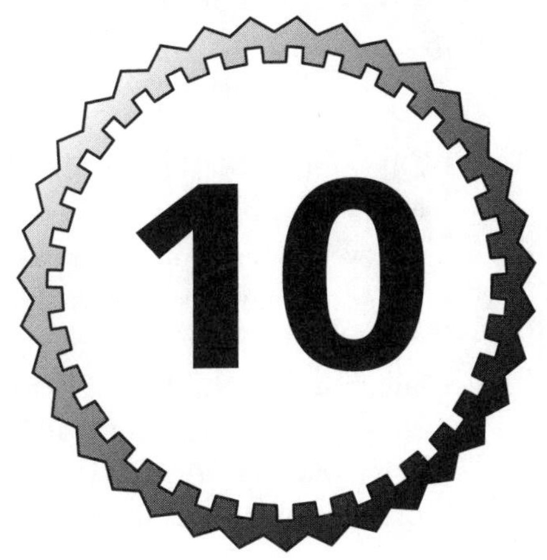

Oracle Recovery Without Archiving

Terms you'll need to understand:

- Restore
- Recover
- **RESTORE** command
- **ALTER DATABASE RENAME FILE** command

Techniques you'll need to master:

- Understanding restoring and recovering data
- Understanding typical steps to recover a database system
- Understanding the implications of media failure in **NOARCHIVELOG** mode
- Recovering **NOARCHIVELOG** databases after media failure
- Restoring files to alternate locations
- Using the **RESTORE** command
- Using Recovery Manager (**RMAN**) to recover a **NOARCHIVELOG** database

One of the critical tasks of an Oracle DBA is to understand database recovery in order to derive an effective recovery strategy that meets site-specific needs. Recovery operations differ depending on the archiving mode of the database. This chapter focuses on database recovery topics relating to databases running in **NOARCHIVELOG** mode. You will learn about the implications of media failure under **NOARCHIVELOG** mode, recovering **NOARCHIVELOG** mode databases, restoring database files to different locations, and using **RMAN** to recover a **NOARCHIVELOG** mode database. Refer to Chapters 11 and 12 for recovery operations with **ARCHIVELOG** mode databases.

Restoring And Recovering Data

Before performing recovery operations, a DBA should understand the following concepts:

- When a file is restored, an original copy of the file is retrieved from a backup.
- When a file is recovered, a restored file is brought current up to the required point in time. The recover process is also known as *rolling forward.*
- Typical steps to recovering a database system include the following:
    1. Detect the failure. Is the database responding to the application? Has the system displayed explicit error messages? Problems such as a corrupt control file might not be detected while the database is online.
    2. Analyze the failure. The recovery procedure depends on the analysis of the type and extent of the failure. The analysis time spent can be significant for large databases.
    3. Determine the database components requiring recovery and the intercomponent dependencies. When a component such as a database table is lost, you need to determine whether you need to recover the tablespace, a data file, or the database. When a table needs recovery, you'll have to re-create the associated indexes.
    4. Determine the location of the backup. Is the backup on disk or tape? Is the backup on-site or off-site? Are mirrored copies available? Is an **RMAN** recovery catalog available?
    5. Perform the restore. You need to restore the physical files from disk or tape to a location where the database can access it for recovery purposes. If **RMAN** is part of the backup and recovery strategy, then

it can be used to perform the restore operation. The amount of time required to restore is affected by the file size, file format, file location, and the parallelization of the restore operation.

6. For archiving databases, apply redo log files and resynchronize the database. RMAN automates this recovery process.

Implications Of Media Failure In NOARCHIVELOG Mode

NOARCHIVELOG mode is the default mode used by an Oracle database instance. In this mode, the filled groups of online redo log files are not archived and therefore no redo history is maintained. No additional administrative overhead or disk space is required, because no archival of the redo log is made. Due to the recycling of the online redo log files, all the work done after the most recent backup is lost, because older redo log files needed for recovery are no longer available. When the database is operating in NOARCHIVELOG mode, recovery from media failure is limited to the most recent full database backup. You need to restore all data files, redo log files, and control files from your backup even if only one file is lost. Your database is unrecoverable if no offline consistent backup is available. Typically, the only databases that run in NOARCHIVELOG mode are those that have a low volume of transactions, such as decision support databases that contain only summarized information from other high activity external databases or a training database that needs to start with a clean slate for each training session.

The only time you don't need to restore all the database files when recovering a **NOARCHIVELOG** mode database after a media failure is when no online redo log files have been overwritten by LGWR since the most recent backup.

Recovering NOARCHIVELOG Databases After Media Failure

In the event of a media failure for a database running in NOARCHIVELOG mode, you must recover from the most recent full database backup. The database is unavailable during the recovery process.

Follow these steps to perform the recovery process:

1. Shut down the database with the SHUTDOWN ABORT statement, as shown here:

```
SVRMGR> SHUTDOWN ABORT;
```

2. Resolve any hardware problems.
3. Restore all data files, redo log files, and control files from applicable offline database backups using operating system copy commands or third-party media management mechanisms. All files must be restored, not just the damaged ones.
4. Open the database, using the code shown here:

```
SVRMGR> STARTUP OPEN PFILE=init_SID.ora;
```

Restoring Files To Alternate Locations

If the disk cannot be replaced after a media failure, then the DBA needs to move the database files to other disks and update the control file accordingly. The following steps restore the database files to alternate locations:

1. Shut down the database if it is open.
2. Restore data files, redo log files, and control files from applicable offline backups using OS copy commands or third-party media managers. All files must be restored, not just the ones that were lost.
3. Update the control file specification in the **CONTROL_FILES** parameter of the *initSID.ora* file. The path and file names need to be changed to reflect a new location for the control file of the Oracle database if the control file was lost in the disk failure.
4. Start up and mount the database but don't open it, as in the code shown here:

```
SVRMGR> STARTUP MOUNT pfile=init_ecsprod.ora
```

5. Update the control file to reflect new locations of data files or redo log files. The DBA typically issues the **ALTER DATABASE** statement with the **RENAME FILE** option from Server Manager. Full path names for the data file at old and new locations should be specified. The following sample code illustrates this operation:

```
SVRMGR> ALTER DATABASE ecs_prod
     2> RENAME FILE '/u1/oradata/ecs_prod/ecs_data.ora'
     3> TO '/u2/oradata/ecs_prod/ecs_data.ora';
```

6. Mimic incomplete recovery, as illustrated by the following code:

```
SVRMGR> ALTER DATABASE RECOVER DATABASE UNTIL CANCEL;
```

7. Cancel the incomplete recovery without applying any redo logs.
8. Open the database:

```
SVRMGR> ALTER DATABASE OPEN RESETLOGS;
```

9. Shut down the database using the NORMAL or IMMEDIATE option, and take a backup.

Using RMAN To Recover A NOARCHIVELOG Mode Database

When performing the restore operation for a NOARCHIVELOG mode database, RMAN uses the recovery catalog or the target database control file to determine which full and incremental backups or image copies it will use. The RESTORE command is used in the restore operation.

RESTORE Command

The RESTORE command enables RMAN to restore files from backup sets or from image copies on disk to the specified location. Files with the same name are overwritten. The RESTORE command syntax applicable to this chapter is as follows:

```
RESTORE <restore_object> <options>;
```

Table 10.1 describes the RESTORE command elements and associated values.

Table 10.1 Elements of the RESTORE command.

ELEMENT	VALUE
Restore_object	Controlfile to <location>; database; datafile <file_spec>; tablespace <ts_spec>; archivelog all
Options	Channel <channel id>; from tag = <tag_name>; parms = <parameters>; from <backupset or datafilecopy>

The following code sample illustrates using the **RESTORE** command to restore a **NOARCHIVELOG** target database in **NOMOUNT** mode:

```
RMAN> Run {
   2> Allocate channel c1 type disk;
   3> Restore controlfile to 'u1/oradata/controlapp1.ora';
   4> Sql "alter database mount";
   5> Restore database;
   6> Sql "alter database open resetlogs";}
```

You should consider the following when using the **RESTORE** command:

- The **RESTORE** command needs to be specified within the **RUN** command.
- At least one channel needs to be allocated preceding the **RESTORE** command.
- The target database must be mounted to perform full database restores.
- **RMAN** only restores backups that were created on the same type of channels that are allocated for the **RESTORE** command.
- You need to open the database with the **RESETLOGS** option after restoring using a backup control file.

The following steps demonstrate the use of **RMAN** to recover a **NOARCHIVELOG** database:

1. Shut down the target database.
2. Start the target database in **MOUNT** or **NOMOUNT** mode.

If the target database is open when you're recovering a **NOARCHIVELOG** database, **RMAN** will return an error.

3. Make sure the recovery catalog database is open.
4. Start **RMAN** by connecting to both the target database and the recovery catalog.
5. Execute a run script that allocates applicable channels, restores control files and data files from offline database backups, opens the database, and releases the applicable channels. You should be aware that both the **RESTORE CONTROLFILE** and the **RESTORE DATABASE**

commands are required when you're performing database restores. The **RESTORE DATABASE** command alone will restore only the data files. To bypass the **RECOVER** command, you should make sure the backups for the control file and the data files were taken at the same time so they are synchronized. The following code sample illustrates an **RMAN** run script for Windows NT that can be used to restore all your database files when your database runs in **NOARCHIVELOG** mode:

```
E:\ORANT\BIN> rman80 target username/passwd@target_db rcvcat
username/passwd@catalog_db

RMAN> run{
allocate channel c1 type disk;
restore controlfile to 'e:\orant\database\control1.ora';
restore database;
sql 'alter database open resetlogs';
release channel c1; }
```

6. Shut down the database and take a full offline database backup. This action is required when you're restoring your database with **RMAN**, because the **RESETLOGS** task has been performed. Using **RMAN** to restore a **NOARCHIVELOG** mode database requires more effort than using OS mechanisms.
7. Open the database for normal use. Inform business users to re-enter data that was lost after the most recent backup.

Practice Questions

Question 1

When a media failure occurs for a test database running in **NOARCHIVELOG** mode, what is the first step the DBA should perform to recover this database after the hardware problem that caused the media failure has been resolved?

- ❍ a. Issue the **RECOVER DATABASE** command.
- ❍ b. Restore all database files from the most recent full offline backup.
- ❍ c. Shut down the database.
- ❍ d. Start the database.

The correct answer is c. DBAs typically perform the following steps to recover from a media failure when the database is running in NOARCHIVELOG mode: (1) issue the SHUTDOWN ABORT command, (2) restore all the database files from the most recent full offline backup, and (3) restart the database. Answer a is incorrect, because this command is not required for this sample scenario. Answers b and d are incorrect, because they are not the first step performed by the DBA under the sample scenario.

Question 2

When a data file has been restored to a new location and you need to issue the **ALTER DATABASE RENAME FILE** command to update the control file, in which state should the database be?

- ❍ a. **OPEN**
- ❍ b. **MOUNT**
- ❍ c. **NOMOUNT**
- ❍ d. **shut down**

The correct answer is b. The database should be mounted and not opened when the control file is being updated with the ALTER DATABASE RENAME FILE command. Answers a, c, and d are incorrect, because these database states don't support the ALTER DATABASE RENAME FILE command.

Question 3

If **RMAN** is part of your backup and recovery strategy and the target database is in **NOARCHIVELOG** mode, the target database should be in what two states when you're restoring data files? [Choose two answers]

- ❑ a. **shut down**
- ❑ b. **NOMOUNT**
- ❑ c. **MOUNT**
- ❑ d. **OPEN**

The correct answers are b and c. When you're using **RMAN** to restore data files for a **NOARCHIVELOG** database, the database must be in **NOMOUNT** or **MOUNT** state. Answers a and d are incorrect, because the database must be started and not opened.

Question 4

What files are required to perform incomplete recovery when a media failure occurs in a **NOARCHIVELOG** mode database?

- ❍ a. All the data files.
- ❍ b. All the data files and the redo log files.
- ❍ c. All the data files and the archived redo log files.
- ❍ d. All the data files, redo log files, and archived log files.
- ❍ e. Valid offline database backup.

The correct answer is e. All the database files—data files, control files, and redo log files—must be restored when a media failure has occurred for a **NOARCHIVELOG** mode database. Answers a and b are incorrect, because they are only a subset of the database files needed. Answers c and d are incorrect, because archived redo log files are not maintained for a **NOARCHIVELOG** mode database.

Question 5

Which of the following files needs to be updated if you've restored the control file to a new location after a media failure?

- ❍ a. Alert log file
- ❍ b. Database initialization file
- ❍ c. Trace file
- ❍ d. Password file
- ❍ e. Data files

The correct answer is b. If the location of the control file has changed, the database initialization file (initSID.ora) needs to be updated with the new location. Answers a, c, and e are incorrect, because DBAs don't update these files. Answer d is incorrect, because the password file does not contain information about control file locations.

Question 6

The disk on which the control file resides has crashed and you need to restore it to a new location. What two steps must you perform before opening the **NOARCHIVELOG** database for general use? [Choose two answers]

- ❑ a. Restore the control file to the new location, all data files, and all redo log files from the most recent offline backup.
- ❑ b. Rename the data files in the init.ora.
- ❑ c. Re-enter the lost transactions.
- ❑ d. Edit the init.ora file to reflect the new control file location.
- ❑ e. Issue the **ALTER DATABASE RENAME FILE** command.

The correct answers are a and d. Answer b is incorrect, because it is an invalid action. Answer c is incorrect, because it is performed after the database is opened for general use. Answer e is incorrect, because the **ALTER DATABASE RENAME FILE** command is used to update the control file with the new location of a data file.

Question 7

Your database is operating in **NOARCHIVELOG** mode. When a disk crashes and the data files for your HR application are lost, which of the following steps should you typically perform to restore the lost data files after you've replaced the faulty disk? [Choose two answers]

- ❑ a. Use OS utilities to restore all the database files from the most recent offline database backup.
- ❑ b. Open the database.
- ❑ c. Issue the **ALTER DATABASE RENAME FILE** command.
- ❑ d. Use OS utilities to restore only the lost data files from the most recent offline database backup.
- ❑ e. Modify the database initialization file.

The correct answers are a and b. When recovering a **NOARCHIVELOG** mode database, you need to restore all the database files using the most recent offline database backup, then open the database for general use. Answer c is incorrect, because the **ALTER DATABASE RENAME FILE** command is only needed when a data file relocation has taken place. Answer d is incorrect, because when performing recovery for a **NOARCHIVELOG** database, you need to restore all the database files from the most recent offline database backup. Answer e is incorrect, because modifications to the database initialization file are needed when a control file relocation has taken place.

Question 8

You are the DBA for a reporting database that is infrequently changed. This database is refreshed monthly and a full offline backup is performed after each refresh operation. To minimize disk space usage, in what database mode could you operate this database?

- ❍ a. **ARCHIVELOG** mode with monthly full offline backups
- ❍ b. **ARCHIVELOG** mode with daily online backups
- ❍ c. **ARCHIVELOG** mode with daily full offline backups
- ❍ d. **NOARCHIVELOG** mode with daily online backups
- ❍ e. **NOARCHIVELOG** mode with monthly full offline backups
- ❍ f. **NOARCHIVELOG** mode with monthly online backups

The correct answer is e. A database running in **NOARCHIVELOG** mode conserves disk space, because no storage space is required for the archived redo log files. Answers a, b, and c are incorrect, because **ARCHIVELOG** mode databases require additional disk space for the archived redo log files. Answers d and f are incorrect, because online backups are applicable to databases operating in **ARCHIVELOG** mode.

Question 9

What does the following Server Manager command accomplish?

```
SVRMGR> alter database rename file
     2> '/disk3/oradata/appl.ora'
     3> to '/disk4/oradata/appl.ora';
```

- ❍ a. Move a data file in the operating system.
- ❍ b. Update the control file with the new location of a data file.
- ❍ c. Rename a data file in the operating system at the same location.
- ❍ d. Update the database initialization file with the new location of a data file.

The correct answer is b. The **ALTER DATABASE RENAME FILE** command is used to update the control file with the new location of a data file after it has been restored. Answer a is incorrect, because the sample command does not physically move the data file in the OS. Answer c is incorrect, because the sample command does not perform the OS rename operation. Answer d is incorrect, because the database initialization file does not contain information about the location of the data files.

Question 10

A media failure occurred for your training database running in **NOARCHIVELOG** mode. You've moved the data files to another drive, because the original drive containing the original data files can't be replaced immediately. What command should you issue to update the database with this location change?

- ❍ a. **ALTER TABLESPACE RENAME FILE**
- ❍ b. **ALTER DATAFILE RENAME**
- ❍ c. **ALTER SYSTEM RENAME FILE**
- ❍ d. **ALTER DATABASE RENAME FILE**

The correct answer is d. When a media failure occurs and you've moved a data file to a new location, the **ALTER DATABASE RENAME FILE** command needs to be issued to update the control file. Answers a, b, and c are incorrect, because they are invalid commands.

Question 11

Evaluate the following **RMAN** command:

```
RMAN> run{
allocate channel c1 type disk;
restore database;
sql 'alter database open resetlogs';
release channel c1; }
```

What command is missing if you need to perform a full database restore for a **NOARCHIVELOG** database?

- ❍ a. **RESTORE CONTROLFILE TO** command
- ❍ b. **RESTORE DATAFILE** command
- ❍ c. **RESTORE TABLESPACE** command
- ❍ d. **RESTORE ARCHIVELOG ALL** command

The correct answer is a. When you're performing full database restores using **RMAN** for a **NOARCHIVELOG** database, you must include the **RESTORE CONTROLFILE** and the **RESTORE DATABASE** commands. Answers b, c, and d are not correct, because they serve other purposes.

Need To Know More?

Dialeris, Connie. *Oracle8 Backup and Recovery Guide Release 8.0*, Part No. A58396-01, Oracle Corporation, 1997.

Lane, Paula. *Oracle8 References Release 8.0*, Part No. A58242-01, Oracle Corporation, 1997.

Leverenz, Lefty. *Oracle8 Concepts Release 8.0*, Part No. A58227-01, Oracle Corporation, 1997.

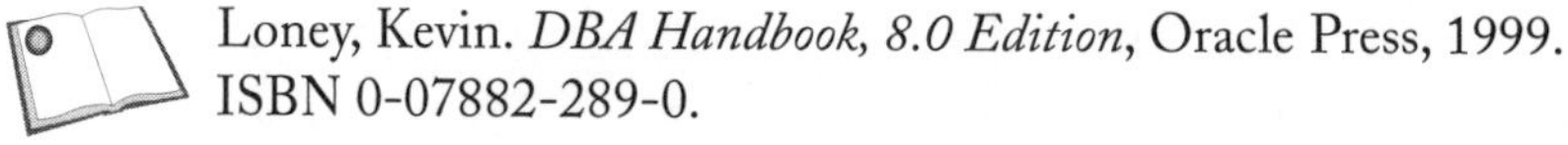

Loney, Kevin. *DBA Handbook, 8.0 Edition*, Oracle Press, 1999. ISBN 0-07882-289-0.

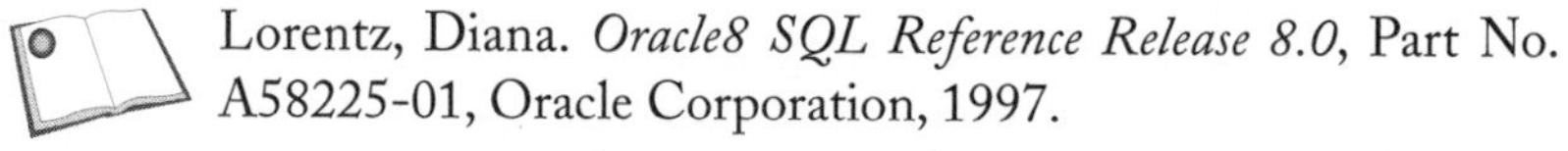

Lorentz, Diana. *Oracle8 SQL Reference Release 8.0*, Part No. A58225-01, Oracle Corporation, 1997.

Velpuri, Rama. *Oracle Backup and Recovery Handbook*, Oracle Press, 1998. ISBN 0-078-82389-7.

11

Complete Oracle Recovery With Archiving

Terms you'll need to understand:

- √ Complete recovery
- √ Incomplete recovery
- √ **RECOVER** command
- √ **ALTER DATABASE RECOVER** command
- √ **V$RECOVER_FILE**
- √ **ALTER DATABASE CLEAR UNARCHIVED LOGFILE** command
- √ **V$RECOVERY_STATUS**
- √ **V$RECOVERY_FILE_STATUS**
- √ **SET AUTORECOVERY ON** command
- √ **V$LOG_HISTORY**
- √ **V$RECOVERY_LOG**
- √ **SET NEWNAME** command
- √ **SWITCH** command

Techniques you'll need to master:

- √ Understanding the implications of instance failure with an **ARCHIVELOG** database
- √ Understanding the pros and cons of recovering an **ARCHIVELOG** database
- √ Understanding complete recovery operations
- √ Using the **RECOVER** command
- √ Performing recovery for an **ARCHIVELOG** database after a media failure
- √ Using Recovery Manager (**RMAN**) to perform complete recovery for an **ARCHIVELOG** database
- √ Understanding pertinent data dictionary views for database recovery

When an Oracle database is operating in ARCHIVELOG mode, the DBA has two recovery options—complete or incomplete recovery. In *complete recovery*, the database is restored and recovered through the application of all redo information generated (in the online and archived redo log files) since the last available backup. This recovery option is typically performed when one or more data files or control files is damaged or lost due to a media failure. The damaged or lost files are fully recovered using all redo information generated since the restored backup. In *incomplete recovery*, on the other hand, the database is restored and recovered through the application of only some of the redo information generated since the last available backup. Incomplete recovery is typically performed when the online redo log files are lost due to hardware problems, a user error requiring recovery to the point in time before the error occurred, or an archived redo log file essential for recovery is not available.

This chapter focuses on complete recovery concepts and procedures. Specifically, you will learn about the implications of instance failure with an ARCHIVELOG database, the pros and cons of recovering an ARCHIVELOG database, complete recovery operations, recovering ARCHIVELOG databases after media failure, and performing ARCHIVELOG database recovery using RMAN.

Implications Of Instance Failure With An ARCHIVELOG Database

An Oracle database typically operates in ARCHIVELOG mode under the following circumstances:

- The backup window doesn't allow for shutting down the database to take an offline backup.
- The organization cannot afford to lose any data.
- The recovery process is simpler when using archived redo log files than manually applying lost transactions.

When a media failure occurs with an ARCHIVELOG mode database and complete recovery up to the time of failure is required, you must make sure the following items are available:

- A valid backup of the damaged or lost data files taken after the database was set to ARCHIVELOG mode
- All the archived redo log files from the time of the restored backup to the present time

Pros And Cons Of Recovering An ARCHIVELOG Database

Operating your database in ARCHIVELOG mode has both pros and cons. The pros include the following:

- You can typically perform the recovery procedures while the database is open. The exception is when the data files for the SYSTEM tablespace or the data file containing rollback segments are being recovered.
- When restoring files from a valid backup, you only need to restore a subset of the valid backup—the damaged or lost files.
- No data loss will be incurred for committed data. When you restore files from a valid backup and apply all the redo information generated via online and archived redo log files, the database will be current up to the present time.
- The total recovery time is dependent on the following factors:
  - The amount of time spent locating the files.
  - The speed of the hardware in restoring the required files and applying all the online and archived redo log files.

The cons include the following:

- Additional disk space is required for the archived redo log files.
- The potential risk of the database to run out of space and subsequently hang is increased.
- Additional DBA maintenance overhead is incurred.
- All the archived redo log files from the time of the last valid backup to the present time must be available. If one file is missing, complete recovery cannot be performed, because all archived redo log files must be sequentially applied.

Complete Recovery Operations

You can use two basic methods to recover physical files, including the following:

- Recovering your database manually by executing the RECOVER or the ALTER DATABASE RECOVER commands.
- Using the RMAN utility to automate recovery.

The following steps are typically performed for a complete recovery up to the time of failure when a valid backup and all the applicable redo log files are available:

1. Determine which data files need recovery. The **V$RECOVER_FILE** view is helpful in this effort.
2. Make sure the status of the damaged or lost file is not **ONLINE**. You can query the **V$DATAFILE** and the **V$TABLESPACE** data dictionary views to obtain the status of the file.
3. Make sure you restore only the damaged or lost file from backup. If you cannot restore a data file to its original location, relocate the restored data file and inform the control file of the new location. Restore any necessary archived redo log files. Also make sure the online redo log files are not restored.

Restoring all the files from the backup will take your database back to a certain point in time, which is not desirable when you're performing a complete recovery up to the time of failure.

4. Make sure the database is in **MOUNT** or **OPEN** mode.
5. Use the **RECOVER** command to recover the restored files.

RECOVER Command

The **RECOVER** command performs media recovery on one or more tablespaces, one or more data files, or the entire database. The following **RECOVER** command syntax examples are typically issued during the recovery process to reconstruct the data files:

- RECOVER [AUTOMATIC] DATABASE—Recovers the entire database. This command is only applicable for a closed database recovery.
- RECOVER [AUTOMATIC] TABLESPACE **<tablespace_specification: number or name>**—Recovers a particular tablespace. The **<tablespace_specification>** is the number or the name of a tablespace in the current database. This command is only applicable for an open database recovery.
- RECOVER [AUTOMATIC] DATAFILE **<datafile_specification: number or name>**—Recovers a particular data file. You can specify any number of data files. This command is applicable for both open and closed database recovery.

The **AUTOMATIC** keyword in the **RECOVER** commands tells Oracle to automatically generate the name of the next archived redo log file needed to continue the recovery operation. Oracle uses the **LOG_ARCHIVE_DEST** and the **LOG_ARCHIVE_FORMAT** parameters to generate the next redo log file name. If the file is found, the contents of the redo log file are applied. If the file is not found, Oracle prompts you for a file name, displaying the generated file name as a suggestion. You can then accept the generated file name or replace it with a desirable fully qualified file name. If you didn't specify **AUTOMATIC**, Oracle prompts you for a file name, displaying the generated file name as a suggestion. You can then accept the generated file name or replace it with a desirable fully qualified file name.

Things To Remember When Using The **RECOVER** Command

You should consider the following when using the **RECOVER** command:

- The **ALTER DATABASE** tokens may be optionally included in front of the **RECOVER** command.
- You must be connected to Oracle as **SYSOPER** or **SYSDBA**.
- You cannot use the **RECOVER** command when connected via the multithreaded server.
- To perform media recovery on an entire database (all tablespaces), the database must be mounted and closed.
- To perform media recovery on a tablespace, the database must be mounted and open, and the tablespace must be offline.
- To perform media recovery on a data file not belonging to the **SYSTEM** tablespace, the database can remain open and mounted with the damaged data files offline.
- You must restore the damaged data files from a valid backup before using the **RECOVER** command. Also, make sure you can access all archived and online redo log files since the restored backup.
- You should restore copies of the archived redo log files needed for recovery to the destination specified in **LOG_ARCHIVE_DEST**, if necessary.
- During recovery, you can accept the suggested log name by pressing Return, cancel recovery by entering Cancel, or enter **AUTO** at the prompt for automatic file selection without further prompting. If you've enabled autorecovery (that is, **SET AUTO RECOVERY ON**), the recovery process proceeds without prompting you with file names. Status messages are displayed when each log file has been applied.

Recovering ARCHIVELOG Databases After Media Failure

You can perform complete recovery for an **ARCHIVELOG** database after media failure using four different techniques:

- Closed database recovery
- Open database recovery with database initially open
- Open database recovery with database initially closed
- Recovery for a data file with no backup

Closed Database Recovery

This recovery technique is typically used under the following circumstances:

- The database does not need to be available 24 hours a day, seven days a week.
- The files that need recovery belong to the **SYSTEM** tablespace or contain rollback segments.
- Recovery is needed for the whole database.
- Recovery is needed for a large number of the data files.

You should be aware that the closed database recovery technique requires the database to be closed, so the database is not available to business users during the recovery process.

Sample Recovery Scenario

Corrupted blocks have been discovered for data file **df3** located on disk **d3**. Data file **df3** belongs to the **SYSTEM** tablespace. The following are steps to recover data file **df3**:

1. Restore the file from the most recent valid backup, as illustrated by this sample code:

```
Unix:
SVRMGR> !cp /ul/backup/df3.ora /u2/oradata/
NT:
SVRMGR> !copy e:\orant\backup\df3.ora d:\orant\database\
```

2. Start the database in **MOUNT** mode, then recover data file **df3** to the point of failure by applying applicable archived log files and online redo log files, as illustrated by this sample code:

```
SVRMGR> startup mount pfile=initTEST.ora
...
SVRMGR> recover datafile '/u2/oradata/df3.ora';
ORA-00279: change 102772 …12/30/99 20:01:22 needed for thread 1
ORA-00289: suggestion : /ul/archive/arch_7.rdo
ORA-00280: change 102772 for thread 1 is in sequence #7
Log applied.
...
Media recovery complete.
```

3. Upon recovery process completion, all the data files are synchronized. The database can be opened for normal use, as illustrated by the following sample code:

```
SVRMGR> alter database open;
```

4. Notify business users to re-enter any uncommitted data before the media failure.

Open Database Recovery With Database Initially Open

This recovery technique is typically used under the following circumstances:

- Minimal downtime can be tolerated, because the database must be available 24 hours a day, seven days a week.
- The files that need recovery don't contain rollback segments or don't belong to the **SYSTEM** tablespace.
- Recovery is needed when a media failure has occurred that didn't cause the database to be shut down.
- Recovery is needed when an accidental file loss has occurred that didn't cause the database to be shut down.
- Recovery is needed when a file corruption has been detected that didn't cause the database to be shut down.

Sample Recovery Scenario

A member of the DBA team accidentally deleted data file **df3** using OS commands. The database is open for normal use. The following are steps to recover data file **df3**:

1. Determine the tablespace to which the data file **df3** belongs, as illustrated by the following code sample:

```
SQL> select file_id FID,
  2> file_name,
  3> tablespace_name TS_NAME,
  4> status
  5> from dba_data_files;
FID  FILE_NAME                        TS_NAME     STATUS
---- -------------------------------- ----------  --------
   1 /u1/oradata/system01.ora         SYSTEM      AVAILABLE
   2 /u2/oradata/df3.ora              APP03_DATA  AVAILABLE
...
```

2. Check to see if data file **df3** is offline. You'll need to take the data file offline if it is currently online. The following sample code illustrates using a SQL query to obtain the current status of all the data files. **OFFLINE** data files may require recovery:

```
SQL> select df.file# file#, df.name, df.status, dh.status
  2> from v$datafile_header dh, v$datafile df
  3> where dh.file# = df.file#;
FILE# DF.NAME                          DF.STATUS DH.STATUS
---- -------------------------------- --------  --------
    1 /u1/oradata/system01.ora         SYSTEM    ONLINE
    2 /u2/oradata/df3.ora              RECOVER   OFFLINE
    3 /u1/oradata/rbs01.ora            ONLINE    ONLINE
...
```

When a tablespace is taken offline, all the data files belonging to the offline tablespace are also taken offline. This means that all the data residing in the offline tablespace is not accessible. To maximize availability for a tablespace comprised of multiple data files, you can take the data file requiring recovery offline so other online data files in the tablespace remain available.

3. Because the data file is offline, you can restore the file from a valid backup, as illustrated by the following code sample:

```
Unix:
SVRMGR> !cp /u3/backup/df3.ora /u2/oradata/
NT:
SVRMGR> !copy e:\orant\backup\df3.ora d:\orant\database\
```

4. Use the **RECOVER** or the **ALTER DATABASE RECOVER** commands to recover the restored data file, as illustrated by the following sample code:

```
SVRMGR> recover datafile '/u2/oradata/df3.ora';
OR
SVRMGR> recover tablespace APP03_DATA;
```

5. Bring the data file **df3** online when the recovery process is finished and all data files are synchronized, as illustrated by the following sample code:

```
SVRMGR> alter database
datafile '/u2/oradata/df3.ora' online;
OR
SVRMGR> alter tablespace APP03_DATA online;
```

When Oracle encounters a file problem, it will sometimes automatically take the data file offline. It is highly recommended that you always check the alert log for any errors and check the current status of data files before you begin the recovery process.

Open Database Recovery With Database Initially Closed

This recovery technique is typically used under the following circumstances:

- A media or hardware failure has caused the database system to go down.
- Minimal downtime can be tolerated, because the database must be available 24 hours a day, seven days a week.
- The files that need recovery don't contain rollback segments or don't belong to the **SYSTEM** tablespace.

Sample Recovery Scenario

You've discovered that the disk controller to disk **u3** failed, which caused the media failure. There is one data file **df3** that resides on disk **u3**. The data file **df3** does not belong to the **SYSTEM** tablespace or contain rollback segments. The data file **df3** also should not prevent users from running their end-of-fiscal-year reports. The following are steps to recover data file **df3**:

1. Start and mount the database, as illustrated by the following code. The database will not open, because data file **df3** can't be opened:

```
SVRMGR> startup mount pfile=$HOME/initTEST.ora
Database mounted.
```

2. Issue the following query to obtain the tablespace number to which the data file belongs:

```
SQL> select df.file# file#, df.ts#, df.tablespace_name TS_NAME,
  2>        df.name, dh.error
  3> from v$datafile_header dh, v$datafile df
  4> where dh.file# = df.file#;
FILE# TS# TS_NAME    NAME                       ERROR
---- -- ---------   ----------------------    ----------------
    1  0  SYSTEM     /ul/oradata/system01.ora
    2  1             /u3/oradata/df3.ora        FILE NOT FOUND
    3  2  RB_DATA    /ul/oradata/rbs01.ora
...
```

3. From the **V$DATAFILE** view, you've determined that the data file **df3** is currently **ONLINE**. The data file **df3** must be taken offline to open the database. The following code sample can be issued to take the data file **df3** offline:

```
SVRMGR> alter database datafile
     2> '/u3/oradta/df3.ora' offline;
```

The **ALTER TABLESPACE** command will not work here, because the database is not opened at this point.

4. Open the database for normal use, as illustrated by the following sample code:

```
SVRMGR> alter database open;
```

5. Restore the data file **df3** to disk **u4** since disk **u3** is no longer available.

```
Unix:
SVRMGR> !cp /u2/backup/df3.ora /u4/oradata/
NT:
SVRMGR> !copy e:\orant\backup\df3.ora f:\orant\database\
```

6. Inform Oracle of the new data file location using the following sample code:

```
SVRMGR> alter database rename file '/u3/oradata/df3.ora'
     2> to '/u4/oradata/df3.ora';
```

7. Issue the following query to obtain the **tablespace name** that owns the data file **df3**:

```
SQL> select file_id f#, file_name,
  2> tablespace_name ts_name,
  3> status
  4> from dba_data_files;
F#   FILE_NAME                     TS_NAME    STATUS
---- ----------------------------- ---------- --------
   1 /ul/oradata/system01.ora      SYSTEM     AVAILABLE
   2 /u4/oradata/df3.ora           APP03_DATA AVAILABLE
   3 /ul/oradata/rb01.ora          RB_DATA    AVAILABLE
...
```

8. Recover the restored data file **df3** using the **RECOVER** or **ALTER DATABASE RECOVER** commands, as illustrated by the following sample code:

```
SVRMGR> recover datafile '/u4/oradata/df3.ora';
OR
SVRMGR> recover tablespace APP03_DATA;
```

9. Bring the data file **df3** online when the recovery process is finished and all data files are synchronized, as illustrated by the following sample code:

```
SVRMGR> alter database
datafile '/u4/oradata/df3.ora' online;
OR
SVRMGR> alter tablespace APP03_DATA online;
```

10. Notify business users to re-enter any uncommitted data before the media failure.

Recovery Of A Data File With No Backup

This recovery technique is typically used under the following circumstances:

- A media or user failure has caused a loss of a data file that has no available backup.
- All archived redo log files from the time the lost data file was created up to the current time are available.
- The files that need recovery don't contain rollback segments or don't belong to the **SYSTEM** tablespace.

During the recovery process, all archived redo log files need to be available on disk. If any archived redo log files are on a backup tape, they must be restored to disk first.

Sample Recovery Scenario

One of the application DBAs created the **TRAINING_DATA** tablespace on disk **u5** yesterday and that tablespace has not been incorporated into the backup strategy. The **TRAINING_DATA** tablespace contains a single data file **df5**, which is now lost. All the archived redo log files generated since yesterday are available. The following are steps to recover data file **df5**:

1. Mount the database if it is closed. Take the data file **df5** offline. Because the **TRAINING_DATA** tablespace contains one data file **df5**, we can optionally offline the tablespace instead of the data file. Make sure the **IMMEDIATE** option is used in the **ALTER TABLESPACE** command to prevent a checkpoint that tries to write to a nonexistent data file. Open the database for normal use. This sample code illustrates this action:

```
SVRMGR> alter tablespace TRAINING_DATA offline immediate;
Statement Processed.
```

2. Query the **V$RECOVER_FILE** view for the status of a backup and to confirm the recovery status, as shown here:

```
SVRMGR> select * from v$recover_file;
FILE# ONLINE  ERROR          CHANGE#   TIME
---- ------- -------------- --------  --------
   5 OFFLINE FILE NOT FOUND           0
```

3. Re-create the lost file, as illustrated by the following sample code:

```
SVRMGR> alter database create datafile '/ul/oradata/df5.ora'
     2> as '/u5/oradata/df5.ora';
Statement Processed.
SVRMGR> select * from v$recover_file;
FILE# ONLINE  ERROR          CHANGE#   TIME
---- ------ -------------- --------  --------
   5 OFFLINE                118249    30-DEC-99
```

4. Recover the re-created data file using the following sample code:

```
SVRMGR> recover tablespace TRAINING_DATA;
```

5. All archived and redo log files are applied and all the data files are synchronized.
6. Upon recovery process completion, bring the tablespace online (or bring the one data file online), as illustrated by the following code sample:

```
SVRMGR> alter tablespace TRAINING_DATA online;
```

7. Incorporate the data file in the backup strategy and notify users the **TRAINING_DATA** tablespace is available for general use.

Additional Recovery Activities

DBAs may encounter several recovery activities in performing their day-to-day functions, including the following:

- Recovery of file in backup mode
- Clearing redo log files
- Re-creating inactive redo log files
- Obtaining recovery status information
- Restoring archived redo log files to a different location
- Enabling automatic application of redo log files
- Locating files that need recovery

Recovery Of File In Backup Mode

While a DBA is performing an open database backup, a failure condition may occur which in turn may cause the database to go down. You should be aware of the following issues when you encounter this situation:

- The backup files will not be valid if the OS backup has been terminated abnormally. A new backup will be required.
- The database files in "hot backup" mode will be out of sync with the rest of the database, because the file headers are frozen at the start of the open database backup.
- You can't issue the **ALTER TABLESPACE** command until the database is open. The database will not open until the database files are synchronized or offline. Taking the database files offline will not help the situation, because the **ALTER TABLESPACE END BACKUP** command used to unfreeze the file headers requires database files to be online.

To perform recovery of a file in backup mode, follow these steps:

1. Query the **V$BACKUP** view to determine which files are in "hot backup" mode:

```
SQL> select * from v$backup;
FILE# STATUS         CHANGE# TIME
---- -------------- ------- --------
    1 NOT ACTIVE           0
    2 ACTIVE          119865 30-DEC-99
    3 NOT ACTIVE           0
...
```

The above listing shows that file #2 is in "hot backup" mode.

2. Issue the **ALTER DATABASE END BACKUP** command to unfreeze the file header:

```
SVRMGR> alter database datafile 2 end backup;
Statement processed.
SVRMGR> select * from v$backup;
SQL> select * from v$backup;
FILE# STATUS         CHANGE# TIME
---- -------------- ------- --------
    1 NOT ACTIVE           0
    2 NOT ACTIVE      119865 30-DEC-99
    3 NOT ACTIVE           0
...
```

3. Open the database for general use:

```
SVRMGR> alter database open;
```

Clearing Redo Log Files

If corruption has been detected for an online redo log file while the database is open, you can use the **ALTER DATABASE CLEAR UNARCHIVED LOGFILE** command to create or clear the online redo log file without shutting down the database. The **ALTER DATABASE CLEAR UNARCHIVED LOGFILE** command is useful when you can't drop the online redo log file because you only have two redo log groups or the corrupt redo log file is a member of the current redo log group. You are not allowed to clear a redo log file that is currently required for recovery.

You should take a backup after using the **ALTER DATABASE CLEAR UNARCHIVED LOGFILE** command, because complete recovery can't be accomplished if the applicable archived redo log file was not generated.

You can also use the **ALTER DATABASE CLEAR LOGFILE… UNRECOVERABLE DATAFILE** command to clear a redo log file even though offline data files require the redo log file for recovery. The offline data files requiring this cleared redo log file will be unusable after this command has been issued. To recover the offline data files, you can restore them and perform an incomplete recovery to the point in time before the required redo log file was cleared or drop the tablespace containing the unrecoverable data files.

Re-Creating Inactive Redo Log Files

When the online redo log files are damaged or lost, you may not be able to perform complete recovery up to the point of failure. However, you will not lose any data under the following conditions:

- The database configuration includes mirrored redo log files.
- The online redo log file has been archived.
- The status of the lost online redo log file is not **CURRENT**.

Sample Recovery Scenario

You've just created the QA database. The **LGWR** background process abnormally terminated and aborted the database instance. You have not taken a backup of this new database and you don't have the resources to re-create the database. To recover from this situation, follow these steps:

1. Restart the database instance:

```
SVRMGR> startup pfile=$HOME/initQA.ora
ORACLE instance started.
...
ORA-00313: open failed for members of log group 1 of thread 1
ORA-00312: online log 1 thread 1: '/u2/oradata/log1a.ora'
```

2. Query the **V$LOG** data dictionary view for the redo log file status:

```
SVRMGR> select GROUP#,THREAD#,BYTES,MEMBERS,
     2> ARCHIVED,STATUS,FIRST_CHANGE#
     3> From v$log;

GROUP#  THREAD#   BYTES  MEMBERS ARC  STATUS  FIRST_CHANGE#
------  -------  ------  ------  --   ------  ------------
     1        1 1048576       1  YES  UNUSED              0
     2        1 104857        1  NO   CURRENT        188128
```

The above listing shows that there is a problem with **log group 1**, because the **FIRST_CHANGE#** is 0. **Log group 1** is not active, because **log group 2** is the current group. The redo log file for **log group 1** has been archived so no recovery information has been lost. You were not successful in locating the redo log file from the file system. Although the redo log file is lost, recovery is not required, because no data has been lost. In this situation, you do need to re-create the lost inactive redo log file so the database can be opened for general use.

When you need to re-create the redo log files, perform the following steps:

1. Obtain the location of the redo log file from the data dictionary:

```
SVRMGR> select * from v$logfile;
GROUP#   STATUS  MEMBER
------   ------  ------------------
1                /u01/oradata/log1a.ora
2         STALE  /u02/oradata/log2a.ora
```

You can't drop **log group 1**, because at least two log groups must exist. You need to create a temporary **group 3**, drop **log group 1**, re-create **log group 1**, drop the temporary **group 3**, and remove the redo log file for **group 3** from the OS. The following code sample illustrates this process:

```
SVRMGR> alter database add logfile group 3
     2> '/u1/oradata/log3a.ora' size 1M;
Statement processed.
SVRMGR> alter database drop logfile group 1;
Statement processed.
SVRMGR> alter database add logfile group 1
     2> '/u1/oradata/log1a.ora' size 1M;
Statement processed.
SVRMGR> alter database drop logfile group 3;
Statement processes.
SVRMGR> !rm /u1/oradata/log3a.ora
```

2. Open the database for general use:

```
SVRMGR> alter database open;
```

3. Implement multiplexing of the redo log files to minimize data loss in the future.

4. When the redo log groups are of the same size, you can optionally re-create the redo log file using two commands, as illustrated by the following code sample:

```
SVRMGR> !cp /u1/oradata/log2a.ora /u1/oradata/log1a.ora
SVRMGR> alter database clear logfile '/u1/oradata/log1a.ora';
```

Obtaining Recovery Status Information

Two data dictionary views provide database recovery status information to the server and user processes performing the media recovery:

- V$RECOVERY_STATUS—Provides overall database recovery information:

```
SQL> desc v$recovery_status;
 Name                            Null?    Type
 ------------------------------- -------- ----
 RECOVERY_CHECKPOINT                      DATE
 THREAD                                   NUMBER
 SEQUENCE_NEEDED                          NUMBER
 SCN_NEEDED                               VARCHAR2(16)
 TIME_NEEDED                              DATE
 PREVIOUS_LOG_NAME                        VARCHAR2(513)
 PREVIOUS_LOG_STATUS                      VARCHAR2(13)
 REASON                                   VARCHAR2(13)
```

- **V$RECOVERY_FILE_STATUS**—Provides information for each data file needing recovery:

```
SQL> desc v$recovery_file_status;
 Name                              Null?    Type
 -------------------------------- -------- ----
 FILENUM                                    NUMBER
 FILENAME                                   VARCHAR2(513)
 STATUS                                     VARCHAR2(13)
```

Restoring Archived Redo Log Files To A Different Location

If you've restored the archived redo log files to a location other than the **LOG_ARCHIVE_DEST** directory, you will need to inform Oracle of the new location during the recovery process. You have three ways to let Oracle know about the new location for the restored archived redo log files:

- You can specify the location and name of the archived redo log file at the **RECOVER** prompt. The following sample code illustrates this:

```
SVRMGR> RECOVER DATAFILE 3;
ORA-00279: change 101109…12/27/99 18:00:05 needed for thread 1
ORA-00289: suggestion : /ul/archive/arch_23.rdo
ORA-00280: change 101109 for thread 1 is in sequence #23
Specify log: {<RET>=suggested | filename | AUTO | CANCEL}
/u2/archive/arch_23.rdo
Log applied.
...
```

- Issue the **ALTER SYSTEM ARCHIVE** command, as illustrated by the following code sample:

```
SVRMGR> ALTER SYSTEM ARCHIVE LOG START TO
     2> <new_location_specification>;
```

- Issue the **RECOVER FROM <location_specification>** command, as illustrated by the following code sample:

```
SVRMGR> RECOVER FROM '<new_location_specification>' DATABASE;
```

Automatic Application Of Redo Log Files

You can perform one of the following actions to tell Oracle to automatically apply the necessary archived and online redo log files before and during the recovery process:

➤ Issue the Server Manager **SET AUTORECOVERY ON** statement before starting media recovery, as illustrated by the following code sample:

```
SVRMGR> SET AUTORECOVERY ON
```

➤ Provide **AUTO** when prompted for a redo log file, as illustrated by the following sample code:

```
Specify log: {<RET>=suggested | filename | AUTO | CANCEL}
/u2/archive/arch_23.rdo
Log applied.
...
```

➤ Provide the **AUTOMATIC** keyword option when issuing the **RECOVER** command, as illustrated by the following sample code:

```
SVRMGR> RECOVER AUTOMATIC TABLESPACE 3;
Media recovery complete.
```

Locating Files That Need Recovery

Three data dictionary views can be used to locate data files that need recovery:

➤ **V$RECOVER_FILE**—This view displays the status of data files needing media recovery:

```
SQL> desc v$recover_file
 Name                              Null?    Type
 -------------------------------   -------- ----
 FILE#                                      NUMBER
 ONLINE                                     VARCHAR2(7)
 ERROR                                      VARCHAR2(18)
 CHANGE#                                    NUMBER
 TIME                                       DATE

SQL> select * from v$recover_file;
FILE#    ONLINE   ERROR      CHANGE#       TIME
----     ------   --------   ----------    --------
    3    OFFLINE                 182173    29-DEC-99
```

➤ **V$LOG_HISTORY**—This view lists information about all the archived redo log files for the database:

```
SQL> desc v$log_history
 Name                          Null?    Type
 ----------------------------- -------- ----
 RECID                                  NUMBER
 STAMP                                  NUMBER
 THREAD#                                NUMBER
 SEQUENCE#                              NUMBER
 FIRST_CHANGE#                          NUMBER
 FIRST_TIME                             DATE
 NEXT_CHANGE#                           NUMBER
```

- **V$RECOVERY_LOG**—This view lists information about archived redo log files that are needed to complete media recovery:

```
SQL> desc v$recovery_log;
 Name                          Null?    Type
 ----------------------------- -------- ----
 THREAD#                                NUMBER
 SEQUENCE#                              NUMBER
 TIME                                   DATE
 ARCHIVE_NAME                           VARCHAR2(513)

SQL> select * from v$recovery_log;
THREAD#  SEQUENCE#  Time       ARCHIVE_NAME
------   --------   --------   ----------------------
     1         21   29-DEC-99  /ul/archive/arch_21.rdo
...
     1         31   31-DEC-99  /ul/archive/arch_31.rdo
     1         32   31-DEC-99  /ul/archive/arch_32.rdo
```

ARCHIVELOG Database Recovery Using RMAN

RMAN can be used to perform complete database recovery, recovery of a data file in an open database, and recovery of a tablespace. For complete recovery of an entire database, the database should be closed. For data file and tablespace recovery, the unaffected portion of the database can remain open and available for normal use.

The basic RMAN recovery commands are **RESTORE** and **RECOVER**. You can use RMAN to restore data files from backup sets or from image copies on disk. You can also restore backup sets containing archived redo logs. The restored files can optionally be directed to a new location. The **RMAN RECOVER** command is used to perform media recovery and apply incremental backups. If you use a recovery catalog, RMAN maintains information on all the essential metadata concerning every backup you have taken. If you do not use a recovery catalog, RMAN uses the control file for the necessary metadata. RMAN completely automates the procedure for recovering and restoring your backups and copies.

Complete Database Recovery

The restore and recovery process for complete database recovery using RMAN is as follows:

1. If the target database is open, perform a shutdown.
2. Start up and mount the target database.
3. Start RMAN and connect to the target database and the recovery catalog:

   ```
   $ rman target rman/rmanpwd@target_db \
   rcvcat rman/rmanpwd@catalog_db
   ```

4. Create and execute the **RUN** command that will perform the restore and recovery operations, as illustrated by the following sample code:

   ```
   RMAN> run {
      2> allocate channel c1 type DISK;
      3> restore database;
      4> recover database;
      5> sql "alter database open resetlogs";
      6> release channel c1; }
   ```

5. Take a backup.

Recovery Of A Tablespace In An Open Database

Perform the following steps to recover a tablespace in an open database using RMAN:

1. Issue a query against the **V$INSTANCE** view to determine the status of the database:

   ```
   SVRMGR> Select status from v$instance;
   ```

2. Issue a query against the **V$DATAFILE_HEADER** view to determine which data files need to be restored/recovered:

```
SVRMGR> select name, file#, tablespace_name,
     2>        status, error, recover
     3> from v$datafile_header
     4> where tablespace_name = 'APP01_DATA';
```

If the error column is not null, then the data file is not accessible and may need to be restored or switched to an associated image copy.

3. Create and execute a **RUN** command script similar to the following sample code:

```
RMAN> run {
   2> allocate channel c1 type disk;
   3> sql "alter tablespace APP01_DATA offline immediate";
   4> restore tablespace APP01_DATA;
   5> recover tablespace APP01_DATA;
   6> sql "alter tablespace APP01_DATA online";
   7> release channel c1; }
```

4. Verify that the tablespace has been recovered.
5. Take a backup.

Recovery Of A Data File In An Open Database

When a data file is not accessible due to a disk failure, it typically will need to be restored to a new location or switched to an associated image copy. For the purposes of this section, we will assume a data file needs to be restored to a new location. Perform the following steps to recover a data file in an open database using **RMAN**:

1. After users reported problems accessing information in data file number 3, which resides on disk number 3, you issued the following query to determine the location of the data file:

```
SQL> select file#, name, bytes from v$datafile;
FILE# NAME                            BYTES
----  ------------------------------  --------
    1 /u1/oradata/system01.ora        31457280
    2 /u2/oradata/app01.ora           10485760
    3 /u3/oradata/app02.ora           10485760
...
```

2. Because there is sufficient disk space on disk **u2**, we will restore the data file to disk **u2** using the **SET NEWNAME** command. We'll also use the **SWITCH** command to tell Oracle the restored data file is now **CURRENT**.
3. Use the **RECOVER** command to begin applying incremental backups, cumulative backups, redo log files, and archived redo log files to synchronize the database.
4. Bring the tablespace online when the recovery process is complete.
5. Inform users that the **APP01** data is available for use and to re-enter any uncommitted data before the system failure.

The following is a sample **RUN** command that can be used to recover a data file that has been restored to a new location:

```
RMAN> Run {
   2> Allocate channel c1 type disk;
   3> Sql "alter tablespace APP01_DATA offline immediate";
   4> Set newname for datafile '/u3/oradata/app03.ora'
   5> To '/u2/oradata/app03.ora';
   6> Restore (tablespace APP01_DATA);
   7> Switch datafile 3;
   8> Recover tablespace APP01_DATA;
   9> Sql "alter tablespace APP01_DATA online";
  10> Release channel c1; }
```

In the restoration process, **RMAN** uses the recovery catalog or the target database control file to determine which backups, archived redo log files, or image copies it will use. The **RESTORE** command does not restore incremental backups with a level greater than 0. **RMAN** will apply these incremental backups to a level 0 backup during recovery.

RMAN will only restore from backups that were taken or registered with **RMAN**.

Practice Questions

Question 1

When you encounter a media failure for your database and you've determined all required archived redo log files are available since the most recent backup, to what point in time should you be able to recover the database?

- ❍ a. To the point in time just before the media failure
- ❍ b. To the point in time of the most recent backup
- ❍ c. To the oldest redo log file sequence number
- ❍ d. To the oldest archived redo log sequence number

The correct answer is a. When a media failure occurs for an **ARCHIVELOG** database and all required archived redo log files are available since the last backup, then the database can be recovered up to the point in time before the media failure. Answers b, c, and d are incorrect, because they are earlier than the point in time just before the media failure.

Question 2

Your production database is operating in **ARCHIVELOG** mode and has been configured with two redo log groups. Which of the following commands needs to be run if you discovered that redo log group #1 is corrupt and it is the **CURRENT** group?

- ❍ a. **ALTER SYSTEM ARCHIVE LOG CURRENT GROUP 1**
- ❍ b. **ALTER SYSTEM ACTIVE LOGFILE GROUP 1**
- ❍ c. **ALTER DATABASE CLEAR UNARCHIVED LOGFILE GROUP 1**
- ❍ d. **RECOVER DATAFILE**

The correct answer is c. The **ALTER DATABASE CLEAR UNARCHIVED LOGFILE** command is used to reinitialize (clear and re-create) an online redo log file that was not archived. This command can be used when there are only two redo log groups or the corrupt redo log file belongs to the current redo log group. Answers a and b are incorrect, because they are invalid command specifications. Answer d is incorrect, because the **RECOVER DATAFILE** command is not applicable to redo log files.

Question 3

Which of the following items must be available when a media failure such as a damaged disk with two HR data files occurs with an open **ARCHIVELOG** mode database and complete recovery up to the time of failure is desired? [Choose two answers]

- ❑ a. Valid backup copies of the damaged or lost data files that were taken in **NOARCHIVELOG** mode
- ❑ b. Valid backup copies of the control file
- ❑ c. Valid backup copies of the damaged or lost data files that were taken in **ARCHIVELOG** mode
- ❑ d. All archived redo log files from the time of last valid backup to the present time

The correct answers are c and d. To perform complete recovery for an archiving database, you only need to restore the damaged or lost data files from the last valid backup and apply all the archived redo log files since the last valid backup. Answer a is incorrect, because the data file backups taken in NOARCHIVELOG mode are not usable in an archiving database. Answer b is incorrect, because it is not required for this sample scenario.

Question 4

Which data dictionary view provides information about all the archived redo log files for a database?

- ❍ a. **V$RECOVERY_LOG**
- ❍ b. **V$LOG_HISTORY**
- ❍ c. **V$LOGFILE**
- ❍ d. **V$REDO_LOGS**

The correct answer is b. The V$LOG_HISTORY data dictionary view provides information on all the archived redo log files in the database. Answer a is incorrect, because the V$RECOVERY_LOG data dictionary view provides information about the archived logs that are needed to complete media recovery. V$RECOVERY_LOG is derived from the log history view, V$LOG_HISTORY. Answer c is incorrect, because the V$LOGFILE data dictionary view provides information on the online redo log files. Answer d is incorrect, because it is an invalid data dictionary view.

Question 5

Your database is operating in **ARCHIVELOG** mode and the available archived redo log files are numbered 102 through 121. In the event archived redo log number 112 is damaged, to what point in time can the database be restored?

❍ a. Through archived redo log number 101

❍ b. Through archived redo log number 102

❍ c. Through archived redo log number 121

❍ d. Through archived redo log number 111

❍ e. Through archived redo log number 112

The correct answer is d. If an archived redo log file is damaged or lost, you can recover up through the previous archived log file, in this case redo log number 111. Answer a is incorrect, because it is not one of the given available archived redo log files. Answer b is incorrect, because subsequent archived redo log files are available. Answer c is incorrect, because archived redo log files beginning with number 112 are not usable. Answer e is incorrect, because redo log number 112 is damaged and therefore unusable.

Question 6

Which of the following tablespaces cannot take advantage of online complete recovery?

❍ a **USER_DATA** tablespace

❍ b. **APPLICATION_DATA** tablespace

❍ c. **INDEX_DATA** tablespace

❍ d. **TEMPORARY_DATA** tablespace

❍ e. **SYSTEM** tablespace

The correct answer is e. When restoring data files belonging to the **SYSTEM** tablespace, the restore operation must be performed while the database is offline. Answers a, b, c, and d are incorrect, because data files belonging to **NON-SYSTEM** tablespaces can be restored while the database is **OPEN**, but the **NON-SYSTEM** tablespaces associated with the restored data files should be offline.

Question 7

Which **RMAN** command points the control file and the recovery catalog to the renamed data files when restoring data files after a media failure?

- ❍ a. **ALTER TABLESPACE**
- ❍ b. **RESTORE DATAFILE**
- ❍ c. **RECOVER DATAFILE**
- ❍ d. **SWITCH**
- ❍ e. **SET NEWNAME**

The correct answer is d. The **SWITCH** command is used to point the control file and the recovery catalog to the renamed data files when restoring data files after a media failure. The **SWITCH** command is similar to the **ALTER DATABASE RENAME DATAFILE** command. Answers a, b, and c are incorrect, because they serve other purposes. Answer e is incorrect, because the **SET NEWNAME** command is used to restore data files to a new location but doesn't point the control file and the recovery catalog to the renamed data files.

Question 8

What does the following command sequence accomplish for a database in **ARCHIVELOG** mode?

```
RMAN> run {
   2> allocate channel c1 type disk;
   3> restore database; }
```

- ❍ a. It recovers the entire database.
- ❍ b. It restores the control file from the last full backup.
- ❍ c. It restores all the files from the last full backup.
- ❍ d. It restores only the data files from the last full backup.

The correct answer is d. The **RESTORE DATABASE** command only restores data files. Answer a is incorrect, because the **RESTORE DATABASE** command does not recover the entire database. Answer b is incorrect, because the **RESTORE DATABASE** command does not restore the control file. Answer c is incorrect, because the **RESTORE DATABASE** command does not restore all files.

Question 9

You've issued the following command sequences:

```
SVRMGR> SET AUTORECOVERY ON
SVRMGR> RECOVER DATABASE;
```

Which part of the database is available for normal use while you perform recovery?

- ❍ a. **READ-ONLY** tablespaces
- ❍ b. Any data file not needing recovery
- ❍ c. Any table unaffected by the recovery procedure
- ❍ d. Any tablespace unaffected by the recovery procedure
- ❍ e. None

The correct answer is e. The sample command sequences will recover the whole database and requires a closed database. Answers a, b, c, and d are incorrect, because they are not accessible for normal use during the recovery of an entire database.

Question 10

Which data dictionary view provides information about data files needing recovery?

- ❍ a. **V$RECOVERY_STATUS**
- ❍ b. **V$RECOVER_FILE**
- ❍ c. **V$LOG_HISTORY**
- ❍ d. **V$DATAFILE**

The correct answer is b. The **V$RECOVER_FILE** view contains the names of data files that need to be recovered. Answer a is incorrect, because the **V$RECOVERY_STATUS** view provides status information on the recovery process. Answer c is incorrect, because the **V$LOG_HISTORY** provides information on all the archived redo log files for the database. Answer d is incorrect, because the **V$DATAFILE** view provides information on all the data files in the database, but does not indicate whether they need recovery.

Need To Know More?

Dialeris, Connie. *Oracle8 Backup and Recovery Guide Release 8.0*, Part No. A58396-01, Oracle Corporation, 1997.

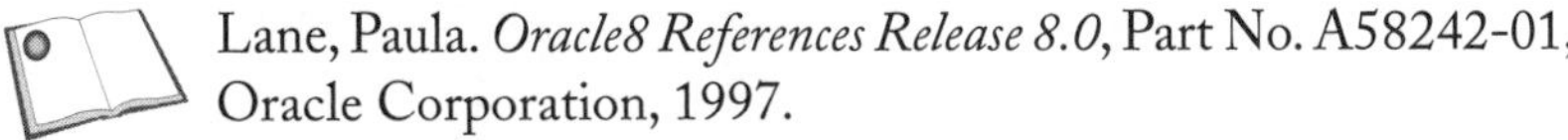
Lane, Paula. *Oracle8 References Release 8.0*, Part No. A58242-01, Oracle Corporation, 1997.

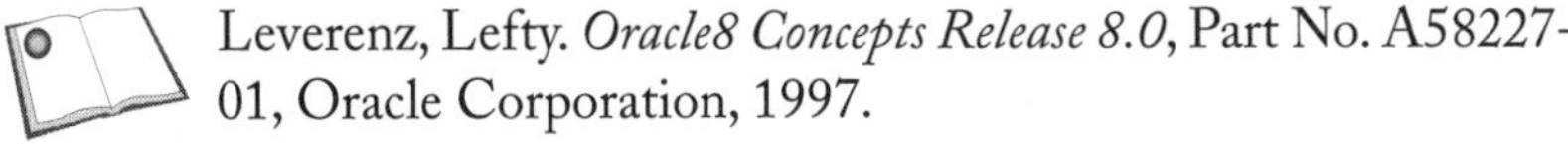
Leverenz, Lefty. *Oracle8 Concepts Release 8.0*, Part No. A58227-01, Oracle Corporation, 1997.

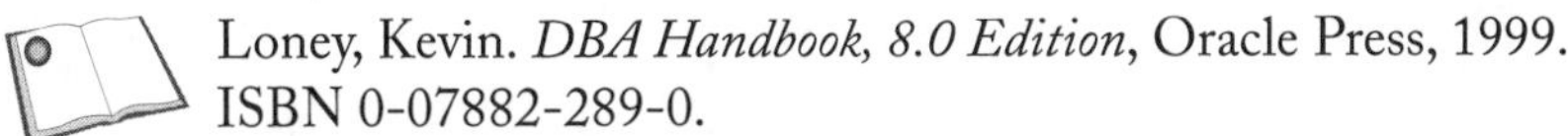
Loney, Kevin. *DBA Handbook, 8.0 Edition*, Oracle Press, 1999. ISBN 0-07882-289-0.

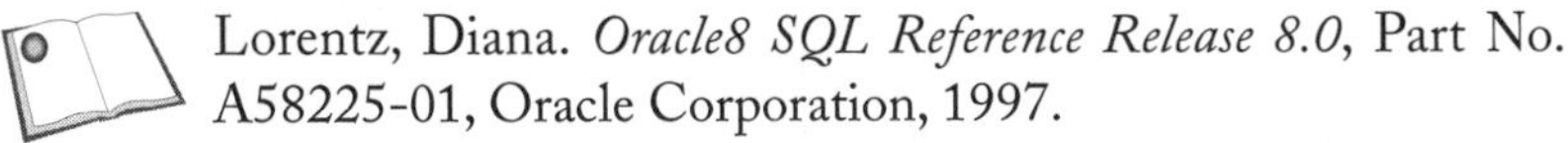
Lorentz, Diana. *Oracle8 SQL Reference Release 8.0*, Part No. A58225-01, Oracle Corporation, 1997.

Velpuri, Rama. *Oracle Backup and Recovery Handbook*, Oracle Press, 1998. ISBN 0-07882-389-7.

12

Incomplete Oracle Recovery With Archiving

Terms you'll need to understand:

- √ Incomplete recovery
- √ **RESETLOGS** option
- √ Cancel-based recovery
- √ Time-based recovery
- √ Change-based recovery
- √ **RECOVER DATABASE** command
- √ Tablespace point-in-time recovery (TSPITR)

Techniques you'll need to master:

- √ Understanding when to use incomplete recovery
- √ Understanding the types of incomplete recovery
- √ Performing incomplete recovery procedures
- √ Understanding recovery implications after losing current and active redo log files
- √ Using Recovery Manager (**RMAN**) in incomplete recovery
- √ Understanding tablespace point-in-time recovery (TSPITR)

When an Oracle database is operating in **ARCHIVELOG** mode and complete recovery cannot be performed or is not desirable after a media failure, incomplete recovery provides DBAs with additional recovery options. In incomplete recovery, the database is restored from a valid backup and recovered through the application of some of the redo information generated since the valid backup. In other words, the database is rebuilt to a point in time before the time of failure. This chapter focuses on incomplete recovery concepts and procedures. Specifically, you will learn when to use incomplete recovery, types of incomplete recovery, incomplete recovery procedures, recovery after current and active redo log loss, using **RMAN** in incomplete recovery, and working with tablespace point-in-time recovery.

When To Use Incomplete Recovery

Incomplete recovery is usually performed under the following circumstances:

- *The control files are lost.* For example, your control file was lost due to a media failure and your database is not multiplexing control files. You don't know the current structure of the database, but you do have a backup copy of an old control file. In this scenario, the database should be restored and recovered to a prior point in time with a different structure than the current database.

- *The online logs are lost due to hardware failure.* For example, your database is not configured for the multiplexing of online redo log files and you lost your redo log files before archiving them along with a data file. In this scenario, the database should be recovered until the last archived log generated before the failure.

- *A user error requires recovery up until just before the error occurred.* For example, a user accidentally deleted accounting transactions before the transactions were sent to the accounting system. In this scenario, the DBA would need to restore the whole database and then perform an incomplete recovery up until the point just before the user deleted the transactions. Other examples include: a user accidentally dropped a table, a user committed data with unwanted values due to a faulty SQL **WHERE** clause construction, and so forth.

- *An archived redo log file required for recovery is missing.* For example, an archive log file needed for complete recovery was lost, damaged, or corrupted (e.g., due to media failure). In this scenario, your option would be to recover up to the missing log.

In all scenarios above, the database must be opened with the **RESETLOGS** option. A RESETLOGS operation invalidates all redo information in the online redo log files, resets the current redo log sequence to 1, and synchronizes the data files with the control files and the online redo log files.

Because incomplete recovery takes a database back to a point in time before the time of failure, data loss may result from committed transactions after the time of recovery. Users may need to manually re-enter data, so a DBA should use incomplete recovery judiciously.

For distributed databases, an incomplete recovery performed at one location requires incomplete recovery to be performed at all the other database locations that are part of the distributed database network.

Performing An Incomplete Recovery

The following items must be in place before you can perform an incomplete recovery:

- A valid offline or online backup of all the database files.
- All the archived redo log files from the valid backup until the designated time of recovery.

There are four types of incomplete recovery:

- Cancel-based recovery
- Time-based recovery
- Change-based recovery
- Recovery using a backup control file

Cancel-Based Recovery

Cancel-based recovery enables the DBA to terminate the recovery process at a desired point in time in the past by entering CANCEL at the recovery prompt. This recovery method is used under the following circumstances:

- A current redo log file or group is damaged and therefore not available for recovery.
- An archived redo log file needed for complete recovery is damaged or lost.

Incomplete Recovery Using **UNTIL CANCEL** Technique

You are the new DBA for a case-tracking database. You discovered that the redo log files are not multiplexed and one of the online redo log files is missing. The missing redo log file (log sequence number 23) has not been archived. The missing redo log file contains approximately 15 minutes of data from 10:00 A.M. A user also informed you that a table was dropped at 10:02 A.M. You've determined that an incomplete recovery should be performed using the **UNTIL CANCEL** technique, as illustrated below:

1. Make sure the database is shut down.
2. Take a full offline database backup.
3. Mount the database.
4. Restore all data files from the most recent valid backup before the backup taken in step 2.
5. Recover the database until log sequence number 23.

```
SVRMGR> RECOVER DATABASE UNTIL CANCEL
...
ORA-00279: change 109101…12/28/99 9:59:01 needed for thread 1
ORA-00289: suggestion : /u2/oradata/archive/arch_23.ora
ORA-00280: change 109101 for thread 1 is in sequence #23
Specify log: {<RET>=suggested | filename | AUTO | CANCEL}
CANCEL
Media recovery cancelled.
```

6. Open the database using the **RESETLOGS** option.
7. Verify that the dropped table exists by querying the database.
8. Take a full offline database backup.
9. Notify users that the database is available and any data entered after 10:00 A.M. will need to be re-entered.

Time-Based Recovery

Time-based recovery enables the DBA to terminate the recovery process at a desired point in time in the past after the database has committed all changes up to the desired point in time. This recovery method is used under the following circumstances:

- An essential table was accidentally dropped.
- Unwanted database changes were made due to faulty SQL constructions.
- A nonmirrored online redo log file was damaged or lost.
- The approximate time of error has been determined.

Incomplete Recovery Using **UNTIL TIME** Technique

You were informed that an essential table was dropped from the QA database two hours ago, at 10:00 A.M. Since the approximate time of failure and the database structure has not changed since 9:59 A.M., an incomplete recovery should be performed using the **UNTIL TIME** technique, as illustrated below:

1. Shut down the database normally if the database is open.

2. Take a full offline database backup.

3. Mount the database.

4. Restore all data files from the most recent valid backup before the backup taken in step 2:

```
UNIX:
SVRMGR> !cp /u2/oradata/backup/*.ora /u1/oradata/

NT:
SVRMGR> !copy d:\orant\database\backup\*.ora d:\orant\database\
```

5. Restore applicable archived redo log files to the location specified by the **LOG_ARCHIVE_DEST** initialization parameter or to a new location by issuing the SQL **ALTER SYSTEM ARCHIVE LOG START TO <location_specification>** or the Server Manager **SET LOGSOURCE <location_specification>** commands.

6. Recover the database using the **RECOVER DATABASE UNTIL TIME '<time specification YYYY-MM-DD:HH24:MI:SS>'** command:

```
SVRMGR> RECOVER DATABASE UNTIL TIME '1999-12-28:10:00:00';
ORA-00279: change 101115 ...12/18/99 15:01:02 needed for thread
ORA-00289: suggestion : /u2/oradata/backup/arch_9.ora
ORA-00280: change 101115 for thread 1 is in sequence #9
Log applied.
...
Media recovery complete.
```

7. Open the database with the **RESETLOGS** option to synchronize data files with control files and the redo log files:

```
SVRMGR> ALTER DATABASE OPEN RESETLOGS;
SVRMGR> ARCHIVE LOG LIST;
...
Oldest online log sequence 0
```

```
Next log sequence to archive 1
Current log sequence 1
```

8. Verify that the dropped table has been restored:

```
SVRMGR> select owner, table_name
     2> from dba_tables
     3> where table_name = 'DROPPED_TABLE_NAME';
OWNER           TABLE_NAME
--------------  --------------
QA              ORGANIZATIONS
```

If the above query returns no rows, then the dropped table has not been restored and you will need to perform incomplete recovery to a different point in time.

9. Take a full offline database backup.
10. Notify users that the database is available and to re-enter data after the recovery point.

Change-Based Recovery

Change-based recovery enables the DBA to terminate the recovery process at a desired point in time in the past after the database has committed all changes up to the specified System Change Number (SCN). This recovery method is used when recovering databases in a distributed database environment.

Query the **V$LOG_HISTORY** view to obtain SCN ranges in the archived redo log files.

Recovery Using A Backup Control File

When performing an incomplete recovery using a backup control file, the DBA can terminate the recovery process when the desired type of recovery (**CANCEL**, **CHANGE**, or **TIME**) has completed or the control files have been recovered. The **RECOVER DATABASE** command should indicate that an old copy of the control file is being used for recovery. This recovery method is used under the following circumstances:

- All control files are lost and can't be re-created. An old copy of the control file is available.
- The database needs to be returned to a prior point in time when the database structure was different.

Incomplete Recovery Using The Backup Control File Technique

You are the new DBA and you accidentally issued the **DROP TABLESPACE APP01_DATA INCLUDING CONTENTS** command that dropped the **PERSONS** table. You've located a backup copy of the control file from yesterday. Using the *alertSID.log* file, you've determined that you made the error at 11:00 A.M. You've also determined that an incomplete recovery should be performed using the backup control file technique, as illustrated below:

1. Shut down the database.
2. Back up control files.
3. Restore all data files and control files for the database at a point in time before the tablespace was dropped.
4. Attempt to open the database and an error indicating that the redo log files and the control files are not synchronized is returned, as illustrated below:

   ```
   ORA-00314: log 1 of thread 1, expected sequence# doesn't match
   ORA-00312: online log 1 thread 1: '/u1/oradata/log1a.ora'
   ```

5. Make sure all offline data files are online, because offline data files may be unrecoverable after recovery.
6. Recover the database using the **RECOVER DATABASE USING BACKUP CONTROLFILE** command, as illustrated by the following code sample:

   ```
   SVRMGR> recover database until '1999-12-29:10:59:00'
        2> using backup controlfile;
   ```

7. Open the database with the **RESETLOGS** option.
8. Verify that the dropped table exists.
9. Take a full offline database backup.
10. Notify users that the database is available and that any data entered after 11:00 A.M. will need to be re-entered.

RECOVER DATABASE Command

Incomplete recovery is typically performed using the following **RECOVER DATABASE** command syntax:

```
RECOVER [AUTOMATIC] DATABASE <option>
```

Table 12.1 describes command elements for the **RECOVER DATABASE** command.

Optionally, you may choose to use the SQL **ALTER DATABASE RECOVER** command syntax.

Instead of using the SQL **RECOVER AUTOMATIC** command, you can use the **SET AUTORECOVERY ON** Server Manager command and enter "AUTO" at the recovery prompt to direct Oracle to automatically apply redo log files during the recovery process.

The following code samples illustrate the **RECOVER DATABASE** command.

- Cancel-based recovery:

```
SVRMGR> RECOVER DATABASE UNTIL CANCEL;
```

- Time-based recovery:

```
SVRMGR> RECOVER DATABASE UNTIL TIME '2000-01-02:10:11:01';
```

- Change-based recovery:

```
SVRMGR> RECOVER DATABASE UNTIL SCN 118110;
```

- Recovery using a backup control file:

```
SVRMGR> RECOVER DATABASE
     2> UNTIL TIME '2000-01-02:10:11:01'
     3> USING BACKUP CONTROLFILE;
```

Table 12.1 Elements and values of RECOVER DATABASE Command.

Element	Value
AUTOMATIC	The **AUTOMATIC** keyword signals Oracle to automatically apply archived and online redo log files.
Option	**UNTIL TIME 'YYYY-MM-DD:HH:MI:SS'; UNTIL CANCEL; UNTIL SCN <integer>**; or **USING BACKUP CONTROL FILE**.

Incomplete Recovery Procedure

Follow these steps to perform an incomplete recovery for an archiving enabled database:

1. Take a full offline backup of the current database.
2. Make sure the database is shut down, because all data files including the system data files will be restored from a prior backup.
3. Restore all the data files to return the database to a past point in time. Don't restore the control file, parameter files, password file, or redo log files.
4. Mount the database.
5. Recover the database to a point in time before the failure.
6. Open the database with the **RESETLOGS** option.
7. Shut down the database cleanly and take a full offline backup of the database.
8. Open the database for normal use.

Things To Consider When Performing Incomplete Recovery

You should remember to do the following when performing incomplete recovery:

- Make sure you perform all recovery steps in the proper sequence. Because the recovery process requires DBAs to manually perform multiple steps, it is prone to operator errors.
- You should take a full offline database backup (including control files and redo log files) before starting the recovery process. The benefits of this activity are as follows:
  - It provides protection in the event of a recovery error or failure. For example, your recovery failed because you mistakenly recovered past the required point of recovery. Unless you have a backup of the control files and the redo log files, the current control files and the redo log files are not usable for future recovery operations.
  - It provides time-savings in the event of a recovery failure. For example, the data files can be restored from the new backup rather than from an older backup, which requires application of archived redo log files.

If taking a full offline database backup is not possible, then it is highly recommended that you archive the current redo log file using the **ALTER SYSTEM ARCHIVE LOG CURRENT** command and back up the control file using the **ALTER DATABASE BACKUP CONTROLFILE TO <location_specification>**.

- You should take a full offline database backup after you've confirmed a successful recovery. This backup can be used if recovery needs to be performed before the next routine backup.
- Make sure the recovery has resolved the failure before opening the database for normal use. If the recovery did not resolve the failure, it needs to be performed again. For example, a user informed you that he dropped a table at 10:10 A.M. You recovered the database to 10:09 A.M. before the table was dropped. You queried the database and the dropped table does not exist. You later learned that the user's clock is ten minutes fast and you should have recovered to 9:59 A.M.
- Take a control file backup whenever the database structure changes. A backup control file will be needed if the current database structure is different from the structure at the desired recovery point.
- Make sure you open the database with the **RESETLOGS** option after each incomplete recovery operation. The **RESETLOGS** option ensures database files are in sync and will automatically re-create missing redo log files when needed.
- Back up archive redo log files from the previous version of the database and remove them from the system to prevent accidental mixing of archive redo log files from two different database versions.
- Be aware that database transactions can only be rolled forward to the desired point in time. Database transactions cannot be rolled back to the desired point in time. This is why all data files must be restored to return the database to a prior point in time. If all data files are not restored, then the database cannot be opened because the database is in an unsynchronized state.
- During recovery, Oracle writes recovery progress information in the *alert_SID.log* file. You should check this file before and after recovery for SCN information, recovery errors, and so forth. The following code sample illustrates recovery progress information recorded in the *alertSID.log* file:

```
...
Media Recovery Log
ORA-279 ... RECOVER   database until time '1999...
Mon Dec 27 10:01:11 1999
ALTER DATABASE RECOVER   CONTINUE DEFAULT
Media Recovery Log /u1/oradata/archive/arch_19.ora
Incomplete recovery done UNTIL CHANGE 100213
Media Recovery Complete
Completed: ALTER DATABASE RECOVER   CONTINUE DEFAULT
Mon Dec 27 10:01:11 1999
Alter database open resetlogs
...
```

Recovery After Current And Active Redo Log Loss

When a current and active redo log file is damaged or lost, the database may be open but in a "hung" state, or the database may be closed because of a media failure or the abnormal termination of a background process. The technique you use for recovery depends on whether the database is open or closed.

If the database is open, follow these steps:

1. Query the **V$LOG** view to determine the redo log file with a status of **CURRENT**.
2. Issue the **ALTER DATABASE CLEAR UNARCHIVED LOGFILE GROUP <number>** command to clear the current log file. This action will cause the log file to be overwritten or re-created, depending on whether it was corrupted or lost.
3. Take a full offline database backup to prevent having to perform incomplete recovery due to media failure before taking the backup, because redo information has just been cleared.

If the database is closed, follow these steps:

1. Start up your instance and mount the database.
2. Obtain the sequence number for the current redo log, as illustrated by the code sample below. You will recover your database up to this redo log.

```
SVRMGR> select sequence# seq_num from v$log
     2> where status = 'CURRENT';
seq_num
-------
     19
```

3. Restore all your data files (but not control files, redo log files, password files, or initSID.ora files) from the most recent backup.
4. Perform incomplete recovery using the cancel-based technique. You will cancel the recovery when Oracle prompts you with the suggested redo log number 19.
5. Open the database using the **ALTER DATABASE OPEN RESETLOGS** command.
6. If you lost a disk containing redo logs, and you do not have the minimum number of logs necessary for Oracle to use, you must create new redo log groups and drop the lost redo log group. You will need to issue a combination of **ALTER DATABASE ADD LOGFILE GROUP** and **ALTER DATABASE DROP LOGFILE GROUP** commands.
7. Take a full offline database backup.
8. Open the database for normal use.

RMAN Usage In An Incomplete Recovery

In RMAN, incomplete recovery is handled the same way as complete recovery. However, you will restore all data files from your most recent backup, not just the damaged ones.

When **RMAN** performs a restore, the files being restored must either be registered with **RMAN** or must have been taken by **RMAN**.

The incomplete recovery procedure using RMAN is as follows:

1. Shut down the target database cleanly.
2. Start up, mount, but do not open the target database. The recovery catalog should also be open.
3. Set the **NLS_LANG** and the **NLS_DATE_FORMAT** environment variable to the appropriate values for your environment. For example, **NLS_LANG=american** and **NLS_DATE_FORMAT='YYYY-MM-DD:HH24:MI:SS'**.
4. Start **RMAN** by connecting to both the target database and the recovery catalog:

```
$ rman target username/passwd@target_db rcvcat username/
passwd@catalog_db
```

5. Create a run script that allocates appropriate channels, specifies the incomplete recovery type using the **SET UNTIL** command, performs the restore and recovery operations, and releases applicable channels.
6. Open the database using the **RESETLOGS** option:

```
...
RMAN> sql "alter database open resetlogs";
...
```

7. Verify the incomplete recovery was successful and take a backup.
8. Notify users that the database is available and to re-enter any uncommitted data before the system failure.
9. If a recovery catalog is being used, register a new incarnation of the database using the **RESET DATABASE** command:

```
RMAN> reset database;
```

The following code sample illustrates a typical **RUN** command used for incomplete recovery:

```
D:\ORANT\BIN> rman80 target user/pass@proddb rcvcat user/pass@catdb
RMAN> run {
   2> allocate channel c1 type disk;
   3> set until time = '2000-01-02:10:05:00';
   4> restore database;
   5> recover database;
   6> sql 'alter database open resetlogs';
   7> release channel c1; }
```

Alternatively, you can restore data files and perform incomplete recovery for an ARCHIVELOG mode database using the OEM Backup Manager.

Working With Tablespace Point-In-Time Recovery (TSPITR)

TSPITR is a type of incomplete recovery that is appropriate when a user error has been discovered and the database cannot be returned to a prior point in time. For example, a defect in an application messed up data in an essential table. The messed up table must be recovered and the database cannot be taken back in time, because other applications are performing other database tasks. You shouldn't have to use TSPITR if you've followed proper backup and recovery procedures. In the unlikely event you need to use TSPITR and because of the complexity associated with TSPITR, you should only perform this task with the assistance of Oracle Worldwide Customer Support Services.

You'll need the following when performing TSPITR:

- All data files associated with the tablespace that needs recovery.
- All data files for the system tablespace.
- All archived redo log files up to the desired recovery point.
- A backup copy of your current control file.
- Sufficient disk space and memory on your machine or another machine to create and run the clone database.

Perform the following steps for TSPITR:

1. Determine if objects will be lost due to TSPITR. Use the **TS_PITR_OBJECTS_TO_BE_DROPPED** view for this purpose.
2. Analyze and resolve any dependencies for the production database. Use the **TS_PITR_CHECK** view for this purpose.
3. Prepare the production database for TSPITR by archiving the current redo log, taking the rollback segments in the recovery set offline, and taking the tablespaces in the recovery set offline. This activity will prevent any modifications to the recovery set during TSPITR.
4. Prepare the parameter files for the clone database. The following parameters should be appropriately specified: **CONTROL_FILES**, **LOCK_NAME_SPACE**, **DB_FILE_NAME_CONVERT**, and **LOG_FILE_NAME_CONVERT**.
5. Prepare the clone database for TSPITR. Copy the applicable recovery files to the clone database, then start and mount the clone database using **ALTER DATABASE MOUNT CLONE DATABASE**.
6. Recover the clone database to the desired point in time via the **USING BACKUP CONTROLFILE** option of the **RECOVER DATABASE** command. Optionally, you can use incomplete recovery techniques such as time-based or cancel-based recovery.
7. Open the clone database using the **ALTER DATABASE OPEN RESETLOGS** command.

8. Export the clone database. You will export the metadata associated with the recovery set tablespaces, as illustrated by the following sample code:

```
$ Exp sys/passwd point_in_time_recovery=y
Recovery_tablespaces=ts1, ts2, ...,tsN
```

9. Copy the cloned files associated with the recovery set to the production database.

10. Import the metadata from the export dump file into the production database. This process will update the file headers and integrate them with the production database:

```
$ imp sys/passwd point_in_time_recover=true
```

11. Back up the recovered tablespace in the production database.

12. Open the production database for normal use.

Refer to Chapter 13 for detailed information on using the **EXPORT** and **IMPORT** utilities.

Practice Questions

Question 1

When an archived redo log file is corrupt and not available for a complete recovery, what type of incomplete recovery should the DBA perform?

❍ a. Recovery using a backup control file

❍ b. Time-based recovery

❍ c. Change-based recovery

❍ d. Cancel-based recovery

The correct answer is d. Cancel-based recovery is appropriate when an archived redo log file that is needed for a complete recovery is damaged or lost. Answer a is incorrect, because it is used when all control files are lost or when you are attempting to restore a database to a prior point in time when the database structure was different. Answer b is incorrect, because the approximate time of error is not known. Answer c is incorrect, because change-based recovery is used for recovering databases in a distributed database environment.

Question 2

Under which of the following circumstances would you open the database with the **RESETLOGS** option?

❍ a. After performing complete recovery of a lost data file using the current control file

❍ b. After restoring and recovering all the database files during complete recovery

❍ c. After restoring and recovering all data files during incomplete recovery

❍ d. After restoring and recovering damaged data files during incomplete recovery

❍ e. After restoring and recovering all database files during incomplete recovery

The correct answer is c. The incomplete recovery procedure requires restoring all data files, mounting the database, recovering the data files before the time failure, and opening the database with the **RESETLOGS** option. Answers a and b are incorrect, because complete recovery operations don't require opening the database with the **RESETLOGS** option. Answers d and e are incorrect, because the incomplete recovery procedure requires that all data files be restored (excluding control file, redo log files, or other configuration files).

Question 3

Which of the following situations requires the DBA to perform an incomplete recovery? [Choose three answers]

- ❑ a. Loss of all control files including corresponding mirrors
- ❑ b. An archived redo log file needed for complete recovery is damaged
- ❑ c. A user mistakenly drops an essential application table
- ❑ d. The archived redo log directory runs out of space
- ❑ e. A media failure occurs in an **ARCHIVELOG** mode database and no data loss is tolerated

The correct answers are a, b, and c. The typical failures that require an incomplete recovery include: user errors that dropped an essential table or committed unwanted data updates, an archived redo log file required for recovery is damaged or missing, all the control files with corresponding mirrors are lost, and an online redo log file is damaged or lost. Answer d is incorrect, because it only requires the DBA to free up space in the archived redo log directory. Answer e is incorrect, because a complete recovery is needed.

Question 4

The QA administrator accidentally dropped an important table in an **ARCHIVELOG** mode database. You need to restore the database to a point in time before the user error was made. What type of recovery should you perform in this situation?

- ❍ a. Complete database recovery
- ❍ b. Tablespace recovery
- ❍ c. Data file recovery
- ❍ d. Incomplete recovery

The correct answer is d. Incomplete recovery is typically performed for databases in **ARCHIVELOG** mode that need to be recovered before the time of failure. Answers a, b, and c are incorrect, because they pertain only to complete recovery situations.

Question 5

When using **RMAN** to perform an incomplete recovery and you want to recover the database to 10:00 A.M. on February 21, 2000, what command should you issue?

- ❍ a. **SET UNTIL TIME = '2000-02-21:10:00:00'**
- ❍ b. **RESTORE DATABASE UNTIL TIME '2000-02-21:10:00:00'**
- ❍ c. **RESTORE DATABASE UNTIL CANCEL**
- ❍ d. **SET RECOVERY UNTIL TIME = '2000-02-21:10:00:00'**

The correct answer is a. When incomplete recovery is managed by **RMAN**, you can set the time to which you want to recover using the **SET UNTIL TIME** command before issuing the **RESTORE DATABASE** command. Answers b, c, and d are incorrect, because they are invalid command specifications.

Question 6

What recovery options enable you to recover to a prior point in time? [Choose three answers]

- ❑ a. Tablespace
- ❑ b. Cancel-based
- ❑ c. Data file
- ❑ d. Complete
- ❑ e. Time-based
- ❑ f. Change-based

The correct answers are b, e, and f. The incomplete recovery types include: cancel-based recovery, time-based recovery, change-based recovery, and recovery using a backup control file. Answers a, c, and d are incorrect, because they apply only to complete recovery.

Question 7

What data files must be restored when performing a cancel-based recovery?

❍ a. Data files for the tablespace

❍ b. Damaged data files

❍ c. Undamaged data files

❍ d. All data files for the database

The correct answer is d. In any type of incomplete recovery for an archiving database, you must restore all the data files from a valid backup. Answers a, b, and c are incorrect, because they are only a subset of the data files required for an incomplete recovery.

Question 8

When performing incomplete recovery, what should you do immediately after shutting down the database?

❍ a. Restore archived redo log files

❍ b. Restore data files

❍ c. Take a full offline database backup

❍ d. Open the database in **MOUNT** mode

The correct answer is c. Oracle recommends that you take a full offline backup of the database after you shut down to protect you in the event of recovery failure. Answers a, b, and c are incorrect, because they are performed after taking a full offline database backup.

Question 9

The database is in a "hung" state and you suspect that a redo log file has been mistakenly dropped. Which view would you use to obtain information about the **CURRENT** redo log group?

❍ a. **V$RECOVER_FILE**

❍ b. **V$LOG**

❍ c. **V$LOGFILE**

❍ d. **V$LOG_HISTORY**

The correct answer is b. The **V$LOG** view provides information on the current redo log group such as the redo log group sequence number. You can use the redo log group sequence number when issuing the **ALTER DATABASE CLEAR UNARCHIVED LOGFILE GROUP** command to reinitialize the damaged or lost file. Answer a is incorrect, because the **V$RECOVER_FILE** view provides information on the status of files needing media recovery. Answers c and d are incorrect, because these views don't indicate whether a redo log group is **CURRENT**.

Question 10

What will the following **RMAN** command accomplish when performing an incomplete recovery?

```
RMAN> RESET DATABASE;
```

- ❍ a. It will synchronize the target database files.
- ❍ b. It will change the database mode of the target database.
- ❍ c. It will reinitialize the redo log files in the target database.
- ❍ d. It will synchronize the recovery catalog database.
- ❍ e. It will register the recovered database in the recovery catalog.

The correct answer is e. The **RMAN RESET DATABASE** command will update the recovery catalog with a new incarnation of the database that has been recovered. Answers a, b, c, and d are incorrect, because the **RMAN RESET DATABASE** command doesn't perform these actions.

Need To Know More?

Dialeris, Connie. *Oracle8 Backup and Recovery Guide Release 8.0*, Part No. A58396-01, Oracle Corporation, 1997.

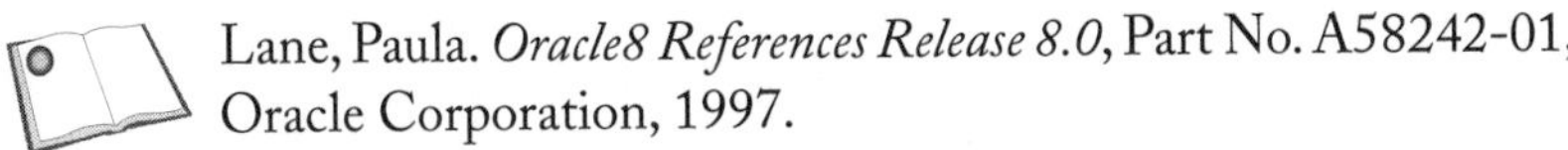

Lane, Paula. *Oracle8 References Release 8.0*, Part No. A58242-01, Oracle Corporation, 1997.

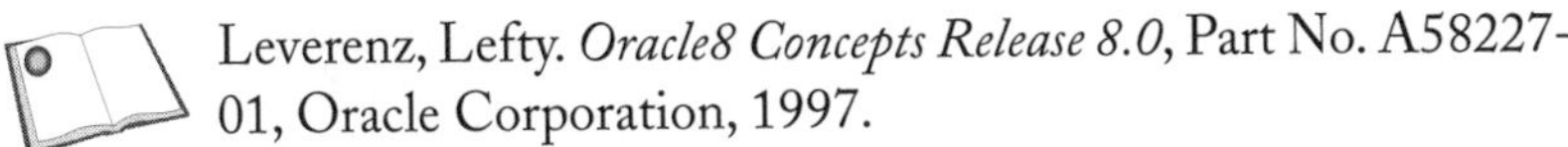

Leverenz, Lefty. *Oracle8 Concepts Release 8.0*, Part No. A58227-01, Oracle Corporation, 1997.

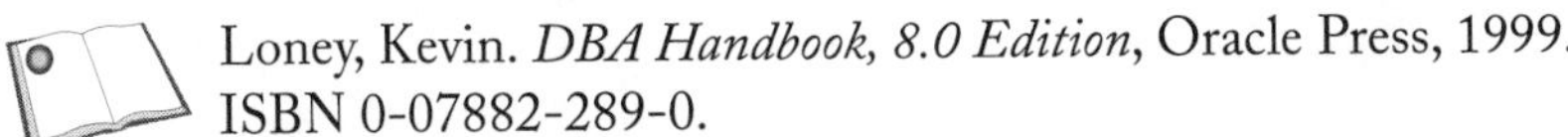

Loney, Kevin. *DBA Handbook, 8.0 Edition*, Oracle Press, 1999. ISBN 0-07882-289-0.

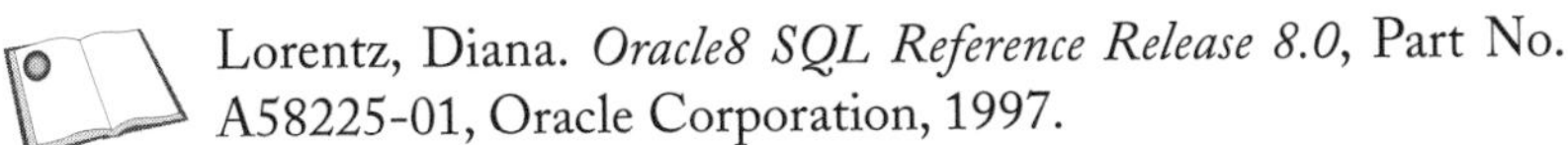

Lorentz, Diana. *Oracle8 SQL Reference Release 8.0*, Part No. A58225-01, Oracle Corporation, 1997.

Velpuri, Rama. *Oracle Backup and Recovery Handbook*, Oracle Press, 1998. ISBN 0-07882-389-7.

Oracle **EXPORT** And **IMPORT** Utilities

Terms you'll need to understand:

- √ Logical backup
- √ **EXPORT** utility
- √ Table mode **EXPORT**
- √ User mode **EXPORT**
- √ Full database mode **EXPORT**
- √ Complete **EXPORT**
- √ Cumulative **EXPORT**
- √ Incremental **EXPORT**
- √ Direct path **EXPORT**
- √ **IMPORT** utility
- √ Table mode **IMPORT**
- √ User mode **IMPORT**
- √ Full database mode **IMPORT**

Techniques you'll need to master:

- √ Using the **EXPORT** utility for logical backups
- √ Understanding the methods to invoke the **EXPORT** utility
- √ Understanding **EXPORT** modes
- √ Understanding **EXPORT** run-time parameters
- √ Using direct path **EXPORT**
- √ Understanding **EXPORT** issues when **EXPORT**ing database objects
- √ Understanding **EXPORT** compatibility restrictions
- √ Understanding the methods to invoke the **IMPORT** utility
- √ Understanding **IMPORT** modes
- √ Understanding **IMPORT** run-time parameters
- √ Using **IMPORT** to recover database objects

EXPORT And IMPORT Utility Overview

The Oracle EXPORT utility enables database administrators (DBAs) to perform logical backups of the database. A logical backup involves making a copy of the logical database structures with or without the associated business data. A logical backup does not involve the physical database files. The Oracle IMPORT utility enables DBAs to read a valid file generated by the EXPORT utility for moving data into an Oracle database and for the recovery of database objects and business data.

Database objects **IMPORT**ed from an **EXPORT** file will not be able to utilize the redo log history.

Oracle DBAs typically use the EXPORT and IMPORT utilities to perform the following tasks:

- Save database object definitions in an alternative Oracle binary format. This may be useful in helping the DBA to maintain a baseline database structure for a particular schema.
- Move data from one Oracle version to another during database upgrades.
- Create a historical copy of an entire database or selective database objects.
- Recover from user failure errors such as accidental drop or truncate of a database table.
- Create the structural definitions for database objects such as tables based on information stored in the EXPORT dump file. This is achieved by configuring the IMPORT process to IMPORT data without rows.
- Create data extractions from a valid EXPORT dump file using the IMPORT modes of table, user or full database.
- IMPORT data from a complete, incremental, or cumulative EXPORT dump file.

Using The EXPORT Utility

Three methods invoke the EXPORT utility:

- An interactive dialog is available when the EXPORT executable name is specified at the operating system prompt with no parameters. The

EXPORT utility prompts the user for input values while providing default values.

- The **EXPORT** page of the Data Manager within the Oracle Enterprise Manager (OEM) administrative toolset invokes the **EXPORT** utility.
- A command line interface is available when the user wishes to explicitly specify **EXPORT** options on the command line. Any missing **EXPORT** options will assume default values. Optionally, the user may use a parameter file to explicitly specify **EXPORT** options. The following code shows an example of using the command line interface of the **EXPORT** utility:

```
Unix:
$ exp scott/tiger tables=(dept,emp) rows=y file=scott.dmp

NT:
D:\ORANT\BIN> exp80 scott/tiger tables=(dept,emp) rows=y
file=scott.dmp
```

Be aware that some **EXPORT** options are available only through the command line interface.

EXPORT Modes

The **EXPORT** modes determine which portion of the database can be **EXPORT**ed. The **EXPORT** utility can be run in three modes:

- Full database mode
- User mode
- Table mode

Full Database Mode

In the full database mode, all database objects except those owned by the **SYS** schema are **EXPORT**ed and written to the **EXPORT** dump file. This file includes the business data and the Data Definition Language (DDL) statements needed to recreate the full database. This mode is available only to privileged database users such as the DBA with the **EXP_FULL_DATABASE** role.

User Mode

In the user mode, all objects owned by a given schema are EXPORTed and written to the EXPORT dump file. Grants and indexes created by users other than the owner are not EXPORTed. Privileged database users including the DBA can EXPORT all objects owned by one or more schemas.

Table Mode

In the table mode, specified tables owned by the user schema are EXPORTed and written to the EXPORT dump file. This mode also enables the user to specify partitions of a table to EXPORT. Privileged database users including the DBA can EXPORT specified tables owned by other database users.

Know how to operate the **EXPORT** utility using the run-time parameters via the command line interface.

EXPORT Run-Time Parameters

The following sections describe typical run-time parameters that can be specified for the EXPORT utility and how to use them to write data from an Oracle database into an operating system file in a proprietary Oracle binary format.

USERID

This parameter specifies the username/password of the user running the EXPORT utility. The USERID keyword does not have to be specified if it is the first parameter following the EXPORT executable name.

BUFFER

This parameter specifies the size of the buffer used to fetch data rows. This parameter applies to the conventional path EXPORT and has no effect on a direct path EXPORT. The default is system dependent.

FILE

This parameter specifies the name of the EXPORT dump file. The default value is EXPDAT.DMP.

COMPRESS

This parameter is a Y/N flag that specifies whether EXPORT should compress fragmented segments into single extents. This parameter affects the storage clauses that will be written in the EXPORT file for the applicable database objects. For the Large Object (LOB) data, extent compression is not performed and the original values of initial extent size and the next extent size will be used. The default value is Y.

ROWS

This parameter is a Y/N flag that specifies whether data rows should be EXPORTed. If set to N, then only the DDL for the applicable database objects will be written in the EXPORT file. The default is Y.

FULL

This parameter is a Y/N flag that specifies whether a full database EXPORT will be performed. The default value is N.

OWNER

This parameter specifies a list of database users whose objects will be EXPORTed in user mode. It has no default value.

TABLES

This parameter specifies a list of tables to EXPORT in table mode. It has no default value.

INDEXES

This parameter is a Y/N flag that specifies whether indexes on tables will be EXPORTed. The default value is Y.

DIRECT

This parameter is a Y/N flag that specifies whether a Direct Path EXPORT should be performed. A Direct Path EXPORT bypasses the buffer cache and the SQL command processing layer during the EXPORT and achieves significant performance gains for the EXPORT process. The default value is N.

INCTYPE

This parameter specifies whether the EXPORT is a complete, cumulative, or incremental EXPORT. There is no default value for this parameter. If the parameter is left unspecified, then the EXPORT cannot be used as part of an incremental backup scheme.

PARFILE

This parameter specifies the name of a parameter file to be read by the EXPORT utility. This file may contain entries for all of the EXPORT parameters described in this section. It has no default value.

HELP

This parameter is a Y/N flag that specifies whether the EXPORT utility displays the EXPORT parameters on the screen with a brief explanation. The default value is N.

LOG

This parameter specifies the file name to which to record the screen output and error messages. By default, no log file is created.

CONSISTENT

This parameter is a Y/N flag that specifies whether a read-consistent version of all the EXPORTed database objects are required. This parameter needs to be set to Y when tables that are related to each other are being modified during the EXPORT process.

STATISTICS

This parameter specifies whether ANALYZE commands for the EXPORTed objects should be written to the EXPORT dump file. It can be set to ESTIMATE, COMPUTE, or NONE. The default value is ESTIMATE.

POINT_IN_TIME_RECOVER

This parameter is a Y/N flag that is used to signal Oracle if you are EXPORTing metadata for use in a tablespace point-in-time recovery.

RECOVERY_TABLESPACES

This parameter specifies the tablespaces whose metadata should be EXPORTed during a tablespace point-in-time recovery.

EXPORT Examples

The following are some examples of using the EXPORT utility:

➤ To execute a table mode EXPORT:

```
$ exp dba9/password9 tables=(test1,test2) file=test.dmp
```

➤ To execute a user mode EXPORT:

```
$ exp dba9/password9 owner=tester file=tester.dmp
```

➤ To execute a user mode EXPORT for a remote database:

```
$ exp dba9/password9@remote_db owner=tester file=tester.dmp
```

- To **EXPORT** only the data definitions without the business data:

```
$ exp dba9/password9 owner=dvlp rows=n file=dvlp0.dmp
```

- To **EXPORT** a user's objects, but not the grants to those objects and excluding indexes:

```
$ exp dba9/password9 owner=prod grants=n indexes=n
file=prodx.dmp
```

- To **EXPORT** only a specific partition of the **PARTTAB** table:

```
$ exp dba9/password9 owner=user1 tables=parttab:a file=parta.dmp
```

Things To Remember About EXPORTs

You should consider the following issues when **EXPORT**ing database objects:

- When sequences are cached, gaps in sequence numbers may occur, because the **EXPORT**ed sequence value is the next sequence number after the largest cached value. Sequence numbers that are cached but unused are lost when the sequence is subsequently **IMPORT**ed.
- When **EXPORT**ing **LONG** data types, there must be sufficient memory available to hold the contents of a row containing the **LONG** column. **LONG** columns can support lengths of up to 2GB. Available system resources may restrict this function.

EXPORTing LOB data does not require as much memory as **EXPORT**ing the **LONG** data, because the LOB data is loaded and unloaded in sections and all sections don't need to be held in memory at the same time.

- When **EXPORT**ing foreign function libraries, only the library specification—name and location—is included in the full database mode and user mode **EXPORT** dump file.
- Directory alias definitions are written to the **EXPORT** dump file in full database mode.
- When **EXPORT**ing **BFILE**s, only the names and the directory aliases are written to the **EXPORT** dump file and subsequently restored by the **IMPORT** utility.

- When **EXPORT**ing array data, sufficient memory must be available to hold the maximum dimensions of the array even though the average dimensions in use may be much smaller.
- In all **EXPORT** modes, the **EXPORT** utility will write object type definitions for a table before writing the table definition. However, the object type definitions may not be complete. For example, if the object type for a column is owned by another user, the full definitions of object types from the other schema are not written to the **EXPORT** dump file.
- When **EXPORT**ing nested tables, the inner nested table is **EXPORT**ed whenever the outer table is **EXPORT**ed. The inner nested tables cannot be **EXPORT**ed by themselves.

Oracle recommends performing full database mode **EXPORT**s on a regular basis to preserve all object type definitions.

The **EXPORT** utility has some compatibility restrictions that you should be aware of:

- You can't run the Oracle6 **EXPORT** against an Oracle8 database.
- You can use Oracle7's **EXPORT** against an Oracle8 database with the exception that the **EXPORT** dump file is in the Oracle7 format and it won't contain any Oracle8-specific database objects. When a lower-version **EXPORT** utility is used against a higher version of the Oracle server, higher version-specific database objects will be excluded from the **EXPORT** dump file.
- The **IMPORT** utility prior to Oracle 7.3 cannot read a Direct Path **EXPORT** dump file.
- Oracle will return an error when you try to use a higher version of **EXPORT** with a lower-version Oracle server.

DBAs typically use the **EXPORT** version that matches the version of the Oracle server.

Using The IMPORT Utility

The **IMPORT** utility is typically used for the recovery of database objects and business data using a valid dump file created by the **EXPORT** utility. Three methods invoke the **IMPORT** utility:

- An interactive dialog is available when the **IMPORT** executable name is specified at the operating system prompt with no parameters. The **IMPORT** utility prompts the user for input values while providing default values.
- The **IMPORT** page of the Data Manager within the Oracle Enterprise Manager (OEM) administrative toolset invokes the **IMPORT** utility.
- A command line interface is available when the user wishes to explicitly specify **IMPORT** options on the command line. Any missing **IMPORT** options will assume default values. Optionally, the user may use a parameter file to explicitly specify **IMPORT** options. The following code shows an example of using the command line interface of the **IMPORT** utility under Windows NT:

```
D:\ORANT\BIN> imp80 scott/tiger tables=(dept,emp) rows=y
file=scott.dmp
```

Be aware that some **IMPORT** options are available only through the command line interface.

IMPORT Modes

The **IMPORT** modes determine which portion of a valid **EXPORT** dump file can be **IMPORT**ed. The **IMPORT** utility can be run in three modes:

- Table mode
- User mode
- Full database mode

Table Mode

In the table mode, all specified tables in the operating user's schema are **IMPORT**ed. A privileged database user such as the DBA can **IMPORT** specific tables owned by other database users.

User Mode

In the user mode, all database objects in the operating user's schema are IMPORTed. A privileged database user such as the DBA can **IMPORT** all database objects owned by one or more schema users.

Full Database Mode

In the full database mode, all database objects except those owned by the **SYS** schema are **IMPORT**ed. Only privileged database users such as the DBA can operate the **IMPORT** utility in this mode.

Know how to operate the **IMPORT** utility using the run-time parameters via the command line interface.

IMPORT Run-Time Parameters

The following sections describe typical run-time parameters that can be specified for the IMPORT utility and how to use them to read information from a valid EXPORT dump file into an Oracle database.

USERID

This parameter specifies the username and password for the user running the IMPORT utility. The format for the command is **username/password**. Optionally, you may use Net8's **@connect_string** format. This parameter has no default value.

FILE

This parameter specifies the name of the **EXPORT** dump file to be IMPORTed. The default value is **expdat.dmp**.

ROWS

This parameter is a Y/N flag that specifies whether rows should be **IMPORT**ed. If set to N, then only the DDL for the database objects will be run. The default value is Y.

IGNORE

This parameter is a Y/N flag that specifies whether the **IMPORT** utility should ignore errors encountered when issuing the DDL **CREATE** commands. This is applicable to **IMPORT**ing database objects that already exist in the target database. The default value is N.

FULL

This parameter is a Y/N flag that specifies whether the full EXPORT dump file is IMPORTed. The default value is N.

TABLES

This parameter specifies a list of database tables to be IMPORTed. It has no default value.

INDEXES

This parameter is a Y/N flag that specifies whether indexes on the database tables will be IMPORTed. The default value is Y.

INCTYPE

This parameter specifies the type of IMPORT being performed. Valid values are COMPLETE, CUMULATIVE, and INCREMENTAL. It has no default value.

PARFILE

This parameter specifies the name of a parameter file to be read by the IMPORT utility. This file may contain entries for all the IMPORT parameters. It has no default value.

HELP

This parameter is a Y/N flag that specifies whether the IMPORT utility will display the available IMPORT parameters on the screen with a brief explanation. The default value is N.

LOG

This parameter specifies the name of the file to spool the feedback from the IMPORT session. Oracle appends an .LOG extension to the file unless the user specifies otherwise. It has no default value.

DESTROY

This parameter is a Y/N flag that specifies whether Oracle will run the CREATE TABLESPACE commands found in the full EXPORT dump file and overwrite any data files that exist. The default value is N.

FROMUSER

This parameter specifies a list of database accounts whose objects should be read from the EXPORT dump file. This parameter is applicable when the FULL parameter is set to N. It has no default value.

TOUSER

This parameter specifies one or more database accounts into which database objects in the EXPORT dump file will be IMPORTed. This parameter value does not need to be set to the FROMUSER parameter value. It has no default value.

INDEXFILE

This parameter specifies that Oracle write all CREATE TABLE, CREATE CLUSTER, and CREATE INDEX commands to a file rather than executing them. All but the CREATE INDEX commands will be commented out. This file is typically run after IMPORTing with INDEXES=N. It is very useful for separating tables and indexes into different tablespaces. This parameter requires that either the FULL parameter is set to Y or a value is specified for the FROMUSER parameter. It has no default value.

POINT_IN_TIME_RECOVER

This parameter is a Y/N flag that specifies whether the IMPORT is part of a tablespace point-in-time recovery. The default value is N.

ANALYZE

This parameter is a Y/N flag that specifies whether the IMPORT utility should execute the ANALYZE commands contained in the EXPORT dump file. The default value is Y.

SKIP_UNUSABLE_INDEXES

This parameter is a Y/N flag that specifies whether the IMPORT utility should skip partition indexes marked as "unusable." This parameter enables you to defer index maintenance on selected index partitions until after row data has been inserted. Without this parameter, inserts that attempt to update unusable indexes will fail. The default value is N.

Understanding The IMPORT Process Flow For Table Database Objects

When you're IMPORTing database tables, the following IMPORT sequence of events takes place:

- The EXPORT dump file is read by the IMPORT utility.
- CREATE TABLE statements are executed, resulting in new tables being created. These newly created tables have the same data and attributes as the original source tables.

- Index structures are created. To increase the performance of the **IMPORT** utility, the DBA can set the **INDEXES** parameter to N, then build the indexes after the **IMPORT** utility has successfully terminated. This approach also minimizes the number of rollback segments needed to support the **IMPORT** process.
- Row data is **IMPORT**ed into the database tables if the **ROWS** parameter is set to Y. If indexes were created along with the table, then indexes are updated along with the row data **IMPORT**.
- Database triggers are **IMPORT**ed.
- Integrity constraints are enabled on the newly created tables.
- Bitmap index structures are created.

The order in which database tables are **IMPORT**ed may be important under certain circumstances. For instance, if the child table contains a foreign key reference to the primary key of the parent table, and the child table is **IMPORT**ed first, then all rows that reference the parent table's primary key that have not been **IMPORT**ed will be rejected if the constraints are in effect. A similar situation exists when a referential constraint on a table references itself. This problem does not apply to full database **EXPORT**s.

When **IMPORT**ing into an existing table, DBAs typically disable the referential constraints, then re-enable them after the **IMPORT** process has been successfully terminated.

Make sure you understand the order in which the **IMPORT** utility loads table objects into the database.

Understanding NLS Implications

When moving data between Oracle databases with different character sets, special consideration should be given to ensure that appropriate data conversion is performed. The **EXPORT** utility writes to the **EXPORT** dump file using the character set specified (such as 7-bit ASCII) for the user session running the **EXPORT** utility. If the character set of the **IMPORT**ing user session is different from the one in the **EXPORT** dump file, the **IMPORT** utility will translate the data to the character set of the **IMPORT**ing user session. After the data is converted to the **IMPORT**ing user session character set, it is then converted to the database character set. During the conversion, any characters in the **EXPORT** file that have no equivalent in the target character set are replaced with a default character that is character set dependent. The **NLS_LANG** environment variable can be set to the character set definition of the source database to protect against undesired data conversions and data loss.

Make sure you understand the National Language Support (NLS) considerations of loading data into the database.

To ensure appropriate data conversion is performed, the target character set should be a superset of the source character set or both character sets should be equivalent.

IMPORT Examples

The following are some examples of using the **IMPORT** utility:

- **IMPORT**ing a table **EXPORT**ed by **USER1** into the **USER2** schema:

```
$ imp dba9/password9 fromuser=user1 touser=user2 file=user1.dmp
tables=user1tab
```

- **IMPORT**ing using a parameter file named **IMPORT.par**:

```
$ imp dba9/password9 parfile=IMPORT.par
```

- **IMPORT**ing in full database mode excluding indexes:

```
$ imp dba9/password9 full=y indexes=n file=dball.dmp
```

- **IMPORT**ing partitions a and b from a table named **parttab** that is owned by **parttabowner**:

```
$ imp dba9/password9 fromuser=parttabtowner
tables=parttab:a,parttab:b
```

Using EXPORT For Logical Backups

When the EXPORT utility is run in the full database mode, you can make a logical backup of the entire database or just the database objects that have changed since the last EXPORT. This mode will EXPORT all table and data definitions. The FULL EXPORT parameter must be set to Y to run in the full database mode. When you're running EXPORT in the full database mode, three types of EXPORTs can be performed:

- Complete
- Cumulative
- Incremental

The INCTYPE EXPORT parameter can be used to specify the desired type of EXPORT. These three types of EXPORTs facilitate backup strategies involving EXPORTs.

Complete EXPORTs

The complete EXPORTs form the basis for a backup strategy involving EXPORTs. A complete EXPORT is equivalent to a full database EXPORT with the additional updates performed against the tables that track incremental and cumulative EXPORTs. The SYS schema owns three tables that enable EXPORT to track incremental and cumulative EXPORTs—INCEXP, INCFIL, and INCVID. A complete EXPORT dump file contains all database objects from the source database and can be used to perform point-in-time recovery up to the time the complete EXPORT was taken. The following example code shows how to invoke the EXPORT utility under Windows NT to create a complete EXPORT file.

```
D:\ORANT\BIN> exp80 DBA9/PASSWORD9 FULL=Y INCTYPE=COMPLETE
FILE='TESTCOMP.DMP'
```

Cumulative EXPORTs

A cumulative EXPORT contains database tables that have changed since the last cumulative or complete EXPORT. A cumulative EXPORT essentially combines several incremental EXPORTs into a single cumulative EXPORT file. You can discard the incremental EXPORT files taken before a cumulative EXPORT, because they are rolled up into the cumulative EXPORT file. The following example code shows how to invoke the EXPORT utility to create a cumulative EXPORT file:

```
D:\ORANT\BIN> exp80 DBA9/PASSWORD9 FULL=Y INCTYPE=CUMULATIVE
FILE='TESTCUM.DMP'
```

Incremental EXPORTs

An incremental EXPORT contains database tables that have changed since the last incremental, cumulative, or complete EXPORT. An incremental EXPORT file contains table definitions with all of the table's data rows. The following example code shows how to invoke the EXPORT utility to create an incremental EXPORT file:

```
D:\ORANT\BIN> exp80 DBA9/PASSWORD9 FULL=Y INCTYPE=INCREMENTAL
FILE='TESTINC.DMP'
```

Incremental **EXPORTs** are more suitable for environments where database changes affect relatively smaller tables.

The incremental and cumulative EXPORTs provide several benefits to DBAs:

- They facilitate in the restoration of accidentally dropped tables.
- Smaller EXPORT files are generated, because only tables that contained changed rows are EXPORTed.
- EXPORT time is reduced, because only database objects that have changed since the last incremental or cumulative EXPORT are written to the current EXPORT file.

Using EXPORT's Direct Path Method

The EXPORT utility uses one of two paths in extracting data from an Oracle database: the *conventional* path or the *direct* path. The conventional path EXPORT uses most of the same mechanisms for extracting data as a SQL SELECT statement would use. Data is read into the buffer cache from disk, evaluated, and passed over to a user such as an EXPORT client, and written to an operating system file. Direct path EXPORTs, on the other hand, run faster because the data is extracted from the Oracle data files and passed directly to the EXPORT client for processing, bypassing the buffer cache and the SQL-command processing layer. The direct-path EXPORT eliminated the need to perform unnecessary data conversions because the data is in the format that EXPORT needs. The IMPORT utility can work with data extracted using either the conventional or direct path EXPORT.

Be aware that the formats of the data and the column specifications in the **EXPORT** dump files generated by direct-path and conventional path **EXPORT**s are different.

Before using direct-path **EXPORT**, the *catexp.sql script* typically located in the **rdbms/admin** directory must be run. Two methods invoke direct-path **EXPORT**:

- Command line option
- Parameter file

Command Line Option

The direct-path **EXPORT** can be invoked by using the **DIRECT** command line parameter at the operating system prompt, as shown by the following code sample under Unix:

```
$ exp dba9/password9 full=y direct=y
```

Parameter File

The direct-path **EXPORT** can be invoked by using a parameter file that contains all the user-specified parameters. The **EXPORT** utility reads the contents of the parameter file at run-time. The following code example shows the contents of a parameter file named **EXPORT.par** and demonstrates how the parameter file is used from the operating system prompt:

```
Contents of the EXPORT.par file:
       USERID=DBA9/PASSWORD9
       TABLES=(TESTTAB1,TESTTAB2)
       FILE=EXP_PAR.DMP
       DIRECT=Y
```

To run the **EXPORT** utility with the **EXPORT**.par parameter file, issue the following command at the operating system prompt for Unix:

```
$ exp parfile=EXPORT.par
```

You can find out whether an **EXPORT** dump file was created using the direct or conventional path by looking in the log file produced by the **EXPORT** session, on the screen while **EXPORT** is running, or when the **EXPORT** dump file is **IMPORT**ed later.

Things To Remember About Direct Path **EXPORT**

When using the Direct Path EXPORT, you should be aware of the following limitations:

- The Direct Path option of EXPORT is not available when you're using the EXPORT utility interactively.
- The Direct Path EXPORT requires matching character sets on the client machine and the server machine, because no character-set conversion will be performed.
- When using the Direct Path EXPORT involving database tables that contain columns defined with Oracle8-specific data types, such as LOB, BFILE, REF, NESTED TABLE, VARRAY, and other object types, only the table definitions are EXPORTed.
- The BUFFER parameter defines the buffer size EXPORT uses when unloading data on the conventional path. This parameter is not used by the direct path EXPORT.

Using IMPORT To Recover Database Objects

The IMPORT utility can be used to recover data and database objects from a valid EXPORT dump file. It is commonly used to support the following recovery activities:

- Creating table definitions from the EXPORT dump file. You need to specify IMPORT without the data rows.
- Extracting data from a valid EXPORT dump file when running in the table, user, or full database mode.
- IMPORTing data from a cumulative, incremental, or complete EXPORT file.
- Recovering an accidentally dropped table.

Restoring Database Objects Using Incremental, Cumulative, And Complete **EXPORT** Files

The order in which incremental, cumulative, and complete EXPORTs are made is IMPORTant. A complete EXPORT must be made before database objects can be restored. Once this has been accomplished, the database object restoration process is as follows:

- Run **IMPORT** with parameter **INCTYPE** set to **SYSTEM** using the most recent incremental **EXPORT** file. Use cumulative **EXPORT** file if no incremental **EXPORT**s have been made. This **IMPORT**s the system objects.
- Run **IMPORT** with parameter **INCTYPE** set to **RESTORE** using the most recent complete **EXPORT** file.
- Run **IMPORT** with parameter **INCTYPE** set to **RESTORE** using all cumulative **EXPORT** files after the last complete **EXPORT**.
- Run **IMPORT** with parameter **INCTYPE** set to **RESTORE** using all incremental **EXPORT** files after the last cumulative **EXPORT**.

Practice Questions

Question 1

Which **EXPORT** parameter is used to specify the location to log **EXPORT** errors?

- ❍ a. **PARFILE**
- ❍ b. **INDEXFILE**
- ❍ c. **HELP**
- ❍ d. **BUFFER**
- ❍ e. **LOG**

The correct answer is e. The **LOG** parameter enables the user to specify the name of the file to which informational and error messages encountered by **EXPORT** are written. Answers a, b, c, and d are incorrect, because they serve other purposes.

Question 2

When you are performing an **EXPORT** of your database, what type of backup is it?

- ❍ a. Physical database backup
- ❍ b. Logical database backup
- ❍ c. It is not a backup

The correct answer is b. The **EXPORT** utility backs up the data and the definitions of all database objects so they can be subsequently recreated via the **IMPORT** utility. Answer a is not correct, because the **EXPORT** utility does not back up the physical file structures of the database. Answer c is incorrect, because the **EXPORT** utility enables users to perform logical database backups.

Question 3

Which two DBA tasks are typically supported by the **EXPORT** and **IMPORT** utilities? [Choose two]

- ❑ a. Creating a historical archive
- ❑ b. Establishing a baseline for complete recovery
- ❑ c. Recreating the control file
- ❑ d. Making physical backups
- ❑ e. Reorganizing database tables

The correct answers are a and e. The **EXPORT** and **IMPORT** utilities can be used to make logical backups of the database. These utilities are typically used to create a historical archive, save database object definitions, reorganize tables, upgrade versions of the Oracle server, and recover from user failure errors. Answer b is incorrect, because the **EXPORT** and **IMPORT** utilities are used for point-in-time recoveries up to the point the **EXPORT** was taken. Answer c is incorrect, because **EXPORT**s are not involved in recreating control files. Answer d is incorrect, because the **EXPORT** and **IMPORT** utilities are not involved in making physical backups.

Question 4

How can **EXPORT**s be incorporated in a backup and recovery strategy?

- ❍ a. Used in conjunction with the redo log files to perform complete recovery
- ❍ b. Instead of operating the database in **ARCHIVELOG** mode
- ❍ c. When a new database needs to be created
- ❍ d. In place of offline backups

The correct answer is c. A logical backup serves to supplement a physical backup, because it can be used to restore a single table, all objects under a user schema, or an entire database. Answer a is incorrect, because redo log files cannot be used with database objects recovered from an **EXPORT** dump file. Answer b is incorrect, because **EXPORT**s should be performed as a safety net and not replace operating the database in **ARCHIVELOG** mode. Answer d is incorrect, because **EXPORT**s should not be used in place of offline backups.

Question 5

Which **EXPORT** parameter enables you to specify the names of database tables to **EXPORT**?

❍ a. **PARFILE**

❍ b. **TABLES**

❍ c. **OWNER**

❍ d. **ROWS**

❍ e. **FILE**

The correct answer is b. The TABLES parameter enables you to specify the names of database tables to be EXPORTed. Answers a, c, d, and e are incorrect, because they serve other purposes.

Question 6

You are **IMPORTing** two tables—**PARENT** and **CHILD**. **CHILD** has a foreign key referencing the primary key of **PARENT**. When database constraints are in effect, what is the correct order in which to **IMPORT** the two tables?

❍ a. The tables must be loaded concurrently.

❍ b. **PARENT** should be loaded first.

❍ c. **CHILD** should be loaded first.

❍ d. No specific load order is required.

The correct answer is b. When IMPORTing two tables with referential integrity defined and enabled, you must IMPORT the table with the foreign key last. Answer a is incorrect, because PARENT should be loaded first, then CHILD. Answer c is incorrect, because CHILD should be loaded after the PARENT so that the CHILD rows referencing the primary key of the PARENT won't be rejected. Answer d is incorrect, because a specific load order (PARENT first, then CHILD) is required in this scenario.

Question 7

What are two limitations when using the direct-path mode of **EXPORT**? [Choose two answers]

❑ a. The **EXPORT** utility will compete with other database users for shared memory.

❑ b. The **BUFFER** parameter will have no effect.

❑ c. The client-side and the server-side character sets must be the same.

❑ d. Tables containing **LONG** columns will not be **EXPORT**ed.

❑ e. The **EXPORT** utility must be run using the interactive interface.

The correct answers are b and c. When using the direct path option of EXPORT, the BUFFER parameter is ignored and the character sets for the client machine and the server machine must be equivalent. Answer a is incorrect, because direct-path EXPORTs bypass the buffer cache and the SQL-command processing layer so they don't compete with other database users for shared memory. Answer d is incorrect, because tables containing LONG columns are supported by the direct path mode of EXPORT. Answer e is incorrect, because direct path EXPORTs require the use of the command line interface.

Question 8

What **EXPORT** mode should be used to **EXPORT** selected tables in a user's schema?

❍ a. Full database

❍ b. Tablespace

❍ c. Table

❍ d. User

The correct answer is c. In the table mode of EXPORT, specified tables are EXPORTed. Answer a is incorrect, because with EXPORTs made in full database mode, all database objects except the database objects owned by SYS are EXPORTed. Answer b is incorrect, because it is an invalid EXPORT mode. Answer d is incorrect, because in the user mode of EXPORT, all the objects in a user's schema are EXPORTed.

Question 9

When **IMPORT**ing database tables, what order does the **IMPORT** utility use to perform the following tasks?

1. Data **IMPORT**ed
2. Indexes created
3. Triggers **IMPORT**ed
4. Integrity constraints enabled
5. Bitmap indexes created
6. Tables created

❍ a. 6,2,5,1,4,3

❍ b. 6,1,2,3,4,5

❍ c. 6,2,1,3,4,5

❍ d. 6,1,2,4,3,5

The correct answer is c. When **IMPORT**ing tables, the **IMPORT** utility will perform the following tasks in order: (1) create the tables, (2) create the indexes, (3) **IMPORT** the data, (4) **IMPORT** the database triggers, (5) enable integrity constraints, and (6) create the bitmap indexes. Answer a is incorrect, because bitmap indexes are performed last. Answers b and d are incorrect, because data is **IMPORT**ed after the indexes are built.

Question 10

What type of **EXPORT** contains only the database objects that have changed since the last **EXPORT** of any type?

❍ a. Complete

❍ b. Incremental

❍ c. Full

❍ d. Cumulative

The correct answer is b. An incremental **EXPORT** will **EXPORT** only the database objects that have changed since the last **EXPORT** of any type. For database tables, it will **EXPORT** the table definition and all the data rows (not just the changed data rows). Answer a is incorrect, because a complete **EXPORT** contains all database objects except those owned by the **SYS** schema. Answer c is incorrect, because it is an EXPORT parameter rather than a type of EXPORT. Answer d is incorrect, because a cumulative EXPORT contains database tables that have changed since the last cumulative or complete EXPORT.

Question 11

What **EXPORT** parameter should be set when you're **EXPORT**ing data and the users are performing updates to the database?

- ❍ a. **CONSTRAINTS=Y**
- ❍ b. **CONSISTENT=Y**
- ❍ c. **DIRECT=Y**
- ❍ d. **IGNORE=Y**

The correct answer is b. When the database is open and in use during an EXPORT, setting the CONSISTENT parameter to Y will enable a read-consistent view of the data. Answer a is incorrect, because it specifies whether constraints will be EXPORTed. Answer c is incorrect, because it specifies whether the direct path EXPORT will be performed. Answer d is incorrect, because it is not a valid EXPORT parameter.

Need To Know More?

Dialeris, Connie. *Oracle8 Backup and Recovery Guide Release 8.0*, Part No. A58396-01, Oracle Corporation, 1997.

Durbin, Jason. *Oracle8 Utilities Release 8.0*, Part No. A58244-01, Oracle Corporation, 1997.

Lane, Paula. *Oracle8 References Release 8.0*, Part No. A58242-01, Oracle Corporation, 1997.

Leverenz, Lefty. *Oracle8 Concepts Release 8.0*, Part No. A58227-01, Oracle Corporation, 1997.

Loney, Kevin. *DBA Handbook, 8.0 Edition*, Oracle Press, 1999. ISBN 0-07882-289-0.

Velpuri, Rama. *Oracle Backup and Recovery Handbook*, Oracle Press, 1998. ISBN: 0-07882-389-7.

Additional Oracle Recovery Issues

Terms you'll need to understand:

- √ Fast warmstart
- √ Parallel recovery
- √ **RECOVERY_PARALLELISM**
- √ **CREATE CONTROLFILE** command
- √ **RESYNC CATALOG FROM BACKUP CONTROLFILE** command

Techniques you'll need to master:

- √ Understanding methods for minimizing downtime
- √ Diagnosing database corruption errors
- √ Recovering from database corruption errors
- √ Reconstructing lost or damaged control files
- √ Understanding read-only tablespace recovery
- √ Recovering from recovery catalog loss

In this chapter, you will learn additional Oracle recovery issues, including:

- Ways for minimizing downtime
- Diagnosing and handling database corruption errors
- Resolving lost or damaged control files
- Read-only tablespace recovery
- Recovery from recovery catalog loss

Methods For Minimizing Downtime

Reducing the amount of time spent in database recovery will minimize downtime and maximize data availability. The Oracle database provides several ways to enhance recovery performance, including:

- Fast warmstart
- Starting Oracle with missing data files
- Parallel recovery

Fast Warmstart

Fast warmstart is an Oracle database feature introduced in Oracle 7.3, that allows for fast instance recovery. There are two main phases in instance recovery: the roll-forward phase and the rollback phase. In the roll-forward phase, Oracle applies transaction data recorded in the online redo log files that have not been recorded in the data files, including the contents of rollback segments. In the rollback phase, instead of waiting for all transactions to be rolled back before making the database available, Oracle enables the database to be opened as soon as cache recovery is complete. This is called fast warmstart. This also means that the database is available at the end of the roll-forward phase of instance recovery and the majority of the rollback activities are essentially deferred to the individual user processes when blocks are subsequently requested. Fast warmstart improves database recovery with minimal performance overhead for subsequent transactions requesting data blocks containing uncommitted data.

Starting Oracle With Missing Data Files

When you lose a data file after your database shuts down, you will not be able to start the database because of the missing file. In this situation, Oracle minimizes downtime by enabling you to bring the unaffected parts of the database up for normal use while you perform recovery operations on the tablespace containing the lost or damaged data file. Follow these steps to start a database that has a missing data file:

1. Start the instance, then mount, but do not open, the database, as illustrated by the following code sample:

```
SVRMGR> STARTUP MOUNT
```

2. Take the missing data file offline using the **ALTER DATABASE DATAFILE <filename> OFFLINE** command. For an **ARCHIVELOG** mode database, you use the **ALTER DATABASE DATAFILE <filename> OFFLINE IMMEDIATE** command, as shown here:

```
SVRMGR> ALTER DATABASE DATAFILE '/u1/oradata/app01.ora' OFFLINE
IMMEDIATE;
```

3. Open the database so users can access the unaffected parts of the database:

```
SVRMGR> ALTER DATABASE OPEN;
```

4. Restore the lost data file from a valid backup.
5. Perform either tablespace or data file recovery. Because the **APP01_DATA** tablespace contains a single data file, which has been lost, we'll use the **RECOVER TABLESPACE** command:

```
SVRMGR> RECOVER TABLESPACE APP01_DATA;
```

6. Bring the tablespace online with the **ALTER TABLESPACE <tablespace_name> ONLINE** command:

```
SVRMGR> ALTER TABLESPACE APP01_DATA ONLINE;
```

The recovery operation for a missing data file will recover through the current online redo log files so that the log sequence number in the headers of the recovered files will synchronize with the rest of the database. This also ensures that no committed transactions are lost.

Parallel Recovery

Oracle's parallel recovery feature enables you to use several processes to apply changes from the redo log files. You can run a recovery in parallel to take advantage of available machine processing power and database resources so the database recovery completes faster and downtime is minimized. Parallel recovery is most beneficial when the data files being recovered reside on different disks. A typical parallel recovery involves a master process (recovery session) that reads and dispatches redo entries from the redo log files to the child processes (recovery processes). The child processes are responsible for applying the changes from the redo entries to the data files.

You can accomplish parallel recovery by performing either of the following activities:

- Setting initialization parameters for parallel recovery.
- Issuing the **RECOVER** command with the appropriate options.

Setting Initialization Parameters For Parallel Recovery

The **RECOVERY_PARALLELISM** initialization parameter specifies the default number of recovery processes per session. The number of recovery processes must not be greater than the value of the **PARALLEL_MAX_SERVERS** initialization parameter. This parameter is typically derived by multiplying one or two processes by the number of disks containing data files. This parameter value determines the degree of parallelism when the **PARALLEL** option is not specified with the **RECOVER** command.

Issuing The **RECOVER** Command With The Appropriate Options

You can use the **RECOVER** command in Server Manager to specify the number of recovery processes for performing media recovery. The **RECOVER** command syntax pertaining to parallel recovery from Server Manager is as follows:

```
SVRMGR> RECOVER OBJECT_LIST [ NOPARALLEL|PARALLEL (DEGREE n)];
```

Refer to Table 14.1 for the **RECOVER** command elements and corresponding actions.

The **NOPARALLEL** keyword and the specification of **PARALLEL (DEGREE 1 INSTANCE 1)** have the same effect.

Multiple OEM sessions can be manually spawned so multiple **RECOVER DATAFILE** commands can operate on a different set of data files at the same time. To enable automatic parallel recovery, you can use Recovery Manager's

Table 14.1 RECOVER command elements and the corresponding actions.

ELEMENT	ACTION
OBJECT_LIST	Specifies that parallel operations will be performed at the **DATABASE**, **TABLESPACE**, or **DATAFILE** levels.
PARALLEL	Specifies parallel recovery is desired.
DEGREE	Used in conjunction with the **PARALLEL** element to specify the number of recovery processes used to apply redo entries to the data files. **DEGREE DEFAULT** tells Oracle to use two times the number of data files being recovered as the desired number of recovery processes.
NOPARALLEL	Specifies serial recovery.

(RMAN) RESTORE and RECOVER commands. In this case, Oracle uses a single process to read the log files and dispatches redo entries to multiple recovery processes, which apply the redo entries to the data files. With RMAN, you only need one session to perform recovery, because RMAN automatically starts the recovery processes.

Handling Database Corruption Errors

Database corruptions resulting from hardware problems or program errors may occur in one of the Oracle data files. The data file corruptions are normally communicated via the "ORA-01578: ORACLE data block corrupted (file # string, block # string)" error when the corrupted block has been read. You can determine which object was corrupted using the following sample SQL statement:

```
SVRMGR> SELECT SEGMENT_TYPE,OWNER||'.'||SEGMENT_NAME
     2> FROM DBA_EXTENTS
     3> WHERE file_num_from_error_message  = FILE_ID
     4> AND block_num_from error_message BETWEEN
     5> BLOCK_ID AND BLOCK_ID + BLOCKS -1;
```

You can resolve data file corruptions three different ways:

- The most effective method is to recover your data files from backup and apply archived redo log information.
- When an index exists for the corrupted table, you can select the corrupted data from the corrupted table using index range scans. The following sample SELECT statement can be used for this purpose:

```
SVRMGR> select distinct(key)
     2> from corrupted_table
     3> where key > (minimum_key_value)
     4> and substr(rowid,1,8) = corrupted_block_id
     5> order by 1;
```

- You can select good data out of the table above and below the corrupted blocks, moving them into another table, and then dropping the corrupted table. The following sample **SELECT** statement can be used for this purpose:

```
SVRMGR> create table new_tab
     2> as select * from corrupted_table
     3> where key > (minimum_key_value)
     4> and key not in (corrupted_key_list);
```

Take a full backup of the data file before taking any corrective actions on the corrupted blocks.

Reconstructing Lost Or Damaged Control Files

Several situations require you to reconstruct or replace a lost or damaged control file for your database, including:

- Loss of all control files for your database due to media failure.
- Needing to change the name of the database.
- Needing to change option settings that are fixed at the time the control file was created (**MAXLOGFILES**, **MAXDATAFILES**, **MAXLOGMEMBERS**, and others).

You can recover from lost or damaged Oracle control files in the following ways:

- Use the multiplexed copy of your control file. This means you didn't lose all of your control files. To recover, just shut down the database using the normal or immediate option, copy your control file, and start the database again.
- Use the **CREATE CONTROLFILE** command to create a new file. You will need to know all the files for your database. The **ALTER**

DATABASE BACKUP CONTROLFILE TO TRACE command can be run periodically to provide a current listing of files for your database.

- When all control files are lost, you can recover by using the backup binary copy of your control file.

Oracle recommends that you mirror your control files to minimize total control file loss.

When the "ORA-01207: file is more recent than control file—old control file" error message is encountered during a recovery operation, it indicates that you need to recover your database using a backup control file. To recover from this situation, follow these steps:

1. Copy the backup control file that was created using the **ALTER DATABASE BACKUP CONTROLFILE** command to the location of the lost control file.
2. Perform database recovery using the backup control file, as shown here:

```
SVRMGR> RECOVER DATABASE USING BACKUP CONTROLFILE;
```

3. Open the database with the **RESETLOGS** option:

```
SVRMGR> ALTER DATABASE OPEN RESETLOGS;
```

Read-Only Tablespace Recovery Issues

A *read-only tablespace* is a tablespace that has its status set to prevent any subsequent updates until the status is reset. The tablespace status was changed by issuing the SQL **ALTER TABLESPACE <tablespace_name> READ ONLY** command. Typically, a tablespace is put into read-only mode to minimize the frequency of backups for the data. A read-only tablespace typically contains static data that infrequently changes, such as lookup tables. The following are types of recovery scenarios associated with read-only tablespaces:

- You are performing a tablespace recovery for a read-only tablespace, TS1. The most recent backup contains the data file for the TS1 tablespace when it was read-only. To recover TS1, you need to restore TS1 from the most recent backup and bypass applying redo entries.

- You are performing a tablespace recovery for a writable tablespace, TS2. The most recent backup contains the data file for the TS2 tablespace when it was read-only. To recover TS2, you need to restore TS2 from the most recent backup and apply redo entries from the point in time when the TS2 tablespace was set to writable.

- You are performing a tablespace recovery for a read-only tablespace, TS3. The most recent backup contains the data file for the TS3 tablespace when it was writable. Because you didn't back up TS3 after setting it to read-only, to recover you need to restore TS3 from the most recent backup and recover up to the point in time when the tablespace was set to read-only.

Things To Consider When Working With Read-Only Tablespaces

You should consider the following issues when working with read-only tablespaces:

- In the event you cannot restore your read-only tablespace data files to the proper location, perhaps because a failed disk cannot be replaced immediately, you can use the **ALTER DATABASE RENAME FILE** command to specify a new location.

- When recovering a read-only tablespace with a backup control file, follow the same procedures as for normal offline tablespaces, with one exception: You need to bring the tablespace online after the database is open.

- When you re-create a control file with the **CREATE CONTROLFILE** command and your database contains read-only tablespaces, you need to follow special procedures. The trace script file produced by the **ALTER DATABASE BACKUP CONTROLFILE TO TRACE** command contains the special handling procedures. The following code snippet is an excerpt from a sample trace script file generated from a database that contains a read-only tablespace:

```
...
# Recovery is required if any of the datafiles are restored
#backups,
# or if the last shutdown was not normal or immediate.
RECOVER DATABASE
# The database can now be opened normally.
ALTER DATABASE OPEN;
```

```
# The backup control file does not list read-only and normal
# offline tablespaces so that
# Oracle can avoid performing recovery on them. Oracle checks
# the data dictionary and finds information on these absent
# files and marks them 'MISSINGxxxx'. It then renames
# the missing files to acknowledge them without having to # #
#recover them.
ALTER DATABASE RENAME FILE 'MISSING0003'
     TO 'D:\ORANT\DATABASE\READONLY.ORA';
# Online the files in read-only tablespaces.
ALTER TABLESPACE "READONLY_DATA" ONLINE;
```

Recovering From Recovery Catalog Loss

The recovery catalog is an important feature in Oracle8 database backup and recovery. The recovery catalog database is no different than any other Oracle database. You should include the recovery catalog database in your regular backup schedule. In the event you cannot recover the recovery catalog using normal recovery mechanisms, you can choose one of the following options to partially rebuild the recovery catalog:

- Use the **CATALOG** command in **RMAN** to catalog all the available data file backups, archived redo logs, and the backup control files.
- Use the **RESYNC CATALOG FROM BACKUP CONTROLFILE** command to repopulate the recovery catalog with information extracted from a backup control file. The **RESYNC CATALOG FROM BACKUP CONTROLFILE** command also enables you to re-create information about backup sets and/or backup pieces.

RMAN does not verify that the files it finds listed in the backup control file actually exist. After resynchronization, you may have recovery catalog records for items that don't exist. To remove these nonexistent items, use the **CHANGE...UNCATALOG** commands.

Practice Questions

Question 1

The data file for a read-only tablespace, TS1, is damaged. The most recent backup was taken when tablespace TS1 was read-only. What action do you need to perform to recover tablespace TS1?

- ❍ a. No recovery action is needed.
- ❍ b. Put tablespace TS1 in read-write mode and restore from the most recent backup.
- ❍ c. Restore from the most recent backup.
- ❍ d. Restore from the most recent backup and apply redo entries from the redo log files.

The correct answer is c. You only need to restore from the most recent backup, because no changes were made. Answer a is incorrect, because you need to restore from the most recent backup. Answer b is incorrect, because you don't need to set tablespace TS1 to read-write mode. Answer d is incorrect, because you don't need to apply redo entries from the redo log files, because no changes were made.

Question 2

Which of the following actions can be used to open an **ARCHIVELOG** mode database with a missing data file?

- ❍ a. Mount the database, take all tablespaces offline, and open the database.
- ❍ b. Restore the data file and open the database.
- ❍ c. Mount the database, take the tablespace with the missing data file offline, and open the database.
- ❍ d. Restore all data files using OS mechanisms, open the database, and perform database recovery.

The correct answer is c. You need to perform the following actions to recover from a lost data file while the unaffected part of the database is available for normal use: mount the database, offline the tablespace with the missing data file, open the database, restore the data file from the most recent backup, recover the data file, and bring the tablespace online. Answers a, b, and d are incorrect, because they don't perform the prescribed recovery actions for starting Oracle with a missing data file.

Question 3

If you tried to open the database and Oracle displayed the following sample error message, what action would you need to take to resolve the error?

```
SVRMGR> ALTER DATABASE OPEN;
ORA-00283:  Recovery session canceled due to errors
ORA-01122:  database file 2 failed verification
     check
ORA-01110:  data file 2: '/u1/oradata/app02/
     app02.ora'
ORA-01207:  file is more recent than control file -
     old control file
```

❍ a. You need to restore a backup data file.

❍ b. You need to recover a data file.

❍ c. You need to restore a backup control file.

❍ d. You need to recover the control file.

The correct answer is c. This error is generated because you restored a data file and tried to open the database with the current control file. The database will not open, because the files are out of sync. To resolve this error, you need to restore the backup control file associated with the backup data file. Answers a, b, and d are incorrect, because these actions don't resolve the given error.

Question 4

When all control files and corresponding mirrors are lost, how would you re-create a control file?

❍ a. You can only restore from a backup control file, because a control file cannot be re-created.

❍ b. Use the **ALTER DATABASE BACKUP CONTROLFILE** command.

❍ c. Use the **CREATE CONTROLFILE** command.

❍ d. Use the **RECOVER DATABASE USING BACKUP CONTROLFILE** command and open the database with the **RESETLOGS** option.

The correct answer is c. You need to use the **CREATE CONTROLFILE** command to create a new control file when all control files are lost. Answer a is incorrect, because a control file can be re-created. Answer b is incorrect, because the **ALTER DATABASE BACKUP CONTROLFILE** command creates a backup control file. Answer d is incorrect, because the **RECOVER DATABASE USING BACKUP CONTROLFILE** command performs recovery using a backup control file.

Question 5

Your **ARCHIVELOG** database has grown by 50 percent within the last month. What can you do to minimize recovery time in the event of a media failure?

- ❍ a. Perform recovery only on the weekend.
- ❍ b. Recover the damaged files only from the most recent backup.
- ❍ c. Perform recovery after hours.
- ❍ d. Recover the database using parallel recovery operations.
- ❍ e. Recover all the data files from the most recent backup and perform point-in-time recovery.

The correct answer is d. Parallel recovery helps to reduce recovery time in the event of a media failure. Answers a and c are incorrect, because recovery time is not reduced when serial recovery operations are deferred to after-hours and weekends. Answer b is incorrect, because this action is a serial operation and a complete recovery requires applying redo information generated since the most recent backup. Answer e is incorrect, because performing point-in-time recovery is a serial operation and requires the application of some of the redo information generated since the most recent backup.

Question 6

What information is needed to create a new control file for an existing database?

- ❍ a. The database name and the names and locations of datafiles and redo log files
- ❍ b. Only the database name
- ❍ c. Only the names of the data files
- ❍ d. Only the location of the parameter file

The correct answer is a. When using the **CREATE CONTROLFILE** command to create a new control file, you need to know the names and locations of all the database files. Answers b and c are incorrect, because they are subsets of the information needed. Answer d is incorrect, because the control file does not record the location of the parameter file.

Question 7

When performing parallel recovery, how many processes per disk drive are typically allocated?

- ❍ a. 5
- ❍ b. 3
- ❍ c. 1 or 2
- ❍ d. 4
- ❍ e. 6

The correct answer is c. To minimize I/O contention during parallel recovery operations, DBAs typically allocate one or two processes per disk drive. Answers a, b, d, and e are incorrect, because they will incur higher I/O overhead with marginal performance benefit.

Question 8

How can you change the **MAXLOGMEMBERS** parameter?

- ❍ a. Use the **ALTER DATABASE** command
- ❍ b. Use the **ALTER SYSTEM** command
- ❍ c. Use the **ALTER SESSION** command
- ❍ d. Re-create the control file using the **CREATE CONTROLFILE** command
- ❍ e. Change the *initSID.ora* parameter file and restart the instance

The correct answer is d. You must re-create the control file to change the **MAXLOGMEMBERS** parameter. Answers a, b, c, and e are incorrect, because they don't support changing the **MAXLOGMEMBERS** parameter.

Question 9

If a data file corruption has been discovered that affects the **ORGANIZATIONS** table and the index on the table is available, how would you recover from this situation?

❍ a. You cannot recover from this situation.

❍ b. Create a new table with data above and below the corrupted block.

❍ c. Restore and recover the data file.

❍ d. Use an index scan to retrieve the data from the corrupted block.

The correct answer is d. When a table is corrupted and an index for the table is available, you can use an index scan to retrieve data from the corrupted block. Answer a is incorrect, because you can recover from this situation. Answer b is incorrect, because you can use an index scan to retrieve data. Answer c is incorrect, because the corruption may exist in the restored files.

Question 10

The data file for a read-only tablespace, TS1, is damaged. The most recent backup was taken when tablespace TS1 was read-write. What action do you need to perform to recover tablespace TS1?

❍ a. Restore from the most recent backup and recover up until the time when the tablespace was set to read-only.

❍ b. Recover to the point in time when the tablespace became read-write.

❍ c. Recovery action cannot be performed for this tablespace.

❍ d. Restore from the most recent backup and set the tablespace to read-only.

The correct answer is a. When a tablespace changes from read-write to read-only, to perform recovery operations, you need to restore from the most recent backup and recover up until the time when the tablespace was set to read-only. Answer b is incorrect, because you need to recover up to the point when the tablespace was set to read-only. Answer c is incorrect, because you can restore and recover this tablespace. Answer d is incorrect, because you should not set the tablespace to read-only.

Need To Know More?

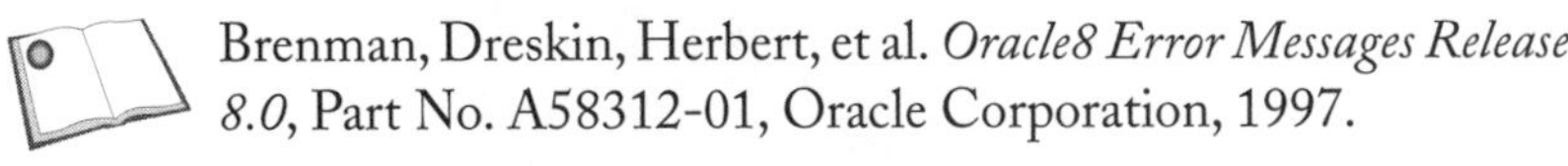
Brenman, Dreskin, Herbert, et al. *Oracle8 Error Messages Release 8.0*, Part No. A58312-01, Oracle Corporation, 1997.

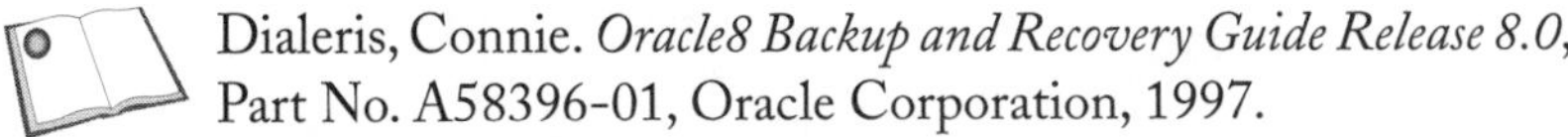
Dialeris, Connie. *Oracle8 Backup and Recovery Guide Release 8.0*, Part No. A58396-01, Oracle Corporation, 1997.

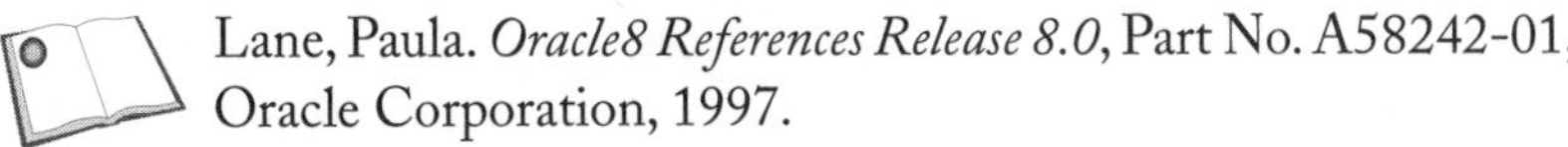
Lane, Paula. *Oracle8 References Release 8.0*, Part No. A58242-01, Oracle Corporation, 1997.

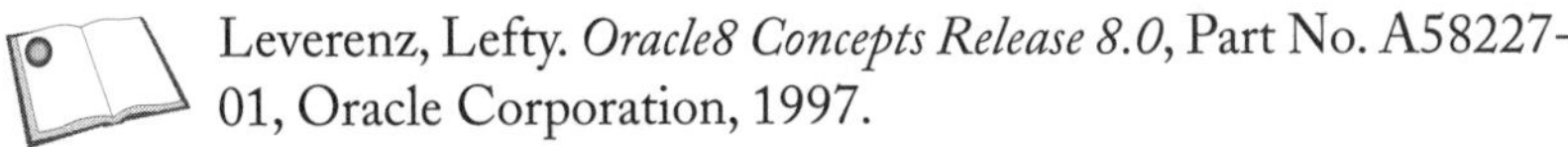
Leverenz, Lefty. *Oracle8 Concepts Release 8.0*, Part No. A58227-01, Oracle Corporation, 1997.

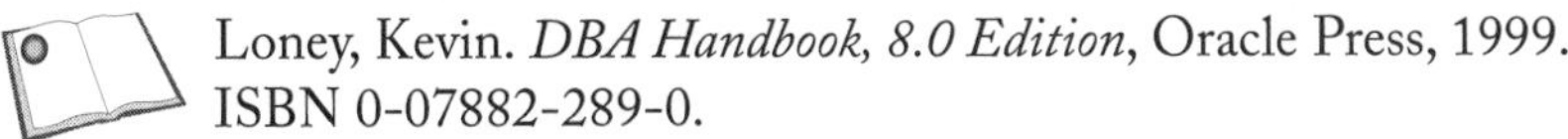
Loney, Kevin. *DBA Handbook, 8.0 Edition*, Oracle Press, 1999. ISBN 0-07882-289-0.

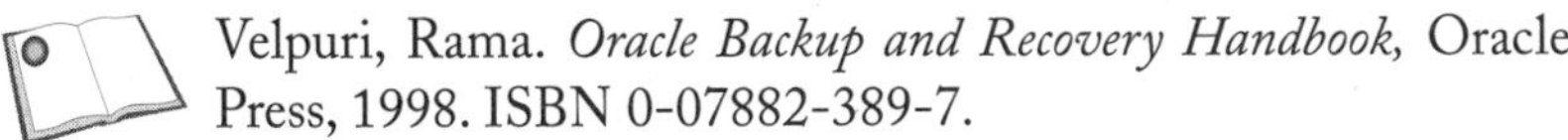
Velpuri, Rama. *Oracle Backup and Recovery Handbook,* Oracle Press, 1998. ISBN 0-07882-389-7.

Sample Test

In this chapter, I provide pointers to help you develop a successful test-taking strategy, including how to choose proper answers, how to decode ambiguity, how to work within the Oracle testing framework, how to decide what you need to memorize beforehand, and how to prepare in general for the test. At the end of this chapter, I include a set of 60 questions on subject matter that is pertinent to Exam 1Z0-015, "Oracle8: Backup and Recovery." In Chapter 16, you'll find the answer key to this test. Good luck!

Questions, Questions, Questions

There should be no doubt in your mind that you are facing a test full of specific and pointed questions. The Oracle8: Backup and Recovery test consists of 60 questions that you must complete in 90 minutes.

Questions belong to one of two basic types: multiple-choice with a single answer, and multiple-choice with two or more answers.

Always take the time to read a question at least twice before selecting an answer, and always look for an Exhibit button as you examine each question. Exhibits include graphics information that pertains to the question. (An exhibit is usually a screen capture of program output or GUI information that you must examine to analyze the question's scenario and formulate an answer.)

Not every question has only one answer; many questions require multiple answers. Therefore, it's important to read each question carefully—not only to determine how many answers are necessary or possible, but also to look for additional hints or instructions when selecting answers. Such instructions often appear in brackets immediately following the question itself (as they do for all multiple-choice questions in which two or more answers are possible).

Picking Proper Answers

Obviously, the only way to pass any exam is to select enough of the right answers to obtain a passing score. However, Oracle's exams are not standardized like the SAT and GRE exams; they are far more diabolical and convoluted. In some cases, questions are strangely worded, and deciphering them can be a real challenge. In those cases, you may need to rely on answer-elimination skills. Almost always, at least one answer out of the possible choices for a question can be eliminated immediately because it matches one of these conditions:

- It does not apply to the situation.
- It describes a nonexistent issue, an invalid option, or an imaginary state.

After you eliminate all answers that are obviously wrong, you can apply your retained knowledge to eliminate further answers. Look for items that sound correct but that refer to actions, commands, or features that are not present or available in the situation that the question describes.

If you're still faced with a blind guess among two or more potentially correct answers, reread the question. Try to picture how each of the possible remaining answers would alter the situation. Be especially sensitive to terminology, because sometimes the choice of words (*remove* instead of *disable*) can make the difference between a right answer and a wrong one.

Only when you've exhausted your ability to eliminate answers should you guess at an answer. An unanswered question offers you no points, but guessing gives you at least some chance of getting a question right. Just don't be too hasty when making a blind guess.

You should wait until the last round of reviewing marked questions (just as you're about to run out of time, or out of unanswered questions) before you start making guesses.

Decoding Ambiguity

Exams are meant to test knowledge on a given topic, and the scores from a properly designed test will have the classic bell-shaped distribution for the target audience, meaning a certain number will fail. A problem with this exam is that it has been tailored to Oracle's training materials, even though some of the material in the training is hearsay, some is old DBA tales, and some is just incorrect. The previous chapters have attempted to present correct information and describe the test topics using available Oracle documentation along with real-world experiences.

The only sure way to overcome some of the exam's limitations is to be prepared. You will discover that many of the questions test your knowledge of something that is not directly related to the issue that the questions raise. This means that the answers offered to you, even the incorrect ones, are as much a part of the skill assessment as the questions themselves. If you do not have a thorough grasp of all the aspects of an exam topic (in this case, backup and recovery), you will not be able to eliminate answers that are obviously wrong, because they relate to a different aspect of the topic than the one the question addresses.

Questions can reveal answers, especially when they deal with commands. So read a question and then evaluate the answers in light of common terms, names, and structure.

Another problem is that Oracle uses some terminology in its training materials that isn't found anywhere else in its documentation sets. Whether this is a deliberate attempt to force you to take its classes to pass the exam or simply a case of sloppy documentation is unknown.

Working Within The Framework

The test questions appear in random order, and many elements or issues that receive mention in one question also crop up in other questions. It's not uncommon to find that an incorrect answer to one question is the correct answer to another question, or vice-versa. Take the time to read every answer to each question, even if you recognize the correct answer to a question immediately. This extra reading may spark a memory or remind you about a feature or function that helps you on another question elsewhere in the exam.

You can revisit any question as many times as you like. If you're uncertain of the answer to a question, check the box that's provided to mark it for easy return later on. You should also mark questions that you think may offer information that you can use to answer other questions. I usually mark somewhere between 25 and 50 percent of the questions. The testing software is designed to let you mark every question if you choose, so use this feature to your advantage. Everything you will want to see again should be marked; the testing software can then help you return to marked questions quickly and easily.

Deciding What To Memorize

The amount you must memorize for an exam depends on how well you remember what you've read, and how well you intuitively know the software. If you are a visual thinker and you can see the drop-down menus and dialog boxes in your head, you won't need to memorize as much as someone who's less visually oriented. Because the tests will stretch your recollection of commands, tools, utilities, and functions related to backup and recovery, you'll want to memorize—at a minimum—the following kinds of information:

- Various utilities and the commands associated with them (for example, Recovery Manager, Server Manager, **IMPORT**, and **EXPORT**)
- How to develop an effective backup and recovery strategy
- The types of failures in an Oracle database
- Taking physical backups with or without **RMAN**
- Understanding Oracle recovery with or without archiving
- The data dictionary views for backup and recovery

If you work your way through this book while sitting at a machine with Oracle8 and Oracle Enterprise Manager (OEM) installed, and you try to manipulate the features and functions of the various commands, tools, and utilities as they're discussed, you should have little or no difficulty mastering this material. Also, don't forget that "The Cram Sheet" at the front of the book captures the material that is most important to memorize, so use it to guide your studies as well.

Preparing For The Test

The best way to prepare for the test—after you've studied—is to take at least one practice exam. I've included one in this chapter for that reason; the test questions are located in the pages that follow. (Unlike the preceding chapters in this book, the answers don't follow the questions immediately; you'll have to flip to Chapter 16 to review the answers.)

Give yourself 90 minutes to take the exam. Keep yourself on the honor system, and don't look at earlier text in the book or jump ahead to the answer key. When your time is up or you've finished the questions, you can check your work in Chapter 16. Pay special attention to the explanations for the incorrect answers; these can also help to reinforce your knowledge of the material. Knowing how to recognize correct answers is good, but understanding why incorrect answers are wrong can be equally valuable.

Taking The Test

Relax. Once you're sitting in front of the testing computer, there's nothing more you can do to increase your knowledge or preparation. Take a deep breath, stretch, and start reading that first question.

There's no need to rush; you have plenty of time to complete each question and to return to those questions that you skipped or marked for return. If you read a question twice and remain clueless, you can mark it. Both easy and difficult questions are intermixed throughout the test in random order. Don't cheat yourself by spending too much time on a hard question early in the test, which deprives you of the time you need to answer the questions at the end of the test.

You can read through the entire test and, before returning to marked questions for a second visit, figure out how much time you've got per question. As you answer each question, remove its mark. Continue to review the remaining marked questions until you run out of time or you complete the test.

That's it for pointers. Here are some questions for you to practice on.

Sample Test

Question 1

Which of the following are roles of the database administrator (DBA) in the development and execution of a backup and recovery strategy? [Choose all correct answers]

- ❑ a. To implement the strategy
- ❑ b. To provide recommendations on how to minimize data loss
- ❑ c. To provide recommendations on how to minimize downtime
- ❑ d. To provide the necessary corporate resources and support for implementation

Question 2

Which of the following *initSID.ora* parameters specifies the number of OS blocks written to the redo logs before a checkpoint is initiated?

- ❍ a. **LOG_CHECKPOINT_TIMEOUT**
- ❍ b. **LOG_CHECKPOINT_INTERVAL**
- ❍ c. **LOG_BUFFER**
- ❍ d. **LOG_CKPT_BLOCKS**

Question 3

What Server Manager command statement will display the current database log mode?

- ❍ a. **SELECT * FROM V$DATAFILE**
- ❍ b. **SELECT * FROM V$LOGFILE**
- ❍ c. **ARCHIVE LOG LIST**
- ❍ d. **SHOW ARCHIVE LOG**
- ❍ e. **ARCHIVE LOG ALL**

Question 4

What file(s) contain all current changes made to the database for recovery purposes?

❍ a. Control file

❍ b. Data files

❍ c. Online redo log files

❍ d. Offline archived redo log files

Question 5

Which of the following are valid **RUN** commands? [Choose all correct answers]

❑ a. **rman> run { host "ls –l"; }**

❑ b. **rman> alter system switch logfile;**

❑ c. **rman> run { sql "alter system switch logfile"; }**

❑ d. **rman> run { execute script DailyBackup; }**

❑ e. **rman> run { sql alter system switch logfile; }**

Question 6

Which of the following functions can be accomplished using **RMAN**'s **REPORT** command?

❍ a. Display the current physical schema of the target database

❍ b. List the number of the copies of each backup set

❍ c. List obsolete data files

❍ d. List obsolete backups

Question 7

What type of **EXPORT** is appropriate when you only need database objects that have changed since the last **EXPORT** of any type?

- ❍ a. Complete
- ❍ b. Incremental
- ❍ c. Full
- ❍ d. Cumulative

Question 8

When a user reboots a PC without disconnecting from the database, what kind of failure occurs?

- ❍ a. Statement failure
- ❍ b. User process failure
- ❍ c. Media failure
- ❍ d. Instance failure

Question 9

Which of the following statements are true about loading data into a table using the **NOLOGGING** option? [Choose all correct answers]

- ❑ a. The inserts are written in the redo log files.
- ❑ b. The inserted data is fully recoverable without taking a backup subsequent to the load operation.
- ❑ c. Processing costs are reduced because the inserts are not recorded in the redo log files.
- ❑ d. The amount of recorded redo will decrease.
- ❑ e. The amount of recorded redo will increase.

Question 10

You are the DBA for a reporting database that is updated monthly. Which backup strategy should you use?

❍ a. Back up before updates are made

❍ b. Back up daily

❍ c. Back up weekly

❍ d. Back up after updates are made

Question 11

Your production database has 15 data files spread across three disk drives. How many backup sets are created by the following command sequence?

```
RMAN> RUN {
   2> ALLOCATE CHANNEL c1 TYPE 'SBT_TAPE';
   3> BACKUP
   4> (DATABASE FILESPERSET = 3);
   5> RELEASE CHANNEL c1; }
```

❍ a. None

❍ b. One

❍ c. Two

❍ d. Three

❍ e. Four

❍ f. Five

Question 12

Which of the following statements is NOT true about the large pool?

❍ a. The **LARGE_POOL_SIZE** parameter configures the size of the large pool.

❍ b. The large pool increases the speed and efficiency of backup and restore operations when using **RMAN**.

❍ c. The large pool is an area of the SGA that **RMAN** uses for buffering information in memory when IO slaves are needed.

❍ d. The large pool is a mandatory memory area.

Question 13

Which of the following would be suitable circumstances in which to operate a database in **NOARCHIVELOG** mode?

❍ a. Control files are multiplexed.

❍ b. Redo log files are multiplexed.

❍ c. The database can be shut down regularly to perform OS backups.

❍ d. You can perform online backups while the database is in use.

Question 14

What is the minimum number of redo log groups you need to configure for your Oracle database?

❍ a. One

❍ b. Two

❍ c. Three

❍ d. Four

Question 15

Which of the following statements is NOT true about the recovery catalog?

❍ a. The recovery catalog should be created in a database that is separate from the target database.

❍ b. The recovery catalog should be used when stored scripts are required.

❍ c. The recovery catalog should be used when incremental block level backups are required.

❍ d. The recovery catalog should be used when historical information about backup, restore, and recovery operations needs to be retained.

❍ e. The recovery catalog should reside in the same database as the target database.

Question 16

Which **EXPORT** mode can be used to export all objects owned by user Steve?

❍ a. Full database

❍ b. Tablespace

❍ c. Table

❍ d. User

Question 17

Which of the following initialization parameter settings will enable check summing for the online redo log files?

❍ a. **DB_BLOCK_CHECKSUM=Y**

❍ b. **DB_BLOCK_CHECKSUM=TRUE**

❍ c. **LOG_BLOCK_CHECKSUM=Y**

❍ d. **LOG_BLOCK_CHECKSUM=TRUE**

Question 18

When one of the Oracle background processes fails and the database shuts down, where are the errors recorded?

❍ a. **CORE_DUMP_DEST**

❍ b. **LOG_ARCHIVE_DEST**

❍ c. **USER_DUMP_DEST**

❍ d. **BACKGROUND_DUMP_DEST**

Question 19

Which of the following commands is used to perform an online backup of the control file?

- ❍ a. **ALTER DATABASE BACKUP CONTROLFILE TO TRACE**
- ❍ b. **ALTER SYSTEM BACKUP CONTROLFILE TO TRACE**
- ❍ c. **ALTER SYSTEM BACKUP CONTROLFILE TO <filename>**
- ❍ d. **ALTER DATABASE BACKUP CONTROLFILE TO <filename>**
- ❍ e. **ALTER SESSION BACKUP CONTROLFILE TO <filename>**

Question 20

How will your backup strategy affect recoverability?

- ❍ a. It will help you determine additional storage device needs.
- ❍ b. It determines whether complete or incomplete recovery can be performed.
- ❍ c. It will help you get management support.
- ❍ d. It will not affect recoverability.

Question 21

After you placed the tablespace **LOOKUP_DATA** in read-only mode, you took a backup of **LOOKUP_DATA**. How often do you need to perform subsequent backups?

- ❍ a. Each time a data file is added to the database.
- ❍ b. Each time the control file is changed.
- ❍ c. Each time a database backup is performed.
- ❍ d. Subsequent backups are not required.

Question 22

Which Oracle background process performs automatic instance recovery?

❍ a. **LGWR**

❍ b. **DBWR**

❍ c. **PMON**

❍ d. **SMON**

❍ e. **ARCH**

Question 23

Which two initialization parameters pertain to the duplexing of archived redo log files? [Choose two answers]

❑ a. **LOG_ARCHIVE_DUPLEX**

❑ b. **LOG_ARCHIVE_DUPLEX_DEST**

❑ c. **LOG_ARCHIVE_DEST**

❑ d. **LOG_ARCHIVE_MIN_SUCCEED_DEST**

❑ e. **LOG_ARCHIVE_START**

Question 24

Which of the following are NOT features of **RMAN**? [Choose all correct answers]

❑ a. It supports incremental block level backups.

❑ b. It is the only way to back up an Oracle database.

❑ c. It is compatible with all versions of Oracle.

❑ d. It detects corrupted blocks.

❑ e. It compresses unused blocks.

Question 25

Which command would you issue to register a new version of the database in the recovery catalog after performing incomplete recovery with the **RESETLOGS** option?

❍ a. **rman> restore database;**

❍ b. **rman> recover catalog;**

❍ c. **rman> restore catalog;**

❍ d. **rman> reset catalog;**

❍ e. **rman> reset database;**

Question 26

What is the first task performed by **IMPORT** when importing data into your database?

❍ a. Enabling database constraints

❍ b. Rebuilding indexes

❍ c. Importing data

❍ d. Creating tables

Question 27

Which file are log switches recorded to?

❍ a. alert.log

❍ b. smon.trc

❍ c. lgwr.trc

❍ d. initSID.ora

❍ e. config.ora

Question 28

The control file is lost because of media failure and you must restore it to a new location. Which steps must you perform before opening the database? [Choose all correct answers]

- ❑ a. Edit the initialization parameter file with the new location.
- ❑ b. Use the **RENAME CONTROLFILE** command to change the control file location.
- ❑ c. Restore the control file to the new location.
- ❑ d. Use the **ALTER DATABASE RENAME CONTROL FILE** command to change the control file location.

Question 29

What types of files will **RMAN** back up? [Choose three answers]

- ❑ a. Archived log files
- ❑ b. Parameter files
- ❑ c. Password files
- ❑ d. Control files
- ❑ e. Data files
- ❑ f. OS files

Question 30

Why do you need to regularly test the validity of your backup and recovery strategy?

- ❍ a. Testing helps management determine the costs associated with downtime.
- ❍ b. Testing reduces the likelihood of media failures.
- ❍ c. Testing helps to identify business, operational, and technical needs that may have changed over time.
- ❍ d. Testing is the only way to ensure optimal database configuration.

Question 31

One of the data files of tablespace **APP2_DATA** has been damaged because of media failure. What recovery should you perform?

❍ a. Tablespace recovery

❍ b. Table recovery

❍ c. Database recovery

❍ d. Import recovery

❍ e. Data file recovery

Question 32

Which of the following database events will trigger a checkpoint?

❍ a. When a user commits a transaction

❍ b. When the **SHUTDOWN ABORT** command is issued by the DBA

❍ c. When the DBA adds a new data file

❍ d. When a log switch occurs

Question 33

What command can you issue to manually archive the oldest online redo log file group that has not yet been archived?

❍ a. **ALTER SYSTEM ARCHIVE LOG SEQUENCE**

❍ b. **ALTER SYSTEM ARCHIVE LOG LOGFILE**

❍ c. **ALTER SYSTEM ARCHIVE LOG CHANGE**

❍ d. **ALTER SYSTEM ARCHIVE LOG NEXT**

Question 34

Which of the following are benefits provided by the Backup Manager? [Choose two answers]

- ❑ a. Compatibility with Enterprise Backup Utility (EBU)
- ❑ b. It is the only option to back up an Oracle database
- ❑ c. It makes it easy to create and schedule backup jobs
- ❑ d. User-friendly GUI interface
- ❑ e. It is provided as part of any client installation

Question 35

What does the following **RMAN** command accomplish?

```
RMAN> CHANGE DATAFILECOPY '/u1/oradata/
     appl1data.bak' delete;
```

- ❍ a. It marks the data file copy as unavailable.
- ❍ b. It removes the data file copy from the control file and the recovery catalog.
- ❍ c. It removes the data file copy from the control file, recovery catalog, and from the physical media.
- ❍ d. It marks the data file copy as available.

Question 36

When you import data into an existing table, what parameter needs to be set to direct **IMPORT** to continue processing if create errors are encountered?

- ❍ a. **CONSISTENT=Y**
- ❍ b. **INDEXES=Y**
- ❍ c. **IGNORE=Y**
- ❍ d. **LOG=Y**

Question 37

What utility enables the DBA to check for data corruption in both online and offline data files?

❍ a. **DBVERIFY**

❍ b. **ANALYZE**

❍ c. **EXPORT**

❍ d. **TKPROF**

Question 38

Which of the following **SHUTDOWN** commands should you use before taking a closed (offline) database backup? [Choose all correct answers]

❑ a. **SHUTDOWN NORMAL**

❑ b. **SHUTDOWN IMMEDIATE**

❑ c. **SHUTDOWN TRANSACTIONAL**

❑ d. **SHUTDOWN ABORT**

Question 39

What will the following command sequence accomplish?

```
RMAN> RUN {
    2> ALLOCATE CHANNEL c1 TYPE DISK;
    3> COPY LEVEL 0
    4> DATAFILE 1 TO '/u1/oradata/backup/app1.ora',
    5> DATAFILE 2 TO '/u1/oradata/backup/app2.ora';
    6> RELEASE CHANNEL c1; }
```

❍ a. It will create an image copy backup that can be used in an incremental backup strategy.

❍ b. It will create an image copy backup of the OS blocks since the last full backup.

❍ c. It will create an OS file copy of two data files.

❍ d. It will create an OS file copy of two backup sets.

Question 40

How will minimizing recovery time benefit the business?

❍ a. It helps to prevent failures from occurring.

❍ b. It reduces the amount of data loss.

❍ c. It reduces the cost of downtime.

❍ d. It reduces the need to regularly update the backup and recovery strategy.

Question 41

Your production database is running in **ARCHIVELOG** mode. Due to a media failure, you need to recover the database and you have a lot of archived redo log files. What command should you issue to direct Oracle to automatically apply the archived redo log files when the recovery process is initiated?

❍ a. **RECOVER DATAFILE**

❍ b. **SET AUTORECOVERY ON**

❍ c. **ALTER DATABASE CLEAR LOGFILE**

❍ d. **ALTER SYSTEM ACTIVE LOGFILE**

Question 42

What takes place when a checkpoint occurs? [Choose two answers]

❑ a. **SMON** coalesces contiguous free extents into larger free chunks.

❑ b. **DBWR** writes all modified data blocks in the database buffer cache to disk.

❑ c. **PMON** frees resources held by failed user processes.

❑ d. **LGWR** writes all modified data blocks in the database buffer cache to disk.

❑ e. **LGWR** writes the redo log entries from the redo log buffer to the online redo log files.

Question 43

You need to perform an incomplete recovery because you've discovered that an archived redo log file is missing. After you've performed incomplete recovery, which of the following statements is true?

❍ a. Committed transactions will be lost prior to the point of recovery.

❍ b. All uncommitted transactions prior to the point of the failure will be committed.

❍ c. All transactions after the point of recovery will be lost.

❍ d. Committed transactions after the point of failure will be recovered when the applicable redo log files are applied.

Question 44

What does the following command accomplish?

```
$rman target scott/pwd@PROD1 rcvcat rman/pwd
```

❍ a. It connects user **SCOTT** to the local **PROD1** database and uses a local recovery catalog.

❍ b. It connects user **SCOTT** to the remote **PROD1** database and uses a remote recovery catalog.

❍ c. It connects user **SCOTT** to the remote **PROD1** database and uses a local recovery catalog.

❍ d. It connects user **SCOTT** to the local **PROD1** database and uses a remote recovery catalog.

❍ e. It connects user **RMAN** to the remote **PROD1** database and uses a local recovery catalog.

Question 45

Which of the following information is contained in the **RC_DATABASE** view?

❍ a. The names of the tablespaces for the databases registered in the recovery catalog.

❍ b. The names of the databases that are registered in the recovery catalog.

❍ c. The names of the users that have read access to the recovery catalog.

❍ d. The names of the stored scripts in the recovery catalog.

❍ e. The names of the data files for the databases registered in the recovery catalog.

Question 46

What **EXPORT** parameter should you set when exporting data while users are performing updates to the database?

❍ a. **IGNORE=Y**

❍ b. **CONSTRAINTS=Y**

❍ c. **DIRECT=Y**

❍ d. **CONSISTENT=Y**

Question 47

When a user enters bad data into a database table that violates integrity constraints, which type of failure is this?

❍ a. Statement failure

❍ b. User process failure

❍ c. Instance failure

❍ d. Media failure

Question 48

What events will occur after you issue the following command?

```
SVRMGR> ALTER TABLESPACE SALES_DATA BEGIN BACKUP;
```

❍ a. Data file header blocks for the **SALES_DATA** tablespace will be updated.

❍ b. An offline backup begins.

❍ c. An online backup ends.

❍ d. Transactions occurring within the **SALES_DATA** tablespace will not be recorded in the redo logs.

❍ e. Data file header blocks for the **SALES_DATA** tablespace are frozen to prevent updates.

Question 49

What will the following command sequence accomplish?

```
RMAN> RUN {
   2> ALLOCATE CHANNEL c1 TYPE DISK;
   3> ALLOCATE CHANNEL c2 TYPE DISK;
   4> COPY
   5> DATAFILE 1 TO '/u1/oradata/backup/app1.ora',
   6> DATAFILE 2 TO '/u1/oradata/backup/app2.ora';
   7> }
```

❍ a. An incremental backup will be performed.

❍ b. Two files will be copied in parallel.

❍ c. A level 2 backup will be performed.

❍ d. One channel will be idle.

Question 50

Which **V$** view is used to query for the names of all data files in the database?

❍ a. **V$CONTROLFILE**

❍ b. **V$DATABASE**

❍ c. **V$DATAFILE**

❍ d. **V$DATABASE_FILE**

❍ e. **V$DATA_FILE**

Question 51

Which of the following circumstances does not require the DBA to perform an incomplete recovery? [Choose two answers]

❑ a. Loss of all control files, including corresponding mirrors.

❑ b. An archived redo log file needed for complete recovery is damaged.

❑ c. A user mistakenly drops an essential application table.

❑ d. The archived redo log directory runs out of space.

❑ e. A media failure occurs in an **ARCHIVELOG** database and no data loss is tolerated.

Question 52

By default, which archive mode is in effect for an Oracle database?

❍ a. **ARCHIVELOG** mode with automatic archiving

❍ b. **NOARCHIVELOG** mode

❍ c. **ARCHIVELOG** mode with manual archiving

❍ d. None of the above

Question 53

The disk in which the **RBS_TS** tablespace resides failed in a **NOARCHIVELOG** database. To what point in time can you recover the database?

❍ a. Last redo log

❍ b. Last export

❍ c. Last full backup

❍ d. Point of failure

Question 54

Which **RMAN** commands will cause an automatic resync of the recovery catalog with its target database? [Choose all correct answers]

❑ a. **BACKUP**

❑ b. **COPY**

❑ c. **RESTORE**

❑ d. **SWITCH**

❑ e. **RESET DATABASE**

Question 55

What does the following command accomplish?

```
Rman> list backupset of datafile '/u1/oradata/
     app01.ora';
```

❍ a. It adds **app01.ora** to the current backup set.

❍ b. It displays the status of the copy of **app01.ora**.

❍ c. It displays all backup sets that contains **app01.ora**.

❍ d. It displays all data files in the same backup set as **app01.ora**.

Question 56

What command is required for **RMAN** to read from or write to the OS?

❍ a. **CHANGE**

❍ b. **CATALOG**

❍ c. **COPY**

❍ d. **BACKUP**

❍ e. **ALLOCATE CHANNEL**

Question 57

Which of the following commands can you use to create the script file for creating a new control file?

❍ a. **ALTER SYSTEM**

❍ b. **ALTER INSTANCE**

❍ c. **ALTER DATABASE**

❍ d. **ALTER SESSION**

❍ e. **ALTER CONTROL FILE**

Question 58

What database components can you recover using the **RECOVER** command with the **PARALLEL** keyword? [Choose all correct answers]

❑ a. Database

❑ b. Data files

❑ c. Tablespaces

❑ d. Tables

❑ e. Control file

❑ f. Redo log file

❑ g. Rollback segments

Question 59

In an Oracle8 instance failure recovery, when are uncommitted transactions rolled back?

- ❍ a. Before the roll-forward is completed
- ❍ b. After the roll-forward is completed
- ❍ c. As soon as the database starts
- ❍ d. When the data blocks associated with the uncommitted transactions are subsequently requested

Question 60

What **V$** view is used to query for processes still connected to the instance before you perform a shutdown?

- ❍ a. **V$SGA**
- ❍ b. **V$INSTANCE**
- ❍ c. **V$DATABASE**
- ❍ d. **V$PROCESS**

16

Answer Key

1. a, b, c
2. b
3. c
4. c
5. a, c, d
6. d
7. b
8. b
9. c, d
10. d
11. f
12. d
13. c
14. b
15. e
16. d
17. d
18. d
19. d
20. b
21. d
22. d
23. b, d
24. b, c
25. e
26. d
27. a
28. a, c
29. a, d, e
30. c
31. e
32. d
33. d
34. c, d
35. c
36. c
37. a
38. a, b, c
39. a
40. c
41. b
42. b, e
43. c
44. c
45. b
46. d
47. a
48. e
49. b
50. c
51. d, e
52. b
53. c
54. a, b, c, d
55. c
56. e
57. c
58. a, b, c
59. d
60. d

This is the answer key to the sample test presented in Chapter 15.

Question 1

The correct answers are a, b, and c. In creating and executing a backup and recovery strategy, database administrators (DBAs) are responsible for providing recommendations to management on how to minimize downtime, minimize data loss, and carry out the strategy. Answer d is incorrect, because providing necessary corporate resources and support for implementation is management's role.

Question 2

The correct answer is b. The **LOG_CHECKPOINT_INTERVAL** initialization parameter specifies the number of OS blocks written to the redo logs before a checkpoint is initiated. Recovery from instance failure starts from the latest checkpoint in the current online redo log file. Answer a is incorrect, because the **LOG_CHECKPOINT_TIMEOUT** initialization parameter specifies the number of seconds passed after the last checkpoint before a new checkpoint is initiated. Answer c is incorrect, because the **LOG_BUFFER** initialization parameter specifies the size of the redo log buffers in bytes. Answer d is incorrect, because it is an invalid initialization parameter.

Question 3

The correct answer is c. The **ARCHIVE LOG LIST** command shows the database log mode, the archive destination, the oldest online log sequence, the next log sequence to archive, the current log sequence, and whether automatic archiving is in effect. Answers a, b, and e are incorrect, because they don't provide information about the current database log mode. Answer d is incorrect, because it is an invalid command specification.

Question 4

The correct answer is c. The online redo log files record current changes made to the database during normal use. Answer a is incorrect, because the control file stores the names and the status of all the data files. Answer b is incorrect, because data files contain the actual business data. Answer d is incorrect, because they contain earlier database changes.

Question 5

The correct answers are a, c, and d. The **RUN** command enables you to execute OS commands, SQL statements, stored scripts, backup commands, and so on. Answers b and e are incorrect, because they are invalid commands.

Question 6

The correct answer is d. The **REPORT** command can be used to list backups that are obsolete. Answers a, b, and c are incorrect, because the **REPORT** command doesn't perform these functions.

Question 7

The correct answer is b. An incremental export will export only the database objects that have changed since the last export of any type. Answer a is incorrect, because a complete export contains all database objects except those owned by the SYS schema. Answer c is incorrect, because it is an invalid export type. Answer d is incorrect, because a cumulative export contains database tables that have changed since the last cumulative or complete export.

Question 8

The correct answer is b. User process failure occurs when a user process that is connected to the Oracle instance terminates abnormally. The sample scenario is an example of an abnormal termination of a user process. Answers a, c, and d are incorrect, because the sample scenario doesn't cause these errors.

Question 9

The correct answers are c and d. When loading data using the direct load operation with the **NOLOGGING** option, the inserts are not recorded in the redo log files. The data should be backed up after the load to ensure the data is fully recoverable. The direct load operation reduces processing costs, because the inserts are not recorded in the redo log files. Answer a is incorrect, because the inserts are not written in the redo log files for direct load operations. Answer b is incorrect, because you need to take a backup after the direct load operation to ensure the data is fully recoverable. Answer e is incorrect, because the amount of recorded redo decreases, not increases, for direct load operations.

Question 10

The correct answer is d. The backup schedule should match the frequency of data updates. Answer a is incorrect, because for this sample scenario you should take a backup after the data has been changed. Answers b and c are incorrect, because more frequent backups of static data are not necessary.

Question 11

The correct answer is f. The **FILESPERSET** option of the **BACKUP** command specifies the number of files included in each backup set. For the sample command, five backup sets with three files in each backup set will be created. Answers a, b, c, d, and e are incorrect, because they don't match the five backup sets the sample command will create.

Question 12

The correct answer is d. The large pool is an optional, not mandatory, Oracle8 memory area. Answers a, b, and c are incorrect, because they are true statements about the large pool.

Question 13

The correct answer is c. If you can regularly shut down a database for backups, then you could consider operating the database in **NOARCHIVELOG** mode if any lost data can be tolerated. Answers a and b are incorrect, because these files should be multiplexed independent of the database log mode. Answer d is incorrect, because **ARCHIVELOG** mode enables you to perform online backups while the database is open and in use.

Question 14

The correct answer is b. The **LGWR** process writes redo log files in a circular fashion, so two redo log groups are required to support this operation. By default, Oracle creates two redo log groups. Answers a, b, and d are incorrect, because they don't match the default number of two.

Question 15

The correct answer is e. The recovery catalog should reside in a database that is separate from the target database. Answers a, b, c, and d are incorrect, because they are true statements about the recovery catalog.

Question 16

The correct answer is d. The **EXPORT** user mode will export all the objects in a user's schema. Users can back up their own schema. A privileged user such as the DBA can export all objects owned by one or more schemas. Answer a is incorrect, because it will export all database objects except those owned by the SYS schema. Answer b is incorrect, because it is an invalid export mode. Answer c is incorrect, because it will only export specified tables owned by the user schema.

Question 17

The correct answer is d. When the **LOG_BLOCK_CHECKSUM** parameter is set to **TRUE**, check summing for the online redo log files will be enabled. Answers a and c are incorrect, because they are invalid parameter specifications. Answer b is incorrect, because **DB_BLOCK_CHECKSUM** parameter applies to check summing of data files.

Question 18

The correct answer is d. When Oracle background processes encounter errors, they will write the error trace files to the location specified by the initialization parameter **BACKGROUND_DUMP_DEST**. Answers a, b, and c are incorrect, because the background processes don't write error trace files to these locations.

Question 19

The correct answer is d. The **ALTER DATABASE BACKUP CONTROLFILE TO <filename>** command is used to take an online backup of the control file. Answer a is incorrect, because it only creates a text script trace file that may subsequently be modified and executed to create the binary control file. Answers b, c, and e are incorrect, because they are invalid command specifications.

Question 20

The correct answer is b. Your backup strategy determines the type of recovery that can be performed. Answers a and c are incorrect, because they don't affect recoverability. Answer d is incorrect, because your backup strategy does affect recoverability.

Question 21

The correct answer is d. The data in a read-only tablespace is static. You only need to back up the **LOOKUP_DATA** tablespace immediately after it becomes read-only. Answers a, b, and c are incorrect, because read-only tablespaces don't need to be backed up under these circumstances.

Question 22

The correct answer is d. The **SMON** process performs instance recovery and free space coalescing. Answers a, b, c, and e are incorrect, because these processes perform other functions.

Question 23

The correct answers are b and d. The **LOG_ARCHIVE_DUPLEX_DEST** parameter specifies the location where copies of the archived log files will be stored. The **LOG_ARCHIVE_MIN_SUCCEED_DEST** parameter specifies the number of archived redo log destinations to which the online redo log files must be successfully written. Answer a is incorrect, because it is an invalid command. Answer c is incorrect, because it specifies the primary archive log destination. Answer e is incorrect, because **LOG_ARCHIVE_START** specifies whether automatic archiving is enabled.

Question 24

The correct answers are b and c. Recovery manager (**RMAN**) is not the only way to back up an Oracle database, because you could choose to use OS mechanisms. **RMAN** does not support backing up pre-Oracle8 databases. Answers a, d, and e are incorrect, because these are **RMAN** features.

Question 25

The correct answer is e. You should issue the **RESET DATABASE** command after you've performed an incomplete recovery and opened the database with the **RESETLOGS** option, so the new version of the database is registered in the recovery catalog. Answers a, b, c, and d are incorrect, because they are invalid commands.

Question 26

The correct answer is d. **IMPORT** performs the following steps when data is imported: It (1) creates the tables, (2) builds the indexes, (3) imports the data, (4) imports the database triggers, and (5) enables the integrity constraints. Answers a, b, and c are incorrect, because they are not the first tasks performed by **IMPORT** when importing data into your database.

Question 27

The correct answer is a. Log switches are recorded in the *alert.log* file. Answers b, c, d, and e are incorrect, because log switches are not recorded in these files.

Question 28

The correct answers are a and c. When your control file is lost due to a media failure, you must restore the control file to the new location and edit the initialization parameter with the new location before opening the database. Answers b and d are incorrect, because they are invalid commands.

Question 29

The correct answers are a, d, and e. **RMAN** will back up data files, control files, and archived redo log files. It will create an image copy or a backup set of either data files or archived redo log files. Answers b, c, and f are incorrect, because **RMAN** will not back up these file types.

Question 30

The correct answer is c. Testing helps to assess the effectiveness of the backup and recovery strategy and to identify any new or changed requirements. Answer a is incorrect, because the costs associated with downtime depends on business, operational, and technical factors and not testing. Answer b is incorrect, because testing does not affect the likelihood of media failures. Answer d is incorrect, because testing is not the only way to ensure optimal database configuration.

Question 31

The correct answer is e. Because only one data file in a tablespace is damaged, you only need to recover the one damaged file. Answers a, b, c, and e are incorrect, because these types of recovery are not appropriate for the sample scenario.

Question 32

The correct answer is d. Checkpoints occur during log switches. Answers a, b, and c are incorrect, because they don't trigger a checkpoint.

Question 33

The correct answer is d. The **NEXT** option of the **ALTER SYSTEM ARCHIVE LOG** command archives the oldest redo log file group that has not yet been archived. Answer a is incorrect, because the **SEQUENCE** option pertains to the Oracle Parallel Server and specifies the thread associated with the redo log group to be archived. Answer b is incorrect, because the **LOGFILE** option specifies the file name of the redo log group member to be archived. Answer c is incorrect, because the **CHANGE** option specifies archiving based on the System Change Number (SCN).

Question 34

The correct answers are c and d. The Backup Manager is a GUI tool within the OEM administrative toolset that can be used to easily create and schedule backup jobs. Answer a is incorrect, because the Backup Manager is not compatible with EBU. Answer b is incorrect, because using the Backup Manager is not the only way to back up an Oracle database. Answer e is incorrect, because the Backup Manager is not provided as part of any client installation.

Question 35

The correct answer is c. The **CHANGE DATAFILECOPY DELETE** command removes specified files from the control file, recovery catalog, and from the physical media. Answers a and d are incorrect, because the **CHANGE... AVAILABLE** and the **CHANGE...UNAVAILABLE** commands mark files as available or unavailable. Answer b is incorrect, because the removal of the data file copy from the physical media has been omitted.

Question 36

The correct answer is c. The **IGNORE** parameter will ignore any create errors encountered during the **IMPORT** process. Answers a and b are incorrect, because these parameters serve other purposes. Answer d is incorrect, because it is an invalid parameter specification.

Question 37

The correct answer is a. The **DBVERIFY** utility is used to verify the structural integrity of data blocks in the online and offline data files. Answer b is incorrect, because **ANALYZE** computes statistics for tables and indexes. Answer c is incorrect, because **EXPORT** is used to perform logical backups of the database. Answer d is incorrect, because **TKPROF** is used for SQL tuning and optimization.

Question 38

The correct answers are a, b, and c. A closed (offline) database backup is an OS backup of the database files that is made after the database has been shut down cleanly using either **SHUTDOWN NORMAL**, **SHUTDOWN IMMEDIATE**, or **SHUTDOWN TRANSACTIONAL**. Answer d is incorrect, because closed database backups performed after a **SHUTDOWN ABORT** are not reliable.

Question 39

The correct answer is a. The sample command sequence allocates the **c1** channel of type disk and copies two data files at level 0. The level 0 copies can be used in an incremental backup strategy. Answer b is incorrect, because the sample command sequence doesn't perform this function. Answers c and d are incorrect, because the sample command sequence doesn't create OS file copies.

Question 40

The correct answer is c. A reduction in recovery time will shorten total downtime and reduce the costs associated with downtime. Answer a is incorrect, because appropriate database configuration prevents failures from occurring. Answer b is incorrect, because the amount of data loss depends on the availability of valid backups. Answer d is incorrect, because minimizing recovery time does not affect the frequency of updates to the backup and recovery strategy.

Question 41

The correct answer is b. Automatic recovery can be enabled using the **SET AUTORECOVERY ON** command. The redo log files must be in the location specified by the **LOG_ARCHIVE_DEST** initialization parameter. You will be prompted for the redo log file names if automatic recovery is not enabled. Answer a is incorrect, because automatic recovery has not been specified via the **AUTOMATIC** keyword of the **RECOVER DATAFILE** command. Answer c is incorrect, because it performs another function. Answer d is incorrect, because it is an invalid command specification.

Question 42

The correct answers are b and e. During a checkpoint event, the **DBWR** process writes all modified data blocks in the database buffer cache of the SGA to the database files, and the **LGWR** process writes all redo log entries in the log buffer to disk. Answers a and c are incorrect, because they are triggered independent of a checkpoint. Answer d is incorrect, because the **LGWR** process writes the redo log entries from the redo log buffer to the online redo log files.

Question 43

The correct answer is c. When you perform an incomplete recovery for an **ARCHIVELOG** database, all the changes made to the data after the point of failure are lost. To recover the lost data, users must manually re-enter the data. Answer a is incorrect, because no committed transactions are lost prior to the point of recovery. Answer b is incorrect, because uncommitted transactions prior to the point of failure will not be committed. Answer d is incorrect, because the archived redo log files after the point of failure are not usable and therefore the committed transactions after the point of failure will be lost.

Question 44

The correct answer is c. The sample command connects user **SCOTT** to the remote **PROD1** database and uses a local recovery catalog. Answers a and d are incorrect, because the sample command connects user **SCOTT** to the remote, not local, **PROD1** database. Answer b is incorrect, because the sample command uses a local, not remote, recovery catalog. Answer e is incorrect, because the sample command connects user **SCOTT**, not user **RMAN**, to the remote **PROD1** database.

Question 45

The correct answer is b. The **RC_DATABASE** view provides the names of the target databases that are registered in the recovery catalog. Answers a, c, d, and e are incorrect, because the **RC_DATABASE** view doesn't provide this information.

Question 46

The correct answer is d. Setting the **CONSISTENT** parameter to **Y** when exporting data from an online database will ensure that the exported data is read-consistent. Answers a, b, and c are incorrect, because these parameters serve other functions.

Question 47

The correct answer is a. Statement failure occurs when a SQL statement fails, such as when a user enters bad data that violates integrity constraints into the database table. Oracle automatically handles these errors. Answers b, c, and d are incorrect, because the sample scenario doesn't cause these failures.

Question 48

The correct answer is e. When a tablespace is placed in backup mode using the **ALTER TABLESPACE BEGIN BACKUP** command, no changes can be made to the data file header blocks associated with the tablespace. Answers a, b, and c are incorrect, because these events don't occur while a tablespace is in backup mode. Answer d is incorrect, because it is a bogus database event.

Question 49

The correct answer is b. The sample command sequence creates two disk channels. The **COPY** command will use the two channels to simultaneously copy the two data files. Answer a is incorrect, because the sample command sequence performs an **RMAN** full backup. Answer c is incorrect, because the sample command sequence does not perform an incremental backup. Answer d is incorrect, because both allocated channels will be used at the same time to copy the two data files.

Question 50

The correct answer is c. The **V$DATAFILE** view provides the names and locations of the data files that comprise the database. Answers a and c are incorrect, because these views don't provide the names of data files for the database. Answers d and e are incorrect, because they are invalid views.

Question 51

The correct answers are d and e. When the archive redo log directory runs out of space, the DBA only needs to free up space for additional redo log files. When a media failure occurs in an **ARCHIVELOG** database and no data loss is tolerated, then complete recovery needs to be performed. Answers a, b, and c are incorrect, because they require the DBA to perform incomplete recovery.

Question 52

The correct answer is b. By default, an Oracle database operates in **NOARCHIVELOG** mode. Answers a, c, and d are incorrect, because they are not the default database mode.

Question 53

The correct answer is c. For a nonarchiving database, you can only restore the database to the last full backup when a failure occurs. Data loss may result, because redo log files are overwritten. Answers a and d are incorrect, because they pertain to archiving databases. Answer b is incorrect, because exports provide logical backups that supplement physical backups.

Question 54

The correct answers are a, b, c, and d. The **BACKUP**, **COPY**, **RESTORE**, and **SWITCH** commands will cause **RMAN** to perform an automatic resynchronization of the recovery catalog with its target database. Answer e is incorrect, because the **RESET DATABASE** command creates database incarnation information in the recovery catalog but does not perform the automatic resynchronization operation.

Question 55

The correct answer is c. The **LIST BACKUPSET** command will display all the backups that contain the specified data file, tablespace, or all the archived log files. Answers a, b, and d are incorrect, because the given command doesn't perform these functions.

Question 56

The correct answer is e. The **ALLOCATE CHANNEL** command must be issued for **RMAN** to read from or write to the OS. Answers a and b are incorrect, because these commands are not required for **RMAN** to read from or write to the OS. Answers c and d are incorrect, because these commands are dependent on the **ALLOCATE CHANNEL** command to read from or write to the OS.

Question 57

The correct answer is c. The **ALTER DATABASE BACKUP CONTROL FILE TO TRACE** command outputs a trace script file that can be used to start the database, re-create the control file, and recover and open the database. Answers a and d are incorrect, because these commands don't generate the trace script file to create a new control file. Answers b and e are incorrect, because they are invalid commands.

Question 58

The correct answers are a, b, and c. Parallel recovery operations can be performed at the database, tablespace, and data file levels. Answer d is incorrect, because tables can be restored only from an **EXPORT** file. Answers e, f, and g are incorrect, because these are not valid levels for parallel recovery operations.

Question 59

The correct answer is d. Uncommitted transactions are rolled back when the data blocks associated with the uncommitted transactions are subsequently requested. Answers a, b, and c are incorrect, because rollback activities don't take place at these times.

Question 60

The correct answer is d. The **V$PROCESS** view provides information on the background and server processes for the instance. Answers a, b, and c are incorrect, because these views don't provide information on the current processes for the instance.

Glossary

ALLOCATE CHANNEL command—A Recovery Manager (RMAN) command that establishes a connection between RMAN and a target database instance. Each connection initiates an Oracle server session on the target database instance that performs the work of backing up, restoring, and recovering backup sets and copies. When multiple connections are established, each connection operates on a separate backup set or file copy.

ALTER DATABASE CLEAR UNARCHIVED LOGFILE command—An SQL command that reinitializes an online redo log without archiving the redo log. This command makes backups unusable if the redo log is needed for recovery.

ALTER DATABASE RECOVER command—An SQL command that is used to perform media recovery for the database, specified tablespaces, or specified data files.

ALTER DATABASE RENAME FILE command—A command that renames data files or redo log files. It renames only files in the control file. It does not rename them on the operating system file system. The file name must be specified using the OS file naming conventions.

ARCH background process—This is an optional background process that copies the online redo log files to a designated archival destination.

archived redo log—A copy of one of the filled members of an online redo log group made when the database is in ARCHIVELOG mode. As each online redo log is filled and before it is overwritten, Oracle copies the log to one or more archival destinations.

ARCHIVELOG mode—The mode of the database in which Oracle copies filled online redo logs to disk. This mode can be set at database creation or by using the **ALTER DATABASE** command.

automatic archiving—The process of automatically performing online redo log group archiving via the **ARCH** background process. You can enable automatic archiving either using the **ALTER SYSTEM** command or by setting the initialization parameter **LOG_ARCHIVE_START** to **TRUE**.

availability—The accessibility of the database for normal business use.

background processes—Noninteractive processes that run in an operating system environment and perform some service or task. The Oracle server uses these processes to consolidate distinct functions of the server that would otherwise be handled by multiple Oracle programs running for each connected client application. The background processes send and receive information to and from the System Global Area (SGA). They asynchronously perform functions such as database writes, monitor other Oracle processes, perform and coordinate tasks on behalf of concurrent users of the database, and provide better database performance and reliability. Oracle has five essential background processes: **SMON**, **DBWR**, **LGWR**, **PMON**, and **CKPT**.

backup—The process of making copies of files on another storage device so that they can be restored if the computer loses that information.

BACKUP command—An **RMAN** command that creates one or more backup sets that contain one or more physical backup pieces.

Backup Manager—One of the DBA tools within the Oracle Enterprise Manager (OEM) administrative toolset. It provides a GUI interface that enables DBAs to manage their database backup and recovery environment.

backup piece—Backup pieces are OS files that contain the backed up data files, control files, or archived redo logs. A backup piece is a physical file in an **RMAN**-specific format that belongs to only one backup set. A backup set usually contains only one backup piece.

backup set—An **RMAN**-specific logical grouping of one or more backup pieces that make up a full or incremental backup of the objects specified in the **BACKUP** command. There are two types of backup sets: *data file backup sets* and *archivelog backup sets*. Data file backup sets are backups of any data files or a control file. This type of backup set is compressed, which means that it contains only data file blocks that have been used; unused blocks are not included. Archivelog backup sets are backups of the archived redo logs.

cancel-based recovery—An incomplete recovery type that enables the DBA to terminate the recovery process at a desired point in time in the past by entering **CANCEL** at the recovery prompt.

CATALOG command—An **RMAN** command that enables you to add information about an OS data file copy, archived redo log copy, or control file copy to the recovery catalog and control file. Specifically, it enables you to perform the following: (1) Catalog a data file copy as a level 0 backup that facilitates performing a subsequent incremental backup, (2) Record Oracle8 database backups created before **RMAN** was installed, and (3) Record Oracle7 backups of read-only or offline normal files made before migrating to Oracle 8.

CHANGE command—An **RMAN** command that is used to set the status of a backup or copy as unavailable or available, delete a backup or copy from the OS and update its status to deleted, and check whether backups, image copies, and archived redo logs are available and, if they are not, mark them as expired.

change-based recovery—An incomplete recovery type that enables the DBA to terminate the recovery process at a desired point in time in the past after the database has committed all changes up to the specified System Change Number (SCN).

channel—A connection between Recovery Manager (**RMAN**) and the target database. Each allocated channel starts a new Oracle server session; the session then performs backup, restore, and recovery operations. The type of channel determines whether the Oracle server process will attempt to read or write and whether it will work through a third-party media manager. If the channel is of type **disk**, the server process attempts to read backups from or write backups to disk. If the channel is of type **sbt_tape**, the server process attempts to read backups from or write backups to a third-party media manager.

checkpoint—A pointer indicating that all changes prior to the System Change Number (SCN) specified by a redo record have been written to the data files by **DBWR**. Each redo record in the redo log describes a change or a set of atomic changes to database blocks. A checkpoint for a redo entry confirms that the changes described in previous redo entries have been written to disk, not just to memory buffers.

closed (offline) database backup—A backup of one or more database files taken while the database is closed. Typically, closed backups are also known as whole database backups. If you closed the database cleanly, then all the files in the backup are consistent. If you shut down the database using a **SHUTDOWN ABORT** or the instance terminated abnormally, then the backups are inconsistent.

complete export—A type of export that can be performed with **EXPORT** in the full database mode. It is equivalent to a full database export with the additional updates performed against the tables that track incremental and cumulative exports.

complete recovery—The process in which a database is restored and recovered through the application of all redo information generated (in the online and archived redo log files) since the last available backup.

CONTROL_FILE_RECORD_KEEP_TIME—The *initSID.ora* parameter that specifies the number of days the **RMAN** information is stored in the control file before being overwritten.

COPY command—An **RMAN** command that creates an image copy of a file. The following types of files can be copied: data files (current or copies), archived redo logs, and control files (current or copies).

CREATE CONTROLFILE command—An SQL command used to re-create a control file under the following circumstances: (1) when all copies of your existing control files have been lost through media failure, (2) when you want to change the name of the database, and (3) when you want to change the maximum number of redo log file groups, redo log file members, archived redo log files, data files, or instances that can concurrently have the database mounted and open.

cumulative export—A type of export that contains database tables that have changed since the last cumulative or complete export. It essentially combines several incremental exports into a single cumulative export file.

data file copy—A copy of a data file on disk created by the **RMAN COPY** command or an OS utility.

database administrator (DBA)—A person responsible for the operation and maintenance of an Oracle server or a database application. The database administrator monitors its use to customize it to meet the needs of the business users of an organization.

database buffers—The memory buffers in the SGA of an instance that hold the most recently used data blocks that are read from the database files.

Direct Path export—One of the two paths used by **EXPORT** to extract data from an Oracle database. In Direct Path **EXPORT**, the data is extracted from the Oracle data files and passed directly to the **EXPORT** client for processing, bypassing the buffer cache and the SQL-command processing layer.

disaster—Any event that creates an inability on an organization's part to provide critical business functions for some predetermined period of time. A disaster could be one of the following representative incidents: natural disasters (flood, fire, earthquake, and so on), blackouts, hardware failure, viruses, theft, and key personnel departure.

disaster recovery plan—The document that defines the resources, actions, tasks, and data required to manage the business recovery process in the event of a business interruption. The plan is designed to assist in restoring the business process following a catastrophic event by minimizing risk and optimizing recovery time.

downtime—Period of time during which a database is unavailable for normal business processing.

dynamic performance views—A set of performance views maintained by the Oracle server. These views are continuously updated while a database is open and in use. By default, these views are available only to the user **SYS** and to users granted **SELECT ANY TABLE** system privilege or the **SELECT_CATALOG_ROLE** role.

EXPORT utility—An Oracle-provided utility that enables DBAs to perform logical backups of the database. A *logical backup* involves making a copy of the logical database structures with or without the associated business data.

fast warmstart—An Oracle database feature first introduced in Oracle 7.3 that allows for a fast instance recovery, meaning that the database can be opened as soon as cache recovery is complete. In other words, the database is available at the end of the roll-forward phase of instance recovery and the bulk of the rollback activities are deferred to the individual user processes when blocks are subsequently requested.

full backup—An **RMAN** backup that is not incremental.

full database mode export—An **EXPORT** of the whole database.

full database mode import—An **IMPORT** of the whole database.

image copy—A copy of a single data file, archived redo log file, or control file that is usable for subsequent recovery operations. It is created by the **RMAN COPY** command or an OS utility such as the Unix dd.

IMPORT utility—An Oracle-provided utility that is typically used for the recovery of database objects and business data using a valid dump file created by the **EXPORT** utility.

incarnation—A separate version of a physical database as used by **RMAN**. The incarnation of the database changes when you open it with the **RESETLOGS** option. The **RMAN RESET DATABASE** command issued after opening in **RESETLOGS** mode will create a new incarnation of the database.

incomplete recovery—The process in which a database is restored and recovered through the application of some of the redo information generated since the last available backup.

incremental backup—An **RMAN** backup in which only modified blocks are backed up. Incremental backups are classified by level. An incremental level 0 backup is equivalent to a full backup in that they both back up all blocks that have ever been used. The difference is that a full backup will not affect blocks backed up by subsequent incremental backups, whereas an incremental backup will affect blocks backed up by subsequent incremental backups.

incremental export—A type of export that contains database tables that have changed since the last incremental, cumulative, or complete **EXPORT**.

initialization parameter file—A file that contains information to initialize the database and instance.

instance failure—The failure that occurs when a problem arises that prevents a database instance from continuing to work. Instance failure can result from a hardware or a software problem.

instance recovery—The recovery of an instance in the event of software or hardware failure, so that the database is again available to users. If the instance terminates abnormally, then instance recovery automatically occurs at the next instance startup.

large pool—An optional Oracle8 memory area. It is used to allocate sequential I/O buffers from shared memory. **RMAN** uses the large pool for performing backup and restore operations. This pool does not have an LRU (least recently used) list.

LIST command—An **RMAN** command that enables you to produce a detailed listing of specified backups or image copies recorded in the recovery catalog or target control file.

log switch—The point at which **LGWR** stops writing to the active redo log file and switches to the next available redo log file. This happens when either the active redo log file is completely filled or a manual switch has been requested by the operator.

LOGGING mode—The default mode that enables full redo or undo data logging for instance and media recovery. In this mode, full recovery is supported from the most recent backup.

logical backup—Backups in which the **EXPORT** utility uses SQL to read database data and then write it into an Oracle-proprietary binary file. Logical backups are typically used to move data into different Oracle databases on possibly different platforms.

manual archiving—The manual process of archiving redo log files using the **ALTER SYSTEM ARCHIVE LOG** command.

media failure—The failure that occurs when the storage device for Oracle files is damaged. This usually prevents Oracle from reading or writing data.

multiplexed archived redo log file—The automated process of maintaining more than one identical copy of a redo log. The *initSID.ora* parameters **LOG_ARCHIVE_DUPLEX_DEST** and **LOG_ARCHIVE_MIN_SUCCEED_DEST** determine whether multiple archived copies of a redo log file are desired.

multiplexed control file—The automated process of maintaining more than one identical copy of a database's control file. You can create multiple entries in the **CONTROL_FILES** initialization parameter to multiplex the control file.

NOARCHIVELOG mode—The mode of the database in which Oracle does not require filled online redo logs to be archived to disk. You can specify the mode at database creation or change it by using the **ALTER DATABASE** command.

NOLOGGING mode—The database mode in which full redo or undo data logging are not performed. Some minimal logging is performed for data dictionary changes and new extent invalidations.

offline backup—An OS backup of the database files that is made after the database has been shut down cleanly.

online backup—A physical file backup of the database made while the database is open and running in **ARCHIVELOG** mode.

online redo log—A set of two or more files that record all changes made to Oracle data files and control files. Oracle generates a redo record in the redo buffer whenever a change is made to the database. The **LGWR** background process is responsible for flushing the contents of the redo buffer into the online redo log. You can create multiple members in each redo log group to enable multiplexing of the online redo logs.

open (online) database backup—A physical file backup of the database made while the database is open and running in **ARCHIVELOG** mode.

operating system backup—A backup of the database files using OS commands or utilities.

Oracle database—A collection of related, physically stored data that is treated as a unit and managed by the Oracle RDBMS. An Oracle database is subdivided into a physical and logical structure that enables the management of physical data storage to be independent from the access to logical storage structures.

Oracle Enterprise Manager (OEM)—A management framework used to manage the complete Oracle environment. OEM consists of a Console, a suite of DBA tools and services, and a network of management servers and Oracle Intelligent Agents.

Oracle instance—A set of memory structures and background processes that access a set of database files.

parallel recovery—An Oracle database feature that enables you to use several processes to apply changes from the redo log files. Parallel recovery is most beneficial when the data files being recovered reside on different disks.

physical database backup—A set of physical database files that have been copied from one place to another. The files include data files, archived redo logs, or control files. You can use **RMAN** or OS commands to make physical database backups.

Program Global Area (PGA)—A memory area reserved for a user process. This memory area is private to the user process and is not shareable. In a Multi-Threaded Server (MTS) configuration, part of the PGA may reside in the SGA.

read-only tablespace—A tablespace whose status has been changed to freeze it from subsequent updates. You put a tablespace in read-only mode by executing the SQL statement **ALTER TABLESPACE <tablespace> READ ONLY**. Typically, you put a tablespace in read-only mode to reduce the frequency with which it is backed up.

recover—The process of applying redo data or incremental backups to database files to reconstruct lost changes and make a file current to a specific point in time.

RECOVER command—An **RMAN** command that applies redo logs or incremental backups to a restored backup set or copy to recover it to a specified point in time.

RECOVER DATABASE command—The Server Manager command used to recover a database that is mounted but not open. This is the Oracle-recommended method of recovering a database, versus using the SQL **ALTER DATABASE RECOVER** command.

recovery catalog—A set of Oracle tables and views used by Recovery Manager (**RMAN**) to store information about Oracle databases. **RMAN** uses this data to manage the backup, restore, and recovery of Oracle databases. If a recovery catalog is not available, **RMAN** uses information from the target database control file.

recovery catalog database—An Oracle database that contains a recovery catalog schema.

Recovery Manager (RMAN)—An Oracle utility that automates the backup, restore, and recovery operations for Oracle databases. You can use it with or without a recovery catalog. If you don't use a recovery catalog, **RMAN** uses the database's control file to store information necessary for backup and recovery operations.

RECOVERY_PARALLELISM—An *initSID.ora* parameter that specifies the default number of recovery processes per session.

redo log buffers—The memory buffer in the System Global Area (SGA) in which Oracle writes redo records. The background process **LGWR** is responsible for flushing the buffers into the current online redo log.

redo log group—The group to which each online redo log belongs. A group has one or more identical members.

REGISTER DATABASE command—An **RMAN** command that is used to register the target database in the recovery catalog.

REPORT command—An **RMAN** command that enables you to perform detailed analyses of the recovery catalog content.

RESET DATABASE command—An **RMAN** command that enables you to create a new database incarnation record in the recovery catalog.

RESETLOGS option—An option that can be used to open the database. This option resets the current redo log sequence to 1. A **RESETLOGS** operation invalidates all redo in the online redo logs.

restore—The process of bringing back an original copy of a file from a valid backup.

RESTORE command—An **RMAN** command that restore files from backup sets or from copies on disk to the current location, overwriting the files with the same name.

RESYNC CATALOG command—An **RMAN** command that enables you to perform a full resynchronization, which creates a snapshot control file and then compares the recovery catalog to either the current control file of the target database or the snapshot control file and updates it with information that is missing or changed.

RESYNC CATALOG FROM BACKUP CONTROLFILE command—An **RMAN** command used to extract information from a backup control file and rebuild the recovery catalog from it.

RUN command—An **RMAN** command that enables you to compile and execute one or more statements within the enclosed braces following the **RUN** keyword.

server process—A process created by Oracle to receive requests from a user process and to carry out the requests.

SET AUTORECOVERY ON command—A Server Manager command that automates the application of the default file names of archived redo logs needed during recovery.

SET NEWNAME command—An **RMAN** command used to specify a new location when restoring files. If you restore data files to a new location, then Oracle considers them data file copies and records the same in the control file and recovery catalog.

shared pool—A memory area in the SGA that holds the library cache and the data dictionary cache.

snapshot control file—A copy of a database's control file taken by Recovery Manager. **RMAN** uses the snapshot control file to read a consistent version of a control file when resynchronizing the recovery catalog or backing up the control file.

stored scripts—A sequence of **RMAN** commands stored in the recovery catalog.

SWITCH command—An **RMAN** command used to specify that a data file copy is now the current data file and the control file reflects this information. A switch is equivalent to using the **ALTER DATABASE RENAME DATAFILE** command: Oracle renames the files in the control file, but does not actually rename them on your operating system. Switching also deletes the data file copy records in the recovery catalog and the control file.

SYSDBA role—A special database administrator role that contains all system privileges with the **ADMIN OPTION**, and the **SYSOPER** system privilege.

System Change Number (SCN)—A stamp that defines a committed version of a database at a point in time. Oracle assigns every committed transaction a unique SCN.

System Global Area (SGA)—A shared memory region that holds data and control information for one Oracle database instance. Oracle automatically allocates memory for an SGA whenever the instance is started. The SGA is deallocated when the instance is shut down. Each Oracle instance has one and only one SGA.

table mode export—An **EXPORT** mode that exports specified tables owned by the operating user's schema. In this mode, privileged database users including the DBA can export specified tables owned by other database users.

table mode import—An **IMPORT** mode that imports all specified tables in the operating user's schema. In this mode, privileged database users including the DBA can import specific tables owned by other database users.

tablespace point-in-time recovery (TSPITR)—A type of incomplete recovery that is appropriate when a user error has been discovered and the database cannot be returned to a prior point in time. In the unlikely event you need to use TSPITR and because of the complexity associated with TSPITR, you should only perform this task with the assistance of Oracle Worldwide Support Services.

tag—A user-specified character string that acts as a symbolic name for a backup set or image copy. A tag can be specified when using the **RESTORE** or **CHANGE** command. A tag is limited to 30 characters.

target database—The database that requires the backup, restore, or recovery operations when using **RMAN**.

time-based recovery—An incomplete recovery type that enables the DBA to terminate the recovery process at a desired point in time in the past after the database has committed all changes up to the desired point in time.

trace file—A file created by the Oracle background processes when a problem or exceptional condition is encountered. It is also known as a *dump file*. The file contains information useful in diagnosing the problem.

unused block compression—The process of copying only used data blocks into **RMAN** backup sets. When **RMAN** creates data file backup sets, it only includes blocks that have been used and omits unused blocks.

user mode export—An **EXPORT** mode in which all objects owned by a given schema are exported and written to the export dump file. Grants and indexes created by users other than the owner are not exported. Privileged database users including the DBA can export all objects owned by one or more schemas.

user mode import—An **IMPORT** mode in which all database objects in the operating user's schema are imported. A privileged database user such as the DBA can import all database objects owned by one or more schema users.

user process—A process that is created when a tool such as SQL*Plus, Oracle Forms, and the like is invoked by the user. A user process could exist on the client machine or the server machine. User processes provide the interface for database users to interact with the database.

V$BACKUP_CORRUPTION—This data dictionary view provides information about corruptions in data file backups from the control file. Corruptions are not allowed in the control file and archived log file backups.

V$COPY_CORRUPTION—This data dictionary view provides information about data file copy corruptions from the control file.

V$LOG_HISTORY—This data dictionary view provides log history information from the control file.

V$RECOVER_FILE—This data dictionary view provides the status of files needing media recovery.

V$RECOVERY_FILE_STATUS—This data dictionary view provides status information on each data file associated with the specified **RECOVER** command. This information is only viewable to the Oracle process doing the recovery. **V$RECOVERY_FILE_STATUS** views will be empty to all other Oracle users.

V$RECOVERY_LOG**—This view provides information about archived logs that are needed to complete media recovery. This information is derived from the **V$LOG_HISTORY view. The relevant information provided by this view is only for the Oracle process doing the recovery. The **V$RECOVERY_LOG** view will be empty to all other Oracle users.

V$RECOVERY_STATUS**—This data dictionary view provides statistics of the current recovery process. This information is useful only for the Oracle process doing the recovery. The **V$RECOVERY_STATUS view will be empty to all other Oracle users.

whole backup—An **RMAN** backup comprised of the control file and all data files.

Index

Bold page numbers indicate sample exam questions.

E

F

H

I